The Complete Vegetable Cookbook

The Complete Vegetable Cookbook

DOLORES CASELLA

Illustrated by Alba Corrado

DAVID WHITE, INC.   PORT WASHINGTON, NEW YORK

By The Same Author

A World of Breads
A World of Baking
The New Book of Breads

Library of Congress Cataloging in Publication Data

Casella, Dolores.

The complete vegetable cookbook.

Includes index.
1. Cookery (Vegetables) I. Title.
TX801.C34 1983   641.6′5   83-14775
ISBN 0-87250-033-0

Published by David White, Inc.

One Pleasant Avenue
Port Washington, N.Y. 11050

Illustrations © 1983 by David White, Inc.
Book design by William Travis
Jacket illustration by Francis Dearden
Manufactured in the United States of America
ISBN 0-87250-033-0

Contents

This book is dedicated to my parents, Evelyn and C.J. Bennett, for the love—and the ideas—and the good things they taught me.

And to the old newsroom companions: Margaret Barkley, Joanne Booth, Rick Bolton, Bob and Sue Evancho, Kent Lauer, Don and Deb Skitt, Larry Slonaker, Bobbie Stephens, and Gene Yoachum. To the hours that we worked together—and to all of the good times and the bad times that we shared.

Preface

I think that I come by my love of good food naturally, having been raised in a Lebanese family. By that I mean not that the Lebanese are better cooks than others, but rather that the cooking is very robust and earthy, laced with the warmth of a Mediterranean sun.

Everyday food for us was very simple, though somewhat exotic, in traditional American terms, and I learned at a very young age not to tell my friends of some of the foods that we ate. They could not be expected to make sense of people who included, much less *enjoyed* such fare as raw lamb, snails, and the tongue and other "innards" of animals on the dinner table.

Festive food was extremely elaborate, requiring days and days of cooking and preparation. I remember my grandmother cooking before a party or picnic, making dozens upon dozens of loaves of pocket bread, mountains of Tabooli, and turkey cooked first in a cinnamon-seasoned broth and then browned in the oven. She used her own garden snails, first purged on lettuce for a week or 10 days before being cleaned and cooked.

Vegetables were a very important part of our diet, as they are for all Mediterranean people. During World War II my mother, along with millions of others, had the requisite Victory garden. Our backyard on Staten Island, New York, seemed to extend straight up to meet the foundation of the building on the street above. The yard was terraced so that she could plant the romaine lettuce, radishes, cucumbers and other vegetables she was familiar with. (I never tasted iceberg lettuce until I was an adult. And although I certainly do not love it, the crisp texture makes up somewhat for its totally bland flavor.)

When I married I literally could not fry an egg. I had been around good food all of my life, but had never learned how to prepare any of it. The man I married, a first generation American as I was, taught me the rudiments of cooking, and I set about learning how to prepare the foods he and I loved.

As with so many things in my life, I learned the answers before I learned the questions. I learned the hows of cooking before I learned the whys. It has been my observation that that is probably the worst thing about self-education. You often build the house before you learn there should be a foundation under it. There is some comfort, though, in considering that during all of those years I spent in my grandmother's kitchen, watching her work and eating the results, I must have absorbed *something*; I probably learned a lot, especially common sense.

Anyway, I have studied cooking and food all of my adult life—but never under a teacher. I have read the manuals as well as the cookbooks and have experimented with techniques as well as with recipes, and have mastered most and given up on a few. I have asked and begged for recipes and ideas, from friends and neighbors, family and acquaintances, and am always picking up ideas from restaurants.

I am appalled by the current idea that you must have a degree as a Home Economist, or have studied at some prestigious cooking school under a famous teacher before you can say that you know anything about cooking. I have had many home economists in my cooking classes, and without exception they have come to learn how to cook. Either a specific type of cooking, or just cooking in general.

About three years ago I decided to teach cooking classes in my home. My intention was to teach the "whys" as well as the "hows" of cooking, as well as flexibility and creativity. If teachers teach recipes alone, they are cheating their students. Recipes can be found in any magazine or newspaper. What must be taught are the "whys" and the "hows" and the process of getting—and applying—new *ideas*. Although I always caution my students to follow a recipe exactly the first time or two, after that I want them to use that recipe as a foundation upon which they will build something that is personal to them. Granted you can't do this with pastry recipes, but we are not talking pastry here—we are talking cooking in general.

This is certainly an age of food. I remember when there was only one regularly published magazine devoted exclusively to food. Now there must be 9 or 10. What bothers me is that while I see an increased interest in food, I don't see any true creativity. The two or three "voices of authority" in the food world are followed slavishly, even though that is certainly not what they intend.

To give an example—a few years ago when I was with a local newspaper, it was suggested that I interview a man who was "a good cook," whatever that means. I did so, and spent a pleasant afternoon with him. Only when I asked for a recipe did I run into any difficulty. He didn't have a recipe of his own. Not even an idea of his own. He used a recipe right out of Julia Child—memorized right down to the last ⅛ teaspoon. He had prepared a marvelous dish—but he had accomplished nothing, only followed a perfect recipe by rote.

That is not good cooking. Neither is the ability to prepare 30 perfect dishes necessarily good cooking. Good cooking is the ability to "wing it," to think of and make changes that are proper and reasonable: the ability to take a recipe and make it your own. And that requires knowledge of food and cooking, not just recipes. My students often laugh at me for not following my own recipes. But flexibility and creativity are necessary. I have had students tell me that they couldn't make a particular dish because they didn't have a particular ingredient. Baloney. You can't make a Béchamel Sauce because you are out of milk? Then make a Velouté Sauce. Think—and then, within reason, be flexible.

Don't be afraid to try new dishes. I frequently include in a cooking class menu a dish that I know most of my students would not try on their own. Like raw fish in a Seviche, for example. Most of them call it my "tricky" food, but in a classroom situation most of them will at least take a bite. Some find that they like it, or at least that it isn't as bad as they thought it might be, and give it another try. If they don't like a dish after trying it, that's fine. But at least they have tried it before deciding. Taste is acquired, period. I don't think that we are born either liking or disliking. And people whom we tend to think of as having strange eating habits, because they are different from ours, think the same of us.

The recipes in this book reflect my own personal preferences, as they must in all cookbooks. But since I have tried to make the book as comprehensive as possible, there are some recipes I tend not to use myself. All, however, have been made in my kitchen. You may detect some omissions, though, as I did not go into some of the more exotic vegetables.

Please read a recipe all the way through before you try it. Remember that no one can really tell you exactly how much salt and pepper to use, as that depends on individual preference. I have students who use no salt at all, and some who salt automatically before they even taste the food. Other seasonings are equally difficult to give exact amounts for, as is an occasional ingredient, such as oil when used for frying. And seasonings, of course, depend entirely on how highly or lightly seasoned you like your food.

The Complete
Vegetable
Cookbook

Beans and Seeds

There are few western vegetables that we cannot buy at the local supermarket in one form or another. Fresh, canned, frozen or dried. Familiarity breeds contempt, or at least a jaded, take-it-for-granted attitude. Green peas are just that. Peas. An ear of corn is an ear of corn. No more. No less. And so we forget, if most of us ever knew, the historical significance and impact of quite a few vegetables and grains.

When the tiny *petit pois* were brought to France from Italy in the 1660s, and presented at the court of King Louis XIV, they created great excitement. A dish of the bright green peas was as much of a luxury as a bowl of caviar or a dish with truffles is today.

Corn, before its debut in Europe, was held in high esteem, having immense religious and mythological significance. We know that corn originated in Peru. But aside from this meager knowledge, its ancestry remains a mystery of the botanical world. And, except for the mutant varieties, all types grown and cultivated today were grown and cultivated literally thousands of years ago.

Corn sustained all Indians, from the Hopi cliff dwellers of Arizona, who used a crude *metate* to grind the corn in, to the Eastern Iroquois who ground corn in wooden mortars, to the great Aztec, Maya and Inca nations of Central and South America.

The more primitive Indians mixed the ground grain with water and made a corn cake similar to the tortilla. Other, more advanced Indians boiled and roasted corn, or cooked it in dishes similar to our corn bread, corn pudding, mush and grits. The highly developed Indian nations of Central America made hominy by parching the corn with lye, and many Indian groups grew a variety of corn that would pop.

Like the date palm in Middle Eastern countries, every part of the corn plant—its husks, leaves and stalks—was used in a variety of ways. To the early colonists, who learned of its culture from friendly Indians, it was daily

1

bread—"the staff of life"—and they completely adopted the Indian method of cultivation.

DRIED BEANS

Dried beans have been a staple food of mankind since the dawn of agriculture, and there are more varieties than you would think possible. Again, many were unknown except in the Americas before the 16th century. In the United States the most popular are navy beans, lima beans, pinto and kidney beans. In the South, blackeyed peas (also called cowpeas) are very popular. Around the Mediterranean, garbanzos (chick peas) and lentils are very popular, and in Italy they also enjoy lupini and fava beans.

Dried beans are frequently available in bulk and can be bought in large quantity for long term storage. Be careful, though. If the beans are faded in color, they are old. And if they are old they will have tougher skins and will require longer cooking. Try to buy only what you would use within a 6-month period. Store beans in a cool, dry area. When ready to use, sort over the beans carefully for clumps of soil and pebbles. Wash and drain.

I prefer to soak beans overnight before cooking them gently in the same water. You can also cover the beans with water (use 3 cups water to each cup of beans), bring to a boil and boil for 2 minutes. Then turn off heat, cover pot and let stand for 1 or 2 hours. Then cook as usual.

Do not cook beans over high heat. Simmer them gently. Remember that the harder the water in which you soak and cook dried beans, the tougher will be the skins and the longer will be the cooking time required to soften them. Many cooks insist on draining off the water in which the beans have soaked and adding fresh water to cook them in. Avoid this if you live in a hard water area. As if the mineral salts from the soaking water were not enough, those in the new water will toughen the skin still further. In hard water areas it is especially important to cook the beans gently so that you will have to add as little water as possible.

For the same reasons, do not salt until beans have softened considerably. For the softer beans such as blackeyed peas and lima beans, this is after about 30 minutes. For the harder beans, allow at least an hour before adding salt.

① Pinto, ② Romano, ③ Yellow wax, ④ Zebra, ⑤ Blackeye, ⑥ Garbanzo, ⑦ Great Northern, ⑧ French Flageolet, ⑨ Lentil, ⑩ Kidney, ⑪ Mung, ⑫ Lima, ⑬ Black Valentine, ⑭ French Horticultural.

If cooking with tomatoes, wine or other acid foods, do not add until the final part of the cooking process as acids also tend to toughen the skins.

Different beans require different cooking times. Blackeyed peas, lima beans and lentils will cook in an hour. The larger beans will take longer, generally from 2 to 2½ hours.

As far as the inability of some people to digest beans properly, there are any number of so-called aids to digestion. Some cooks swear by a good-sized pinch of ginger in the cooking water. Others add beer to the water. One lady told me that she always boiled a potato with the beans. Supposedly the potato absorbed whatever it is that makes beans difficult. Still others add vinegar to the water. It's a 50-50 proposition no matter what you do. Just don't add baking soda to the water as it kills vitamins.

YIELD: 2 cups of dried beans approximate a pound. 1 pound of dried beans, cooked, makes 5 or 6 cups. With ¾-cup servings, 1 pound will serve 7 or 8.

Blackeyed Peas

This was one of my mother's better dishes. She always used onions and garlic, some bay leaves and some kind of pork product. Occasionally it was ham, more often it was a ham hock or pork hock or pork chops. In the South, they take this same dish, add a cup of rice to it and call it Hopping John. Blackeyed peas are creamy smooth and have a lovely flavor and texture to them. Soaking is not necessary.

2 cups dried blackeyed peas
1 onion, minced
2 cloves garlic, crushed
2 tablespoons pork fat or butter
1 bay leaf
1 or 2 ham hocks, or pork chops, or pigtails
and ears
¼ teaspoon crushed red pepper
salt and pepper to taste

Cover peas with water, using 3 cups water to each cup of beans. Cook gently.

Sauté the onion and garlic in the fat until limp and add to the peas along with the bay leaf and pork or ham and the crushed red pepper. Let cook gently until tender, about 1 hour. Salt and pepper to taste. This amount will serve 5 or 6.

Southern Baked Blackeyed Peas

Make as above. Remove meat from the bones when tender. Turn cooked peas into a casserole and stir in ½ cup honey. Bake for an hour at 325°F (165°C).

Burgundy Beans

This is another nice dish for a buffet, and is as simple to make as it is delicious.

2 pounds dried pinto or small red or pink
beans
1 pound ham, cut into cubes
2 tablespoons or more chili powder
6 to 8 cloves garlic, crushed
1 onion, minced
¼ cup olive oil
salt and pepper to taste
1½ cups burgundy wine

Soak beans overnight. Then cook gently in water to cover for an hour before adding the ham. At the end of the second hour stir in the chili powder and the garlic and onion that have been sautéed in olive oil until limp. Salt and pepper to taste at the end of the third hour. Then stir in the wine and

simmer for another hour, making 4 hours cooking time in all. Serves 10 to 12.

Homemade Baked Beans

These are truly excellent baked beans, more traditional in their ingredients than some. Don't forget to serve with a deep, brown bread, or with corn bread. And remember that baked beans are great for a crowd. You can use either the small navy beans, or the large whites (marrow beans). The small beans will require a longer cooking time, but the large whites are creamier.

2 cups white beans (*see above*), soaked
overnight
½ pound salt pork
1 bay leaf
½ cup dark molasses
¼ cup brown sugar
1 large onion, minced
1 teaspoon dry mustard
freshly ground black pepper

Simmer beans for 2 hours, or until just *barely* tender. Drain, reserving the liquid. Then, using a 2-quart casserole, make a layer of the beans. On this put the bay leaf, another layer of beans, the molasses and another layer of beans. Then add the minced onion, the dry mustard and a sprinkling of cracked black pepper. Over this put the last of the beans. Place the piece of salt pork in the center and then sprinkle with the brown sugar and pour on 2 cups of the reserved bean liquid. Cover and bake in a 300°F (150°C) oven for from 4 to 6 hours. Check occasionally to see if the beans need the addition of more liquid. Remove cover for the last 45 minutes. Serves 6 to 8.

Variations

You can add ¼ cup of vinegar. Some cooks like to add catsup. I don't. Still others omit the salt pork and place slices of bacon across the top of the beans. The bacon slices become crisp when the lid is removed.

Latin Beans

This is a great party dish and can be kept warm in the oven for several hours. Serve with a large tossed green salad or a spinach salad, and garlic bread or tortilla chips with hot sauce.

 1 pound small red beans
 2 pounds beef cut into tiny dice
 2 teaspoons salt (*less if desired*)
 2 large onions, minced
 2 cloves garlic, minced
 1 green pepper, minced
 salt and pepper to taste
 3 or 4 California green chilis, roasted,
  peeled and diced
 2 or 3 tomatoes, seeded and diced
 1 10-ounce can tomato sauce
 1 tablespoon chili powder (*you may wish to
  use more*)
 1 teaspoon dried oregano
 1 teaspoon dried rosemary
 ½ teaspoon powdered cumin

Soak beans overnight. Then cook until tender, adding salt towards the end of the cooking time. Drain.

Brown the meat with the onions, garlic, and green pepper. Season with salt and pepper to taste and add remaining ingredients to the meat mixture. Cover and simmer for 1 hour, or until it forms a thick, rich sauce.

To serve, pour beans into a large serving bowl. Mexican pottery would be ideal. Pour meat sauce over and stir together. Serves 10 to 12.

Using Canned Baked Beans

Most of us keep a couple of cans of good baked beans (the list of ingredients should include no tomato product if you are using *good* canned baked beans) on an emergency shelf. Following are a few nice ways to use them. All recipes are based on using 2 large (*28-ounce*) cans.

1. Sauté 1 onion and 1 clove garlic, minced, in oil until limp. In a casserole, combine the beans, onions and garlic and any leftover chicken or poultry that you might have. Sprinkle with some parsley and add ½ cup burgundy wine. Bake in a 350ºF (175ºC) oven for 20 minutes, or until hot.

2. Combine beans with ⅓ cup brown sugar, 1 cup apple juice, pinch of sweet basil, thyme and marjoram and place in casserole. Arrange 6 pieces of bacon on top. Bake in a 350ºF (175ºC) oven for 1 hour, adding more apple juice if necessary.

3. Arrange in a casserole in layers the following: the canned beans, 1 minced, cooked onion, some nice fat franks, and chili sauce that has been spiked with chili powder to taste. Top with more beans and a final layer of grated cheese. Bake in a 350ºF (175ºC) oven for 30 to 40 minutes.

4. My mother used to cook up an onion, several cloves of garlic and a sliced green pepper until all were limp. To this she would add the canned beans and Worcestershire sauce to taste. I occasionally still prepare canned beans this way.

Ranch Style Beans

These are great with barbecues. Use the canned red-chili sauce that is made with red chili peppers, not the bottled condiment that is called chili sauce.

 2 cups dried pink beans
 1 pound beef stew meat, in small cubes
 1 tablespoon fat of some kind
 1 large onion, minced
 2 cloves garlic, minced
 1 cup canned red-chili sauce (*see above*)
 1 cup burgundy
 8 ounces tomato sauce
 1 tablespoon salt
 1 teaspoon oregano
 1 bay leaf

Cover beans with 6 cups water and let soak overnight. Then cook beans gently for an hour. While the beans are cooking, brown the meat in the fat with the onion and garlic. Add the meat, onions and garlic to the beans and simmer for another 30 minutes, or until the beans are almost tender. Then stir in the remaining ingredients and simmer for another hour, or until tender and richly flavored. Serves 8.

Chili with Beans

I worked this recipe out for the local Ski Club's annual chili party. This amount will serve a large group, so if it makes too much the recipe is easily halved. However, chili freezes well for up to 3 months.

   1 cup each: dried kidney beans, pinto beans
      and chili beans
   1 can (*1 pound 13 ounces*) Italian plum
      tomatoes, crushed
   1 7-ounce can green chili sauce
   1 6-ounce can ripe olives
   ½ to 1 cup diced green chilis
   1 tablespoon ground cumin
   1 cup red wine
   3 or 4 dried red chilis, crushed
   1 tablespoon oregano
   3 bay leaves
   5 pounds stewing beef, cubed, or ground
      beef
   2 onions, minced
   4 or 5 cloves garlic, crushed

Soak beans overnight in 9 cups of water. In the morning cook the beans in the same water gently for an hour and a half. Then add the tomatoes along with all of the ingredients up to the beef. Simmer gently.

Brown the meat in its own fat if you are using ground beef. If you are using cubed beef you will need to add some fat. When meat is almost browned, add the onions and garlic and cook and stir until limp. Add to the beans and stir to mix well. Cover the pot and simmer gently for another 1½ to 2 hours. Stir occasionally. Season to taste with salt, pepper and more crushed red chilis if desired.

Serve with sour cream, shredded cheese, chopped onion, sliced ripe olives and some chopped jalapeño peppers if desired. This amount should serve 10 to 12.

Cooked Pinto Beans

If you like pinto beans, it would be a good idea to make this up in quantity. The beans freeze very well and can be served hot, as is, or added to soups or chili, or even made into refried beans.

   2 cups dried pinto beans
   3 or 4 slices thick bacon, cut into dice
   2 small onions, minced
   2 cloves garlic, minced
   1 teaspoon ground cumin
   1 teaspoon salt

Soak beans in 6 cups water overnight. In the morning cook the bacon until it begins to crisp. Then add onions and garlic and cook until limp.

Cook beans for an hour, gently. Then add the bacon, bacon fat, onions and garlic. Stir in the cumin and the salt and simmer until tender, 1 to 1½ hours. Serve hot to 4 to 6.

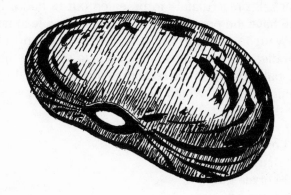

Refried Beans

A Mexican staple, these are delicious and can be used in all manner of ways. Simply make the above recipe, omitting the bacon. Use ⅓ cup lard instead. The beans can be refried as soon as they are cooked, or they can be frozen for future use. Thaw before attempting to refry.

To refry the beans, heat 2 tablespoons lard in a large, heavy skillet until very hot. Use a slotted spoon to place beans in the skillet. Add a little cooking liquid. Mash beans with a potato masher or the back of a large spoon. Beans may be partially or completely mashed. Add more salt to taste and simmer beans to desired consistency, adding more cooking liquid if needed. Stir frequently. Serves 4.

Felafel & Pocket Bread

Falafel

Falafel is an Egyptian bean dish. Traditionally it is made with fava beans, but I much prefer chick peas. On the west coast many of the college communities have stands, similar to hot dog stands, that sell only Falafel—to be eaten out of hand. If you have the opportunity to try it this way, lean far forward to take the first bite, which is bound to dribble. A more genteel method is to serve the little balls as an appetizer, surrounding a bowl of Tahini Sauce in which to dip them.

>   **1 cup dried chick peas**
>   **3 or 4 green onions**
>   **½ cup parsley sprigs**
>   **3 cloves garlic**
>   **1 large egg**
>   **salt and pepper**
>   **½ teaspoon ground cumin**
>   **½ teaspoon baking soda**
>   **sesame seeds**
>   **Tahini Sauce** (*see below*)

Soak the chick peas in water to cover overnight. Drain in the morning and put through a food processor (do *not* cook first), with the onions, parsley and garlic. Add the egg and just a little salt and pepper. Add the cumin and the baking soda. Let the mixture stand for 15 minutes. Then shape the soft mixture into balls or patties. Pat a pinch of sesame seed onto each.

I deep fry these in an electric wok at 385°F (195°C), but they can be pan fried. Fry until golden brown and crisp. Be careful when first adding to the hot oil as the balls can fall apart fairly easily.

Once fried, however, they hold together very well. This will make enough for 4 to 6 people. Serve with Tahini Sauce.

Note. *Use also as a filling for pocket bread sandwiches with shredded lettuce, chopped tomatoes and Tahini Sauce.*

Tahini Sauce

You will need tahini, a canned paste made of ground sesame seeds. It is available in health food stores as well as in markets that sell Middle Eastern products. This recipe is on the can, and is the best. Mix together (the food processor works best, but a heavy spoon will do, as will a blender) 1 cup of tahini with ½ cup fresh lemon juice, 3 crushed cloves of garlic, ½ cup cold water and ½ teaspoon salt. This will make a creamy sauce which is excellent drizzled over Falafel sandwiches, on many vegetables, and on fish.

Hungarian Style Lentils

Lentils are not properly appreciated in this country. They would be better appreciated if people would try recipes other than lentil soup with franks. This method is good.

>   **½ pound lentils**
>   **1 large onion, minced**
>   **2 tablespoons bacon fat**
>   **2 tablespoons flour**
>   **¼ cup cold water**
>   **2 teaspoons sugar**
>   **1 teaspoon salt if desired**
>   **2 tablespoons wine vinegar**

Soak the lentils in water to cover for an hour if you wish. This is a step that I do not consider necessary either with lentils or blackeyed peas. Simmer just until tender and then drain and keep warm. Sauté the onion in the bacon fat until limp. Then stir in the flour, stirring until it is golden. Add the remaining ingredients and cook until thickened. Pour over lentils and serve immediately. Serves 4.

Hints and Ideas for Lima Beans

Frozen lima beans are almost as good as the fresh, and can be used in any of the following ways.

1. Melt ¼ cup butter or chicken fat and in it sauté 4 minced green onions just until limp. Add to 1½ pounds fresh cooked lima beans, or 2 10-ounce packages of the frozen. Season to taste with salt and pepper.

2. Combine 1 cup cooked limas, 1 cup whole kernel corn and ½ to 1 cup cooked peas. Add ½ cup cream and ½ teaspoon each salt and sugar. Simmer gently just until hot. This can be baked in a 350ºF (175ºC) oven for 20 minutes if desired.

3. Sauté 1 cup sliced or whole mushrooms in 2 tablespoons butter just until soft. Add to 2 cups cooked limas with ½ cup cream and salt and pepper to taste. Bring to a boil and serve.

4. Sauté 1 minced onion and ½ cup sliced mushrooms in butter until limp. To this, add the contents of 1 10-ounce package frozen lima beans, 2 shredded lettuce leaves, 3 or 4 coriander seeds and just a little water. Cook just until the limas are tender.

5. This goes for limas or lentils. Cook them just until tender. Drain and marinate in a mixture of tarragon wine vinegar and olive oil with a touch of garlic and some fresh herbs to taste.

6. Make 2 cups Bechamel Sauce (see page 122) and heat it with a cup of shredded cheese until the cheese is melted. Then add ½ cup diced pimiento, 1 tablespoon grated onion, and ⅓ cup sliced ripe olives. Pour over the contents of 2 10-ounce packages of cooked lima beans. Turn into a casserole and bake in a 350°F (175°C) oven for 30 minutes.

Baked Dried Lima Beans

This is one of those marvelous bean recipes that made the rounds during the 1960s. During that decade, I seldom went to a party that did not feature a casserole of these beans.

1 pound baby dried lima beans
2 teaspoons salt if desired
½ cup butter

½ to ¾ cup brown sugar
1 tablespoon dry mustard
1 tablespoon molasses
1 cup commercial sour cream

Wash the beans and soak overnight. In the morning cook the beans in the same water in which they were soaked, for about 2 hours, or until the beans are tender and the liquid has almost evaporated. There should be a little less than 1 cup of liquid on the beans.

Add remaining ingredients and stir together. Turn into a deep casserole. Bake, uncovered, in a 350°F (175°C) oven for 45 minutes to 1 hour. This will serve about 6.

Note. *You can use navy beans instead of the dried limas if you wish.*

Italian Style Chick Peas

Marvelously Italian, this dish can be served either chilled or at room temperature.

⅓ cup olive oil
1 bunch green onions, sliced
½ teaspoon dried thyme
2 cloves garlic, crushed
salt to taste
1 teaspoon freshly ground black pepper
¾ to 1 cup dry white wine
juice of 3 or 4 lemons
2 20-ounce cans chick peas, drained and rinsed

Heat oil in a skillet. Add the green onions, thyme, garlic, a little salt and the pepper. Sauté gently for 5 minutes. Add the wine and lemon juice and bring to the boil. Reduce heat and simmer for 5 minutes. Add chick peas and more wine or lemon juice if needed. Taste as you go. Heat for 5 minutes and then remove from heat. Serve chilled as part of an antipasto, or at room temperature. The beans keep well and can be tossed into salads if desired. Serves 6 to 8 as a side dish.

CORN

The only grain that has its origins in the New World, varieties of corn have been found in ancient tombs in Peru. It is the most popular vegetable in the United States.

There is absolutely no argument about the virtues of homegrown corn. The difference between corn that is picked and immediately husked and boiled for 5 minutes until tender, and the days-old corn that we buy at the market is enormous. Fresh-picked corn needs nothing other than butter, perhaps a seasoned herb butter, and some salt. If you must buy corn, cook it in water with some milk or a bit of sugar in it. *Never* salt the water.

At the market, look for snug green husks, with brown silk. The kernels should be plump and close together. Avoid ears with missing rows of kernels, or with dried out stem ends.

YIELD: Allow 1 or 2 ears per serving. Two ears of corn will yield about 1 cup corn kernels.

Tips and Ideas for Corn

When boiling corn, do not salt the water as this toughens the corn.

Add some milk to the water to help the corn taste just-picked—or at least more like it.

To roast corn, run a little water inside the husks and place the corn in a 325°F (165°C) oven for 15 to 20 minutes. Remove husks and serve with butter and salt.

This way is extra good. Wash a head of romaine lettuce. Drain. Combine 2 or 3 tablespoons of soft butter with ¼ teaspoon paprika, a pinch of marjoram and some salt and pepper. Spread on husked corn. Wrap 3 or 4 leaves of romaine around each ear of corn to completely cover. Tie with a string and place in a shallow, buttered baking dish. Cover with foil. Bake in a 350°F (175°C) oven for 45 minutes.

To steam corn, Yankee style, remove husks from ears of corn and line a pot with the husks. Cover bottom of pot with water. Lay corn on top of husks and cover. Steam for 20 minutes.

Soak corn in seawater or, lacking that, in salt water for an hour before barbecuing or oven roasting. Do not husk or remove silk until after

soaking. Then pull back husks, remove silk, and pull husks back over the corn for cooking.

Butter for Corn on the Cob

For 6 ears of corn, combine the following, either melting the butter and adding the juice and paprika, or by mixing all to a paste: ¼ pound butter; juice of 1 lime; ½ teaspoon hot or sweet paprika.

Succotash

This is an American Indian dish. The name is a corruption of the Indian *m'sickquatash*.

**½ cup water
2 cups fresh or frozen baby lima beans
½ teaspoon salt if desired
freshly ground black pepper to taste
2 cups fresh or frozen corn kernels
⅓ cup half and half or heavy cream**

Bring water to a boil with 2 tablespoons of butter or bacon fat. Then add the beans, salt and pepper and simmer until the beans are tender, about 10 minutes. Add corn and simmer another 4 or 5 minutes, or until corn is tender. Stir in the half and half and let heat, but do not boil. Taste for seasoning and adjust to taste. Serves 6.

Note. *Early settlers boiled the corncobs in water and used the water for soup and vegetable dishes.*

Barbecued Corn

First make a seasoned butter by blending ⅓ cup of melted butter with one of the following: ¼ teaspoon red pepper, 2 tablespoons soy sauce, ½ teaspoon chili powder, ¼ teaspoon oregano, ¼ teaspoon cumin or a crushed clove or 2 of garlic. Set aside.

Remove husks and silk from 8 ears of corn. Place each ear on a piece of heavy-duty aluminum foil. Pour several teaspoons of butter mixture over each ear. Wrap securely and place right in the barbecue coals·for 15 minutes, turning occasionally. Serves 4 to 8.

California Indian Corn

This recipe is another one that made the rounds during the 50s and early 60s. It is very good.

½ cup melted butter
1 cup cornmeal
1 can (*1 pound 13 ounces*) Italian plum tomatoes
1 1-pound can cream-style corn
1 tablespoon chili powder
1 4-ounce can or bottle of olives, either black or green
salt to taste if desired

Combine all ingredients, stirring together. Pour into a buttered casserole and bake, uncovered, in a 375°F (190°C) oven for 1 hour. Serves 4 to 6.

Baked Corn and Tomatoes

This is a lovely August dish when you are tired of corn on the cob, barbecued corn and other corn delights.

2 cups raw corn kernels
2 cups diced, seeded tomatoes
4 or 5 green onions, minced
⅓ cup minced green pepper
¼ cup butter
salt and pepper
1 tablespoon fresh chives, minced
1 cup fresh bread crumbs
4 or 5 slices bacon, cut into dice

Layer the corn, tomatoes, green onions and green pepper in a buttered casserole. Dot with the butter and sprinkle with the salt, pepper and chives.

Strew the top with the bread crumbs and the diced raw bacon. Bake in a 350°F (175°C) oven for 50 minutes. Serves 6.

Corn Salad

This is a lovely combination. In the summertime I use the fresh corn and in the winter I use frozen corn kernels which, while not as good as the fresh, are still good.

2 cups corn kernels, steamed until barely tender
1 can hearts of palm, cut in ½-inch slices
3 or 4 green onions, minced
¾ cup good vinaigrette
2 heads butterhead, Boston or Bibb lettuce
⅓ to ½ cup thinly sliced Provolone cheese strips
salt and pepper to taste

Combine the corn, hearts of palm and green onions with the vinaigrette. Let marinate for a while. Then toss with the lettuce and the cheese. Add salt and pepper to taste. Serves 6 to 8.

Note. If I use frozen corn kernels in this salad, I do not cook them at all. Just thaw and drain and use.

Fried Corn

Try this method if you have some extra ears of corn. The recipe is supposed to serve 4, but is so good that you should not count on serving more than 3.

4 ears of corn
4 strips of bacon
½ cup heavy cream
salt and pepper to taste

Cut corn off the ears. Fry the bacon until crisp. Discard all but 2 or 3 tablespoons of the fat. Add the corn to the bacon fat and cook and stir for 5 minutes. Add the cream, salt and pepper and the crisp bacon pieces. Simmer for another 5 to 10 minutes. Serve immediately.

Note. You can add some minced green onions and use 1 cup of commercial sour cream in place of the heavy cream.

Sour Cream Corn Pudding

Try this old-time recipe using either fresh, frozen or canned corn.

**3 cups corn kernels
3 large eggs
1 cup milk or half and half
2 teaspoons sugar
½ teaspoon salt if desired
¼ teaspoon freshly ground black pepper
1 cup sour cream
2 tablespoons melted butter**

Combine ingredients, whisking together. Turn into a buttered 1½ to 2-quart casserole. Bake in a 350°F (175°C) oven for 30 to 45 minutes, or until firm. Test as you would a custard. Serves 4.

California Style Hominy

Hominy is a parched corn that is also known as samp. Ground it is known as grits. Available dried or canned; canned white hominy is found in the Mexican/Spanish food department.

**1 #2½ can white hominy (*1 pound 13 ounces*)
4 green onions, minced
¾ cup commercial sour cream
¾ cup grated Monterey Jack cheese
3 California green chilis, roasted, peeled
   and diced
dry bread crumbs
2 tablespoons butter**

Drain the hominy and mix with the onions, sour cream, cheese and green chilis. Turn into a buttered 1½-quart casserole. Sprinkle the top with bread crumbs and dot with the butter. Bake in a

350°F (175°C) oven for 30 minutes, or until hot. Serves 5 or 6.

Hominy and Tomatoes

Butter a shallow baking dish. Drain a #2½ can of hominy (*1 pound 13 ounces*) and turn the hominy into the baking dish. Add 2 cups drained canned tomatoes and cover with a mixture of ½ cup fine dry bread crumbs and ½ cup grated Parmesan cheese. Bake in a 350°F (175°C) oven for 30 minutes.

GREEN BEANS

Green beans, or yellow wax beans, are just two of an enormous variety of beans. Available year round, the peak season is from May through October. To buy, choose beans that are bright, firm and crisp-feeling. They should snap. Avoid wilted looking, flabby beans. The beans can be cooked whole, or cut into pieces. They might be sliced French style in long slivers, or cut Chinese style in long, slanting slices. How they are cut will affect the cooking time. The thinner the cut, the less time will be required, since ideally the beans should remain bright green and tender/crisp. Thin cut beans will often cook in 3 or 4 minutes, while whole beans might take up to 15 or 20 minutes. If you grow your own beans, pick them while they are tiny and just barely cook them.
YIELD: 1 pound green beans will serve 3 or 4.

Green Bean Tips and Ideas

Frozen green beans can substitute for the fresh. But do not cook them as long as the package directions state. Generally, the frozen beans need only to be added to boiling water and then immediately removed if they are the French cut, or removed as soon as the water returns to the boil if they are regular cut.

Combine cooked and drained green beans with thin slices of raw onion and some vinaigrette. They will keep in the refrigerator for several days. Serve cold or at room temperature.

Braise cooked green beans in garlic-flavored olive oil.

Green Beans with Bacon Dressing

This is an old-fashioned method of cooking green beans.

1½ pounds green beans
½ pound bacon, cooked until crisp, and crumbled
¼ cup drippings
2 large eggs
⅓ cup wine vinegar
½ cup water
1 or 2 tablespoons sugar
pinch salt
some diced pimiento

String the beans if necessary. Drop into ¼ cup boiling water and stir and cook over low heat for 10 to 15 minutes, or until beans are just tender, with still some bite to them. The time depends on the size of the beans. Large ones will take more time than young, small beans.

Prepare bacon as directed and set aside. Pour off all but ¼ cup drippings. Combine eggs, vinegar, water, sugar and salt and whisk together. add to drippings and cook over low heat, stirring, until thickened. Turn beans out onto serving plate and pour sauce over them. Garnish with bacon pieces and diced pimiento. Serves 4 to 6.

Green Beans with Sour Cream

This way of dressing up the beans is special.

1½ pounds green beans
1 medium onion, minced
2 tablespoons olive oil
½ cup commercial sour cream
salt and pepper if desired

Prepare green beans. Drop into ¼ cup boiling water and stir and cook over low heat for 10 to 15

minutes, or until beans are barely tender. Drain. Meanwhile sauté onion in the oil. Add onion to beans and stir in sour cream, salt and pepper. Mix lightly. Serves 4 to 6.

Stewed Green Beans with Tomatoes

This fine dish is prepared the same way in Greece, Turkey, Syria and Lebanon, and probably much the same way in Italy. The Italians will add some sweet basil in place of the thyme and sprinkle the top with grated Parmesan cheese. If you are lucky enough to have a garden, pick the beans whily they are tiny. Otherwise, snap the beans into pieces about 1½ inches long.

1 to 1½ pounds green beans
1 pound fresh tomatoes
2 medium onions, peeled and sliced
1 or 2 cloves garlic, crushed
2 tablespoons olive oil
salt and pepper to taste
½ teaspoon dried thyme

Prepare beans and set aside. Peel and quarter the tomatoes. Sauté onion and garlic in the oil. When golden, add the tomatoes and a little water if the mixture is too thick. Add the beans. Cover and simmer just until tender, about 25 to 30 minutes. Serves 4 to 6.

Indian Green Beans

This method results in a dry vegetable dish that is excellent with lamb or any other rich meat.

1 medium onion, minced
2 medium potatoes, peeled and cut into dice
2 or 3 tablespoons olive oil
2 teaspoons curry powder
½ teaspoon salt if desired
1 to 1½ pounds green beans
¼ cup water
juice of 1 lemon or lime

Sauté onion and potatoes in the oil. Add the curry powder, salt, beans and water. Cover and cook until beans and potatoes are tender. Add the lemon or lime juice. Serves 6.

Chinese Style Green Beans

Take a pound of fresh, trimmed green beans and blanch them for 4 minutes. Then plunge into cold water to stop the cooking. Toss with a mixture of 3 tablespoons soy sauce and 1 teaspoon Oriental sesame oil.

PEAS

Green peas, an edible seed, and snow peas, an edible pod, are among the most popular of vegetables. The field pea is used for split peas.

A cool season crop, the best peas of all are the tiny ones that you must grow yourself, and the snow peas which are mainly used in Oriental cooking.

To buy, choose well-filled, brightly colored crisp pods. When buying snow peas look for bright green, crisp pods.

YIELD: 1 pound peas in the shell will yield 1 cup shelled peas. Allow ¾ cup per serving. 1 pound snow peas will serve 4.

Frozen Peas

Frozen peas, while not as good as the fresh, are still quite good indeed. Ignore the cooking instructions in favor of undercooking the peas. Frozen snow peas are disappointing. If you use them, thaw and add to your dish at the last minute, just to heat them.

One 10-ounce package frozen green peas will equal 1 pound in the shell, or a little over 1 cup shelled peas.

Cold Curried Peas

This can be traced back to some of the cold curried Indian dishes. This one, however, comes by way of England, with snow peas substituted for the more typical corn and celery.

2 cups fresh peas, blanched 1 minute
1 cup fresh snow peas, blanched 1 minute
½ cup sour cream
¼ cup mayonnaise
some fresh chives
½ teaspoon curry powder
salt and pepper to taste
dash Tabasco
lettuce leaves

Prepare peas and snow peas as directed and chill. Combine remaining ingredients, adding chives to taste and a dash of Tabasco to spice things up. Taste and adjust seasoning. Toss with the peas and snow peas gently so as not to mash the peas. Serve in a glass bowl garnished with more chives. Chill. Serve individual servings on lettuce leaves. Serves 6.

East Indian Peas with Ginger

1 quarter-sized slice of fresh ginger
½ cup corn or peanut oil
¼ teaspoon whole black mustard seeds
5 whole fenugreek seeds
¼ teaspoon turmeric
1 cup packed chopped fresh coriander (cilantro)
1 fresh jalapeño pepper, sliced
3 cups shelled fresh or frozen, thawed peas
1 teaspoon ground coriander
1 teaspoon powdered cumin
1 teaspoon Garam Masala (see following recipe)
½ teaspoon salt

Mince the ginger very fine and add it to 2 tablespoons water. Reserve.

Heat oil in a skillet and when very hot add the mustard and fenugreek seeds. The mustard seeds will pop, at which time add the ginger mixture and the turmeric. Watch out for spattering. Turn the heat down and stir in the chopped fresh coriander and the sliced pepper. Cook, stirring, for another 2 or 3 minutes. Then stir in the peas and cook, stirring, for 5 minutes.

Now stir in remaining ingredients and 3 table-spoons warm water. Lower heat and cook slowly for 25 to 30 minutes. Serves 6.

Garam Masala

This is an Indian spice mixture which varies from cook to cook and from region to region. I've tasted some that had quite a lot of fennel in them. This is a good mixture, though, and one which I keep in the house.

    **2 parts ground coriander
    1 part coarsely ground black pepper
    1 part powdered cumin
    ½ part powdered cloves
    ½ part powdered cinnamon**

Combine and keep in a tightly stoppered jar. Use where a recipe calls for it, or combine with commercial curry powder using 1 part Garam Masala to 2 parts curry powder.

Venetian Rice and Peas
(Risi en Bisi)

This is a delicious Italian way of preparing green peas.

    **1 tablespoon olive oil
    ¼ cup butter
    1 small onion or 3 or 4 green onions,
      minced
    2 cups green peas
    ¾ cup long-grain white rice
    1¾ cups chicken stock
    salt and pepper to taste
    1 or 2 tablespoons grated Parmesan cheese**

Heat the olive oil and butter and in it sauté the onion until limp. Add the peas and cook for just a minute, stirring. Then add the rice and stir to coat the rice with the butter and oil. Then add the chicken stock and a little salt and pepper. Cover and cook over low heat for 15 to 20 minutes, or until rice is just tender and each grain separate. Taste for seasoning. Serve sprinkled with grated Parmesan cheese to 3 or 4.

Peas and Lettuce

The French line the cooking pot with wet lettuce leaves when cooking peas. The lettuce leaves provide all of the moisture that is needed. In this recipe the lettuce is cooked right with the peas.

    **⅓ cup butter
    4 cups shelled peas
    1 teaspoon sugar
    ¼ cup water
    small head Boston or Bibb lettuce, shredded
    16 small, precooked onions
    1 cup heavy cream
    salt and pepper to taste**

Melt the butter in a heavy pot with a lid. Add the peas, sugar, water, lettuce and onions. Cover and cook, shaking occasionally, for 5 to 10 minutes, or until peas are tender. Boil the cream down to ½ cup and season with the salt and pepper. Add to the peas and serve to 6.

Italian Snow Peas

I serve this as part of a buffet as it is better at room temperature and holds up very well.

    **3 pounds fresh snow peas, trimmed
    ¼ cup olive oil
    1 bunch green onions, sliced
    2 cloves garlic, crushed
    ½ cup dry white wine
    juice of 2 lemons
    ¼ teaspoon dried thyme
    1 bay leaf
    ½ cup water or very clear chicken broth
    salt and pepper to taste**

Prepare snow peas and set aside. Heat the oil and sauté the onions and garlic until limp. Add remaining ingredients and heat to simmering. Cover the pot and simmer for 7 or 8 minutes at the most. I test at the end of 4 or 5 minutes as I do not want the snow peas overdone. Remove snow peas and reduce liquid until there is no more than ¼ cup. Remove bay leaf and pour liquid over snow peas. Chill or serve at room temperature to 8 to 10.

Hawaiian Pea Pods

This delicious dish has Oriental origins. It goes especially well with ham, pork or poultry.

¼ cup butter
½ teaspoon curry powder
½ cup chopped green onions

1 pound fresh trimmed snow peas
1 20-ounce can pineapple chunks
3 tablespoons cornstarch
¼ cup rice wine vinegar or white wine vinegar
1 cup chicken stock
1 tablespoon soy sauce
2 tomatoes, cut in wedges
½ cup sliced water chestnuts

Heat butter and curry powder until bubbly. Add onions and snow peas. Cook, stirring, just until they begin to wilt. Blend ½ cup syrup from the pineapple with the cornstarch and vinegar. Add to vegetables. Add broth. Cook, stirring gently, until the sauce thickens. Stir in soy sauce, tomatoes, water chestnuts and pineapple chunks. Heat a few minutes longer and serve hot to 8.

The Entire Cabbage Family

A Rainbow of Cabbage

Of the various relatives of the cabbages, broccoli is my particular favorite. But I am very fond of the rest of the *Brassica* family of vegetables, which includes broccoli, Brussels sprouts, cauliflower, cabbage, kale and kohlrabi. At least one of these is readily available.

Cabbage has always been a staple of everyday cooking. Many of the recipes we use today have their origins in old methods, from many countries.

Broccoli is not mentioned in older English-language cookbooks. Indeed it did not begin to become familiar or popular with Americans (the Italians have loved it for centuries) until well after the 1930s.

Broccoli is a native of the Mediterranean and there are several varieties. The Italians like the purple variety; here we eat the green. There is a little-known white variety, as well.

For my cooking purposes, I prefer to separate the flowers and cut off the thick stalk, leaving the flowers attached to some of the tender stalk. The thick stalk can be peeled and used in Oriental cooking, in a pasta sauce, or marinated to use in salads or by itself. The flowers are used in the recipes in this section.

Cauliflower was cultivated in Europe by at least the 16th century. However, it is another vegetable that was not much mentioned in the early years of this country. The white variety of broccoli is so similar to cauliflower that most people do not differentiate between them.

One of the biggest thrills of my early gardening years was in monitoring the growth of my first planting of Brussels sprouts. The tiny heads grow at the base of the leaves. Until then I had only seen them in small, expensive packages at the market.

I knew even then that vegetables were at their best when picked small. I picked the Brussels sprouts tiny, and we loved them. When you buy them, as most of you must, pick out the smallest sprouts you can find.

Kale is similar to wild cabbage, and consists of a "head" of loose curly or frilled leaves.

Kohlrabi, sometimes called "cabbage turnip," is popular in eastern Europe. Unfortunately, people here do not seem to know what to do with it, except for letting it get too big. The small ones, at their best when no larger than 2 inches in diameter, are so crisp and delicious that they are best, to my taste, eaten raw. I have one friend who grates them and mixes the shredded bulb with sour cream and a little horseradish.

BROCCOLI

As with any of the heading members of the cabbage family, buy firm, solid heads. Avoid broccoli that is limp, or with flowers which are loose or fading. Try and choose heads that have stalks that are not too thick. Do not wash until you are ready to use. Store in a plastic bag in the refrigerator for use within 3 or 4 days.

Broccoli can also be stored by the same method used for spinach. Wash and trim the broccoli and cut into flowers with just a little of the stem attached. Place in a large glass jar—I generally use a gallon jar—and put the lid on. It will keep in the refrigerator for 2 weeks, and possibly a little longer. The broccoli will smell *very* strong when you remove the lid. There is nothing wrong with it, it is just that the odor of cole vegetables gets very strong when trapped.

Most broccoli plants have a branching habit so that when you harvest the central head the plant will continue to produce side shoots that greatly extend the harvest. This is unlike cauliflower which makes just one head and the plant is done. YIELD: Allow ½ pound per serving. Some recipes include the complete stems. I do not. I use the thick part of the stems for other purposes and just include an inch or so of the tender stems with the flowers. Available year round.

Broccoli and Artichoke Casserole

This casserole dish is one of the most popular cooked vegetable dishes that I prepare for catering. I find it quite simple since so much of it can be done ahead. The original recipe called for canned cream of mushroom soup, which I used until just recently. However, making the sauce from scratch *does* make a more flavorful dish.

SAUCE

4 tablespoons butter
6 tablespoons flour
1 cup chicken broth
⅓ cup heavy cream
⅓ cup Madeira wine

CASSEROLE INGREDIENTS

1 or 2 bunches (*depending on size*) broccoli, cut into small flowers with some of the tender stems
1 10-ounce package frozen artichoke hearts
½ cup or more sliced mushrooms
2 tablespoons butter
1 cup commercial sour cream
¾ cup grated Cheddar cheese

First make the Sauce. Melt the butter and stir in the flour, cooking it until it bubbles. Add the chicken broth and the heavy cream. Cook until sauce is thick and smooth. Stir in the wine and cook very gently for another 4 or 5 minutes. Remove from heat and set aside.

Cook the broccoli and artichoke hearts in boiled, salted water until just tender, about 8 minutes for the broccoli and a little less for the artichoke hearts. Drain and place in a greased, shallow baking dish. Sauté the mushrooms lightly in the butter and pour over the top of the vegetables. Combine the Sauce with the sour cream and blend well. Pour over the vegetables and then strew the cheese over all. Season to taste with salt and pepper, if desired. Bake in a 350°F (175°C) oven for 20 minutes, or until bubbly. Serves 4 to 6.

Broccoli and Mushroom Casserole

In the above recipe, use half the broccoli amount, omit the artichoke hearts, and use 1 to 1½ *pounds* of mushrooms, sliced and sautéed gently in butter until tender, but still firm. You can also use whole button mushrooms. Occasionally I omit the cheese and sprinkle the top with bread crumbs instead and bake until they are browned and the entire dish bubbly. Serves 4 to 6.

Note 1. You can use frozen broccoli if fresh is unavailable. Just use 2 10-ounce boxes and cook for no more than 5 minutes.

Note 2. The dish can be made ahead and reheated. Or you can prepare it ahead and bake it at the last minute. Not too far ahead though, or it might become watery, especially if you have used the larger amount of mushrooms.

Broccoli with Lemon Cream

This makes a nice luncheon dish. It also holds up well for buffet serving, making it a nice party dish.

**2 pounds broccoli flowers with some of the
   tender stems attached
6 large eggs**

**¾ cup half and half
¾ cup mayonnaise
2 or 3 tablespoons lemon juice
salt and pepper to taste
¼ cup each: grated Parmesan cheese and
   fine bread crumbs**

Cook the broccoli in boiling water for 8 to 10 minutes, or until tender but still bright green. The broccoli must not be overcooked. Arrange over the bottom of a shallow buttered baking dish. Beat the eggs with the half and half, mayonnaise and lemon juice. Add salt and pepper to taste. Bake in a 350°F (175°C) oven for about 25 minutes, or until nice and bubbly. Combine the cheese and crumbs and sprinkle over the casserole. Bake for another 10 minutes. Serves 4 to 6.

a broccoli side shoot

Broccoli with Lemon

A simple dish. Broccoli and lemon juice marry well.

**1½ to 2 pounds broccoli flowers with some
   of the tender stems attached
1 clove garlic, crushed
¼ cup olive oil
salt and pepper
2 tablespoons lemon juice**

Cook the broccoli in boiling water for 8 to 10 minutes, or until broccoli is tender/crisp. While it is cooking prepare the sauce. Cook the garlic in the oil until golden. Add salt and pepper and lemon juice. Heat. Reserve. When broccoli is done remove it to a serving dish. Heat the sauce until bubbly and pour over broccoli. Serves 4 to 6.

Broccoli Provençal

This is very French and very good.

**1 large bunch broccoli flowers with about 2
  inches of stem attached
¼ cup lemon juice
2 tablespoons olive oil
4 or 5 fresh tomatoes, cut into thickish slices
chopped fresh parsley and chives
½ teaspoon dried basil**

SAUCE

**3 egg yolks
pinch each of salt and red pepper
1 tablespoon white wine vinegar
1 tablespoon heavy cream
¼ cup frozen butter
1 tablespoon fresh herbs: use parsley,
  chives, chervil, marjoram and a little
  thyme**

Steam or cook broccoli until just tender, 8 to 10 minutes. Sprinkle with the lemon juice and keep warm.

Make the sauce: In a heatproof bowl, whisk egg yolks with a pinch of salt and red pepper and the vinegar and cream. Place bowl in a shallow pan half filled with hot water and place over low heat. Beat mixture until it thickens. Then whisk in the frozen butter, a little piece at a time, beating constantly. Then whisk in the herbs. Add a dash of lemon juice if desired. Cover bowl with plastic wrap or waxed paper and leave in the warm water until needed.

Heat the olive oil in a skillet and quickly sauté the tomato slices over high heat. Place tomato slices on a warm serving platter and sprinkle with more fresh herbs and the dried basil. Place broccoli on top and pour the sauce over all. Serve immediately. Serves 4 or 5.

Broccoli with Anchovies

This is Italian, a beautiful marriage of broccoli and anchovies with leeks, although I occasionally use small whole onions in place of the leeks. For a lovely surprise, prepare this dish and while it is cooking cook some pasta. When ready, toss the two together and serve with some grated Parmesan cheese.

**2 to 3 pounds broccoli flowers with some of
  the tender stems attached
⅓ cup olive oil
3 to 6 leeks (*depending on size*), washed and
  cut into lengths using the white part only
salt and pepper
1 or 2 2-ounce cans anchovy fillets, drained
  (*use the oil either in this dish, or add it
  to a salad dressing*) or 8 to 10 salted
  anchovies, rinsed and drained
½ cup dry white wine**

Use a fairly large skillet with a lid. Add the oil. Cover with the broccoli and then the leeks. Season with a little salt and quite a bit of freshly ground pepper. Top with the anchovies and then cover the pan. Cook over low heat for 25 minutes, or until broccoli and leeks are done. Add the wine, uncover and turn the heat to high to reduce the liquid. Serve as is or with pasta, as mentioned above. Serves 4 to 6.

Broccoli Pie

This is another of my favorite ways of preparing one of my favorite vegetables. People are always surprised, and then delighted by it.

**5 cups cut-up broccoli (*the flowers and some
  of the tender stems*)
salt if desired
freshly ground black pepper
¼ cup plus 2 teaspoons olive oil
⅓ cup bread crumbs
¼ cup grated Parmesan cheese**

Steam the broccoli or cook it in boiling water to cover until almost tender, about 8 minutes. Drain and turn into a bowl. Add seasonings and then add the ¼ cup olive oil, ¼ cup of the bread crumbs and 3 tablespoons of the cheese. Toss lightly to mix well.

You will need a 10 or 11-inch skillet with a lid. I use a skillet with a nonstick finish. Rub it with the remaining 2 teaspoons oil. Then sprinkle it with the remaining bread crumbs and cheese. Turn the broccoli into the skillet, adding it carefully so as to disturb the crumbs as little as possible. When all of the broccoli is added, tamp it down until it is fairly tightly packed.

Cover the skillet and place over low heat. Cook for 20 minutes. Check it every 5 minutes or so and either shake the pan to see if the "pie" will move, or loosen it with a spatula. At the end of 20 minutes, remove the lid and raise the heat to about medium. Continue to cook for another 4 or 5 minutes. Drain off any excess juices. Now place a serving plate over the skillet and invert. The pie should hold its shape nicely on the plate. Cut into wedges to serve to 6.

Sharon's Broccoli

This can be served as a salad or as a side dish. I like it either way.

**1 or 2 bunches broccoli, cut into small
 flowers with some of the tender stem—
 save the rest of the stems
1 or 2 cloves garlic
1 cup mayonnaise
2 tablespoons wine vinegar
freshly ground black pepper
4 hard-cooked eggs, quartered**

Cook the broccoli in boiling salted water, with the garlic, just until tender, about 8 minutes. Plunge into cold water to stop the cooking immediately. Remove garlic, crush it and add to the wine vinegar.

Peel the reserved stems and cut them into thin slices. Cook until tender and cool immediately. Arrange the broccoli flowers in a circle on a serving plate. Mound the cooked, cooled stalks in the center. Combine the mayonnaise with the wine vinegar and some freshly ground pepper and pour over the broccoli. Circle with hard-cooked egg quarters. Serve at room temperature. Serves 4 to 6.

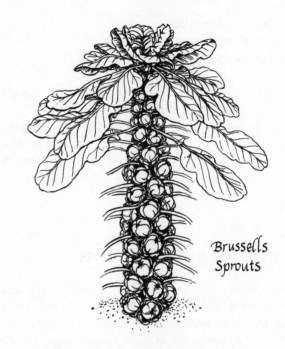

Brussells
Sprouts

BRUSSELS SPROUTS

Sprouts are generally picked far too large—a product perhaps of our conviction that bigger means better. The smaller the sprouts, as with carrots, green beans and so many other vegetables, the more delicate the flavor will be. Buy, or pick, only those that are small and compact, and a vivid green. Avoid large, loose heads. Store sprouts in a plastic bag in the refrigerator. Use within a week. Do not wash until ready to use.

You can use frozen sprouts in any recipe. To cook them, just add the frozen sprouts to boiling water, allow the water to return to the boil and remove the sprouts. Any further cooking will overcook them. If you are using frozen sprouts, use 1 or 2 10-ounce packages for each pound of sprouts called for.

My favorite method of preparing sprouts is to marinate them (*see page 135*) to serve as a side dish or cut in half and toss in a salad.

You can also halve sprouts lengthwise and add to a stir-fry.

YIELD: One pound of sprouts will serve 4.

Fried Brussels Sprouts

Even people who don't like sprouts will like these.

1 pound Brussels sprouts
1 large egg
1 tablespoon milk
¾ cup fine dry bread crumbs
oil for deep frying

Cook the sprouts in boiling water until barely tender/crisp, about 8 minutes. Drain well.

Beat the egg with the milk. Dip the sprouts in the milk mixture and then roll in the bread crumbs. Deep fry at 375°F (190°C) until golden brown. Drain and serve hot. Serves 4.

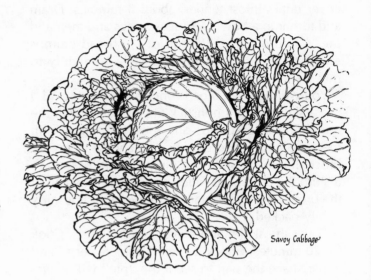

Savoy Cabbage

Meat-basted Brussels Sprouts

Try this when you are preparing a roast—chicken, beef or pork. Simply cook the sprouts in boiling water to cover until just tender/crisp. Remember that sprouts lose color as well as develop a strong flavor when overcooked. Drain and arrange around the roast during the last 4 or 5 minutes of cooking. Baste with the pan juices and serve surrounding the roast.

Italian Style Brussels Sprouts

The Italians prepare many vegetables this way.

1 pound Brussels sprouts
¼ cup olive oil
2 cloves garlic
2 tablespoons butter
2 tablespoons lemon juice
⅓ cup grated Parmesan cheese

Clean the sprouts and cook them in boiling water to cover for 6 to 8 minutes, or until tender/crisp. The smaller the sprout the less the cooking time. The larger sprouts may require up to 10 minutes. Drain and reserve.

Heat the oil in a skillet and sauté the garlic until golden. Remove garlic if desired. Add the sprouts to the hot oil and cook for just a minute or two. You really just want them to pick up the flavor of the oil and garlic. Remove sprouts to a serving dish. Add the butter and lemon juice to the skillet and heat until butter is melted. Pour over sprouts and sprinkle with the cheese. Serves 4.

Brussels Sprouts and Celery

2 cups Brussels sprouts
2 cups celery cut into thin slices
1½ cups Bechamel Sauce (*see page 122*)
½ cup bread crumbs
2 tablespoons grated Parmesan cheese

Clean the sprouts. Cook the sprouts and the celery in boiling water to cover until just tender/crisp, about 8 minutes. Large sprouts may require 10 minutes or longer, while tiny sprouts require less than 8 minutes. Drain and place in a buttered shallow baking dish. Pour the sauce over the vegetables and sprinkle with the crumbs and cheese. Dot with butter if desired. Bake in a 350°F (175°C) oven for about 10 minutes. Serve immediately to 4.

CABBAGE

When buying domestic green cabbage, buy firm, *green* solid heads, as the whiter heads are generally more mature and thus less tender. Store, unwashed and uncooked, in a plastic bag. Refrigerated, the firm-headed cabbages will keep for several weeks. When buying red cabbage, wrap and store it as for the green cabbage. It will also keep for several weeks. I have kept these cabbages in a seldom-opened refrigerator for well over a month with little or no loss of flavor. With its loose head and crinkly leaves, Savoy cabbage is more mellow in flavor than the other cabbages. It can be used in any recipe that calls for green cabbage, and makes a fine sauerkraut. Wrap tightly in plastic and keep refrigerated. Fresh, unblemished cabbage will keep over the winter in a cold cellar. The critical aspect is freshness at the time of storage. Savoy cabbage does not keep as well as the others, however.

Some books call bok choy Chinese cabbage. It is a member of the mustard family. And Napa (Chinese cabbage) is an entirely different cabbage. The confusion arises because Chinese *Mustard* Cabbage is another name for bok choy. Anyway, they are both good and we use them exclusively in the stir-fry recipes in that chapter. However, one friend tells me that she takes fresh Napa and tears it up to use as a salad green. Wrap and store as directed for the other cabbages. Use within several days.

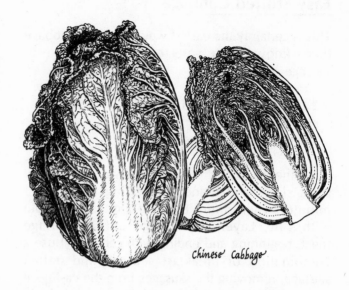

Chinese Cabbage

If you have the interest and patience you can brighten the platter further by judiciously filling the spaces between the quarters with flowerets of cooked cauliflower and broccoli, a sprinkling of Brussels sprouts, baby kohlrabi, and shredded raw cabbage in all colors, thus bringing the *Brassicas* together in something akin to a family reunion.

A Rainbow of Cabbages

I have prepared this dish several times over the years. I serve it with a pork roast and a hearty salad and solid bread. The visual appeal is enormous, and my guests have always enjoyed it tremendously. It is from *The Vegetable Cook Book,* by Cora, Rose and Bob Brown, published by Lippincott in 1939.

Boil white, green, savoy and purple (red) cabbages separately, using freshly cut heads and cooking rapidly. Cut into steaming quarters and lay on a platter in a rainbow of shades, leaving half of the purple cabbage in its natural cooked color and sprinkling the other half with lemon juice to turn it flaming crimson.

Danish Stuffed Red Cabbage

This is another recipe idea from the Browns' book.

I enjoy preparing this, as it looks lovely and surprises people when you cut it into wedges.

Use a large (4 to 5-pound) "red" or purple cabbage. Cut off top to use later as a cover, and scoop out most of the inside. Fill with the following blended mixture: 2 pounds hamburger, 3 slices bread soaked in hot water, 1 grated onion, pepper, salt, nutmeg and 2 eggs. Replace cover you cut from top, tie securely in cheesecloth and boil in slightly salted water for 2 hours. Serve with melted butter or gravy.

Note: *I generally use a combination of sausage and hamburger. The bread is from an honest loaf, which usually means homemade. I add garlic, plenty of it, to the onion and instead of soaking the bread in hot water, I soak it in wine.*

Easy Stuffed Cabbage

This is certainly the easiest way of stuffing cabbage that I know of. Be sure to use good, flavorful sausage meat.

    2 to 3-pound head of cabbage
    salt if desired
    1½ to 2 pounds sausage meat

Slice the head of cabbage crossways into fairly thick slices and blanch in boiling water for 3 minutes. Then drain. Butter a 2-quart casserole with a lid. Layer the cabbage and the sausage meat, beginning and ending with cabbage. I use a combination of breakfast sausage and Italian sausage, removing the sausages from the casings if they are in links. Salt if desired. Cover and bake in a 300°F (150°C) oven for 2 to 2½ hours. Serves 4 or 5.

Golden Fried Cabbage

    1 medium head cabbage
    ¼ cup butter or margarine
    1½ cups half and half
    salt and pepper to taste

Shred the cabbage. Heat the butter in a large skillet and brown the cabbage lightly. Add 1 cup half and half and salt and pepper if desired. Add remaining half and half only if necessary. Cover skillet and simmer for another 4 or 5 minutes. Serves 6.

Cabbage Cheese Casserole

This dish is especially nice for winter buffets, along with ham, cheese, a salad and a crusty bread.

    1 medium head cabbage
    1 teaspoon salt, if desired
    ¼ teaspoon black pepper
    ½ teaspoon paprika
    ¼ cup butter or margarine
    ¾ cup grated Cheddar cheese
    4 large eggs
    1 cup milk or half and half

Shred the cabbage and cook in a small amount of boiling water for 6 minutes. Drain well. Butter a casserole and in it layer half of the cabbage. Sprinkle with half of the salt, pepper, paprika, butter and cheese. Repeat, ending with cheese. Beat the eggs with the milk and pour over the top. Bake in a 350°F (175°C) oven for 35 minutes. Serves 4 to 6.

Cabbage and Sausage Casserole

    1 pound pork sausage
    1 medium head cabbage
    salt and pepper to taste
    ½ cup onion, minced
    ¾ cup bouillon

Brown the sausage. Coarsely chop the cabbage and place in a greased casserole. Sprinkle with a little salt and pepper and the minced onion. Pour the bouillon over all and top with the sausages. Cover and bake in a 350°F (175°C) oven for 1 hour. Serves 4 to 6.

Cabbage Custard

This is another simple dish, as cabbage recipes seem to be. I just serve it with some good sausages and some crusty bread and a red wine. The recipe can also be baked as a quiche. Just pour the custard into a 10 or 11-inch Quiche Shell (*see page 168*).

    ¾ cup butter
    6 cups shredded cabbage
    1 onion, minced
    5 large eggs
    2 cups half and half
    ¼ teaspoon nutmeg (*optional*)
    salt and pepper if desired

Melt butter in a heavy skillet. Add the cabbage and onion and sauté gently until golden and tender. Stir frequently.

Whisk the eggs with the half and half and the nutmeg. Add salt and pepper if desired.

Arrange the cabbage mixture in a shallow baking dish. Pour custard mixture over it. Set in a pan of hot water (a *bain-marie*) and bake in a 350°F (175°C) oven for 45 minutes, or until custard is set and golden. Serve hot to 4 to 6.

Stuffed Cabbage Rolls

This is a more traditional stuffed cabbage in that the leaves are separately stuffed and rolled. The use of gingersnaps makes this distinctly German. In India they frequently stuff the cabbage rolls with a mixture of potatoes and onions, seasoned with cumin and fennel. Remember that stuffed cabbage freezes very well. And since they are too much work to make for two or three people, I make several casseroles of the plump rolls at a time. Any dish of this type benefits from reheating. I prepare the stuffed rolls a day or even two days ahead of serving. The flavors mellow and blend together. Any of the cabbages can be used, but I especially like the Savoy cabbage for this dish.

1 large head cabbage
1 pound ground lean beef
1 pound pork sausage
1 cup cooked rice
1 large onion, minced
2 large eggs
3 large cloves garlic, minced
1 teaspoon salt if desired
freshly ground black pepper to taste
4 cups chopped fresh or canned tomatoes, drained
2 cups brown gravy
½ cup crushed gingersnaps
⅓ cup lemon juice
2 tablespoons brown sugar

Blanch the cabbage in boiling water until the leaves are pliable, about 5 minutes. If you are using a regular cabbage you might remove the core before blanching the head. The boiling water penetrates faster and the leaves become pliable faster. If you are using a Savoy cabbage, just blanch it for 5 minutes. In either case, drain the cabbage and cool it enough to handle. Remove the

good leaves. You should have about 16 of them. Reserve. Chop the remaining cabbage and set aside.

Combine the beef, sausage, rice, onion, eggs, garlic, salt and pepper. Mix well. Place about ¼ cup of the meat mixture in the center of each cabbage leaf. Fold the bottom of the leaf over the filling, then fold the sides over to the center. Roll. (Cabbage leaves are rolled in the same manner as are grape leaves. These are illustrated in the Leafy Vegetables chapter.) Secure with a toothpick.

Now take half of the reserved chopped cabbage and cover the bottom of a large pot with it. You can add a couple of cloves of garlic to this layer. Arrange the cabbage rolls over the chopped cabbage. Cover with the remaining chopped cabbage. Combine the tomatoes, gravy, gingersnaps, lemon juice, and brown sugar. Pour over cabbage rolls. Cover the pot and simmer gently for 2½ hours. Will serve 8, allowing 2 rolls per serving.

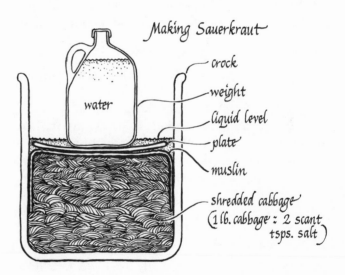

Making Sauerkraut
crock
weight
liquid level
plate
muslin
water
shredded cabbage
(1 lb. cabbage = 2 scant tsps. salt)

Sauerkraut

Made by one of the oldest methods of preservation, sauerkraut is a self-fermented, cured product which is really quite simple to make, provided you follow directions carefully and work with small batches. As always, the homemade product is superior to the store product and, since it isn't difficult to make, you might want to give it a try.

Pick firm, solid heads of cabbage, either green or Savoy, and wash and drain carefully. The cabbage must be completely dry when you work with it, so let it drain and dry overnight.

Shred the cabbage thinly. The shreds should be no thicker than a dime. It doesn't matter if they are long or short, as long as they are thin.

You will need a little less than 2 teaspoons of non-iodized salt for each pound of cabbage. And you will go by weight, not by volume.

Turn a pound at a time into a large bowl and add the salt. Alba, who taught me how to make sauerkraut, uses a 2-pronged fork to mix the two thoroughly. However, you can use clean hands. Too little salt, or too poor distribution of the salt, results in soft kraut. Too much salt can result in pink kraut. After distribution, turn the kraut into another bowl. Then begin again with one pound of cabbage and the salt, continuing until you have 3 pounds worth.

Then tamp it down into a crock. Place sterilized muslin over the cabbage and tamp it down all the way around. On top place a plate and on top of the plate place a weight. The liquid must cover the kraut so that no air touches it.

Every day for 7 to 9 days remove the weight, plate and cloth and resterilize the cloth. Place each back on the kraut. Remove the scum each day.

After 9 days check the kraut by tasting it. The scum will have diminished appreciably after the 7th day. When it has reached the peak of flavor that you like, turn the kraut into jars and steam-can for 15 minutes. At first I questioned this step. After all, sauerkraut has been made for probably a thousand years before canning. The answer however, makes sense. If the fermentation process is not stopped, it will continue until the kraut becomes overly sour, past the point where it appeals to modern tastes. Canning it stops it at the peak of flavor, and of course eliminates the need for continual checking. Alba cans the kraut, places the jars on a rack over boiling water, covers the pot and places a weight on the lid so that no steam can escape, and lets it steam for 15 minutes. Then the jars are removed. Any whose lids do not pop are checked. If the kraut is good, it is cooked and eaten. If there is any off odor or flavor, it is discarded. That's why it is best to work with small batches. If there is a mistake, or a batch goes bad, it isn't as heartbreaking as it is if you have done up gallons.

To Cook Sauerkraut

This is the way I always cook sauerkraut. I have seen people who professed not to like sauerkraut take second helpings when it was cooked this way.

Drain the sauerkraut and rinse it well in cold water. Drain again. Now heat it in a mixture of ½ chicken broth and ½ dry white wine with a few cloves of garlic. Heat just until hot, or let it simmer for 30 minutes or so. Either way the flavor is marvelous—not at all sour.

A friend of mine, who spent many years in Germany, drains the sauerkraut and braises it in meat drippings. He braises it until it is golden brown all over and it is really quite delicious.

Cabbage and Noodles

This dish is what, in my cooking classes, I call one of the "homely dishes." One of those stand-by dishes that we faithfully serve to family, and which they remember with nostalgia all their lives, but which we never think good enough to serve to friends or company. A winter stand-by, I always served it with sausages, hot rolls and milk. Now I serve it with corned beef or with roast pork, and it is served to company as well as to family. A Hungarian dish, it is a marvelous blend of flavors.

2 or 3-pound head of cabbage
1 large onion, sliced
¼ pound butter
½ pound egg noodles
salt and pepper

Core the cabbage and cut it into thin slices. In a large skillet, brown the onion in the butter until just transparent. Add the cabbage, cover, and cook over medium heat, stirring occasionally. While this is cooking, cook and drain the noodles. Add to the onion and cabbage with just a little salt and pepper. You can always add more if it is needed. Toss together lightly. Heat, covered, over low heat for 10 minutes. Serves 6.

Red Cabbage
(Blue Kraut)

This is traditionally German, although it is made in basically the same way throughout the eastern European countries. In Hungary they use bacon and, in place of the apple, they use firm winter pears. The liquid is red wine and a clove or two of garlic is added.

Adding the cabbage to the hot fat and then adding the vinegar sets the color and the finished dish will be a deep purple color, rather than the mushy pink cabbage that is so often served in restaurants. As with most dishes of this type, it will actually be better the second day.

1 2 to 3-pound head red cabbage, trimmed, cored and shredded
¼ cup butter, lard or bacon fat
1 tablespoon sugar
1 large apple, peeled, cored and chopped
1 onion, minced
¼ cup wine vinegar
salt to taste
1 to 2 cups beef stock
roux made with 2 tablespoons butter kneaded with 2 tablespoons flour

Prepare the cabbage as directed and set aside. Heat the fat in a heavy pot. Add the sugar and let it turn a golden brown. Add the apple and onion and sauté over low heat for 5 minutes.

Toss in the cabbage and stir until well coated with the fat. Now pour the vinegar over the cabbage and stir well. Cover the pot and sauté slowly for 10 minutes. The cabbage should be a bright purple. Now add a little salt and 1 cup of the stock. Cover and simmer slowly for 1 hour, or until cabbage is very tender. Add more liquid as needed. If there is too much liquid, thicken with some of the roux at the very end. Just add little balls of roux to the sauce and let thicken for 3 or 4 minutes. Serves 6.

Note. *I've given the Hungarian version in the foreword to the recipe. However, some Hungarian friends have told me that their mothers used to add a handful of raisins to the cabbage.*

Something that I occasionally do, and which my sons like enormously, is to add some fresh pork hocks at the beginning, and cook the whole thing for about 2 to 2½ hours. It makes a delicious meal.

Sweet and Sour Red Cabbage

This is a simpler way with red cabbage and is from a cook who was willing to share ideas with me.

1 head red cabbage
lemon juice
1 tablespoon butter, bacon or chicken fat
1½ to 2 teaspoons flour
1 cup dry red wine
salt and pepper to taste
½ cup beef broth
1 teaspoon brown sugar
some roux if necessary

Shred the cabbage and dip in boiling water for a minute. Then drain and sprinkle with a little lemon juice. Melt the butter in a skillet with a lid. Add the flour and stir and then add the wine, stirring. Cook and stir until smooth. Add the cabbage and season to taste with salt and pepper. Add beef broth and brown sugar. Cover and simmer for 45 minutes to an hour. Add more broth if necessary. When cabbage is tender and done, thicken with some of the roux if necessary. Serves 4 to 6.

CAULIFLOWER

Buy only those heads that are firm, white and compact. Avoid spreading heads. Cauliflower should be stored, unwashed, in a plastic bag in the refrigerator, and used within a week. In a very cold refrigerator I have kept cauliflower for up to three weeks. Good cauliflower is available year round.

For a nice flavor touch when cooking cauliflower, add a clove or two of garlic or a bay leaf to the cooking water. For added flavor cook in chicken broth.

Parboil or steam the flowerets and then fry them in garlic-flavored olive oil until lightly browned.

Add ½ cup small shrimp to a cup of Bechamel Sauce and pour over cooked cauliflower.

Or serve cooked flowerets with a sauce made by sautéing 2 tablespoons chopped green onion in 3 tablespoons olive oil for a minute and then adding ¼ cup soy sauce.

To cook frozen cauliflower, simply turn it into boiling water and then remove as soon as the water returns to the boil. Use frozen cauliflower in stir-fried dishes; add the cauliflower to the stir-fry *before* it has completely thawed.

YIELD: A medium-sized head (*about 1½ pounds*) will serve 4 or 5.

Note. *A number of the recipes for cauliflower and broccoli are interchangeable. A nice touch, and one with great visual appeal, is to cook some of each, separately, and combine them in a dish.*

Cauliflower au Gratin

I like to serve this dish with a simple rotisseried chicken that has been basted with a combination of butter, white wine and garlic, some tomato wedges, sprinkled with lime juice and salt, and of course, a nice crusty bread. For dessert, some fresh or frozen berries with cream. I much prefer the combination of cream with grated cheese to the standard cream sauce.

**1 medium head cauliflower, boiled or
 steamed until tender
1 cup heavy sweet cream
1 cup grated Cheddar cheese
salt if desired
freshly ground black pepper**

Separate the cooked cauliflower into flowerets and place in a shallow buttered baking dish. Combine the cream with the cheese and season as desired. Pour over the cauliflower and bake in a 350°F (175°C) oven until bubbly and lightly browned, about 20 minutes. Serves 4 or 5.

Cauliflower with Tomatoes

Zucchini and okra as well as cauliflower are prepared this way around the Mediterranean from Italy to Lebanon and Egypt. Occasionally the cauliflower is first dipped in batter and deep fried without any prior cooking, and then cooked in the tomato sauce. It is often served chilled as an appetizer or first course.

**1 medium head cauliflower, separated into
 flowerets
1 onion, minced
1 or 2 cloves garlic, minced
3 tablespoons olive oil
3 tablespoons parsley, minced
½ teaspoon basil
pinch of oregano
salt if desired
pepper to taste
2 or 3 medium to large ripe tomatoes, diced**

Prepare cauliflower as directed and reserve. Sauté the onion and garlic in the oil until golden. Stir in the herbs and stir around for a half minute. Then add remaining ingredients and simmer until cauliflower is tender and the sauce is reduced slightly, about 30 minutes. Serves 4 to 6.

Deep-fried Cauliflower

Cauliflower is a favorite vegetable for deep frying. All recipes call for first cooking the flowerets in boiling water until barely tender, then dipping in some kind of batter and frying. In the Middle East the cauliflower is dipped in beaten egg, rolled in bread crumbs and deep fried. The crisp flowerets are served with Tahini Sauce (*see page 6*). The Italians take the tender cauliflowerets and fry them in garlic-scented olive oil. I use the following method.

**1 medium head cauliflower, broken into
 flowerets
juice of 1 lemon
flour for dredging
Batter
oil for deep frying**

Blanch cauliflowerets in boiling water until barely tender. Drain and sprinkle with the lemon juice.

Dip in flour (mixed with a little garlic powder, if desired) and shake off any excess. Dip in either of the Batters (*see below*) and deep fry at 375°F (190°C) until golden brown. Drain on paper towels and serve with or without a sauce. Serves 4 to 6.

Note. You can substitute for the cauliflower any of the following: broccoli flowers; sliced zucchini; asparagus tips; peeled and sliced eggplant; sliced okra.

For onion rings, peel and slice large onions and separate into rings. Proceed as above, using Beer Batter.

Cauliflower

Egg White Batter

½ cup flour
1 tablespoon oil
¾ cup dry white wine
2 egg whites, stiffly beaten

Combine first three ingredients and fold in the stiffly beaten egg whites. This batter should be used immediately.

Beer Batter

12 ounces light beer
1 cup flour
1 teaspoon salt
1 tablespoon paprika

Combine ingredients and whisk until light and frothy. This batter can be used at once or it can stand for several hours. Whisk it from time to time to keep it mixed. The batter will keep for a week or more stored in a covered container in the refrigerator.

Note. Beer Batter is also very good for chicken, meat or fish. It is especially good for small fish such as small trout or smelt. Follow instructions for the vegetables, first dipping the fish in the flour, shaking off the excess and then dipping in the batter.

Cauliflower Mousse

Surprisingly easy to make, especially if you have a food processor in which to purée the vegetable. Vegetable mousses can be decorated very attractively, and baked in containers large or small for family or individual servings.

2 smallish heads cauliflower (*2 pounds*) cut
    into large pieces
water or chicken broth
pinch of red pepper
pinch of freshly grated nutmeg
1 cup medium Bechamel Sauce (*see page
    122*)
6 large eggs
salt if desired
pepper to taste
½ cup grated Parmesan cheese
butter to grease molds

Cook cauliflower in boiling water or chicken broth to cover until tender. Drain and add the red pepper and nutmeg and purée. Add the Bechamel Sauce to the purée. Beat the eggs and seasonings and cheese and add to the purée. Pour into a well-greased 6 to 8-cup mold. You can use a soufflé dish or a heavy, oven-proof serving bowl. If desired the mold can be decorated (*see illustration*) before adding the purée. When unmolded, the mousse makes a lovely presentation. Set the mold in a pan of hot water (*bain-marie*) and bake in a 350°F (175°C) oven for 45 to 55 minutes, or until the mousse begins to pull away from the edge of the mold or an inserted knife comes out clean.

Do not overcook as the mousse will become watery. The mousse can be served right from the dish, or it can be unmolded and garnished. I like to serve this without any sauce, but you can serve it with a lightly browned butter. Serves 8.

Note. Individual molds surrounding a roast, or served on individual serving plates, are especially festive and nice. You will need from 6 to 8 small molds, well-greased. The molds can be decorated before pouring the purée in if desired. Bake in a pan of hot water at 350°F (175°C) for 20 minutes. Test as for the larger mold.

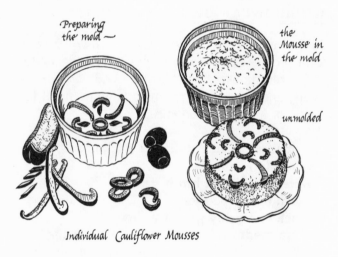

Individual Cauliflower Mousses

Marinated Cauliflower

A simple peasant dish. One of my favorite ways of preparing one of my favorite vegetables.

1 head cauliflower
2 cloves garlic, crushed
⅓ cup olive oil
juice of ½ lemon
salt and paprika

Cut cauliflower into flowerets. Cook in boiling water until stems are tender but still firm. Cool by plunging into ice water to stop the cooking im-

mediately. Drain and place in serving dish. Sauté the garlic in the olive oil until golden. Pour over the cauliflower and add the juice of ½ a lemon. Salt to taste and sprinkle with paprika. Let marinate for several hours before serving. Also good made a day ahead. Serves 4 to 6.

Debu's Cauliflower

This recipe is from a friend of mine who married into an Indian family. Debu and Catherine had two ceremonies, one an American wedding with white gown and reception, and the other a typically Indian wedding with the bride radiant in a red sari and wearing a clip-on ring in her nose.

Indian food is spicy, but it does not have to be hot. This recipe makes a dish that is typically Indian and thoroughly delicious. Colored a deep yellow by the turmeric, it is also lovely to look at. I serve it occasionally as a vegetable dish, but I most often serve it as a vegetable appetizer to be picked up with the fingers for easy munching.

1 2-pound head cauliflower
3 tablespoons butter
1 tablespoon oil
2 dried red chilis
1 teaspoon whole cumin seed
2 bay leaves
1 tablespoon whole peppercorns
a quarter-sized piece of fresh ginger, grated
½ teaspoon turmeric
½ teaspoon salt if desired

Prepare cauliflower by washing, trimming and cutting into flowerets. Set aside.

Heat the butter and oil (for a pungent dish use Indian mustard oil, otherwise, use any salad oil) and to it add the spices and the ginger. Fry gently. Do not allow the spices to burn; however, the chilis should pop. This will take about 1 minute. Then stir in the cauliflower and the turmeric and salt. Stir to coat the cauliflower all over with the color. Cook over medium-low heat and turn occasionally until the cauliflower is cooked through, about 25 to 30 minutes, depending on the size of the flowerets. Serves 6.

Cauliflower in Meat Sauce
(Kahnabahar Yemegi)

This is a Turkish recipe and simply means "cooked cauliflower."

2 medium onions, minced
2 cloves garlic, minced
¼ cup olive oil
¼ pound ground beef
1 small head cauliflower, trimmed and
  separated into flowerets
1 cup chopped tomato, either fresh or
  canned
freshly ground black pepper
salt if desired

Combine onions and garlic and sauté in the oil until transparent. Add meat and brown and break up. Then add the cauliflower, the tomato and seasonings.

Cook, covered, over medium heat until the cauliflower is tender. Turn into a serving dish. If there is too much liquid from the tomatoes, reduce it by boiling quickly and then pour the reduced sauce over the cauliflower. Serves 4.

Italian Fried Cauliflower and Broccoli

The following is a typical Italian method of frying the vegetables. It is especially delicious.

Prepare the cauliflower and broccoli by cleaning, trimming and cutting into flowerets. Cook in boiling, salted water until tender, but not at all mushy. This will take about 7 minutes for the broccoli and about 10 minutes for the cauliflower, depending on the size of the flowerets. Drain thoroughly and then dust with flour, dip in egg and then in a mixture of bread crumbs and grated Parmesan cheese. Fry in shallow oil in a skillet, turning until flowerets are browned all over. Serve mounded on a platter, garnished with lemon wedges.

KALE

There are two varieties of kale, a cold-hardy vegetable. One variety has bluish green leaves that are finely curled. The other variety has broad, thick, grayish green leaves that are frilled at the edges. A strongly flavored vegetable, it is best served with pork products like bacon and sausages. Store in a plastic bag in the refrigerator and use within 4 or 5 days. Any brown edges can be trimmed off. Peak season is from December through April.
YIELD: One pound will serve 2 or 3.

Steamed Kale

Kale is generally boiled or steamed until tender and then seasoned with butter or meat drippings and salt and pepper. The Italians steam it until tender, and then sauté garlic in olive oil until golden and add both the garlic and the oil to the kale. They then add bread crumbs and grated Parmesan cheese and let it cook for another minute before serving.

Braised Kale

Cut up a bunch of kale and measure it. You should have between 8 and 10 cups of chopped vegetable. Heat 3 or 4 tablespoons meat drippings from a roast, or bacon or sausage fat. Stir in the chopped kale and add ¼ to ⅓ cup stock, and salt and pepper to taste. Simmer, covered, until tender, about 15 to 20 minutes. Serves 6.

KOHLRABI

Buy small bulbs. Avoid if large or blemished. The young bulbs do not need peeling but larger ones do. Kohlrabi keeps, refrigerated, for a week.
YIELD: Allow 1 medium or 2 small bulbs per serving.

Kohlrabi Hints

Young kohlrabi is best eaten raw. Slice it, or cut in thin strips and serve as part of an hors d'oeuvre tray with mayonnaise or another dip.

Shred some and add to the Shredded Beet Salad in the Salads chapter.

Cut into julienne strips and marinate in Basic Vinaigrette. Add some thinly sliced radishes and you have a nice salad to serve in lettuce cups.

Kohlrabi can be diced and cooked in boiling water until tender, about 10 to 15 minutes, depending on the age of the bulbs. Add the leaves the last 3 minutes. Drain and dress with several tablespoons of lightly browned butter. Add pepper and salt if desired.

In Europe they use slightly larger bulbs and stuff them.

Stuffed Kohlrabi
(*Tolcott Kalarabe*)

This is the way kohlrabi is prepared in eastern Europe. It is similar to the Middle Eastern method in that the insides of the vegetable to be stuffed are chopped and used to provide moisture and prevent the vegetable itself from burning.

**6 medium kohlrabies
⅓ cup finely chopped kohlrabi leaves**

**1 or 2 cloves garlic
1 slice firm bread soaked in milk
⅓ to ½ cup ground beef
⅓ cup ground sausage
1 large egg
pepper
salt if desired
2 green onions, chopped
½ cup chicken broth
1 tablespoon flour**

Cut a lid off of the top of each kohlrabi and scoop out the insides. Combine with the chopped kohlrabi leaves and place in the bottom of a heavy pot; add the garlic. Combine the bread with the meats, egg, pepper, salt if used, and chopped onions. Use this to stuff the kohlrabies. Arrange the filled bulbs over the filling in the pot. Any leftover meat mixture can be made into small meatballs and added to the pot. Add the chicken broth if you think it needs more liquid. Cover the pot and cook over low heat until tender. This will take about 25 to 30 minutes depending on the size of the bulbs. When tender, remove kohlrabies to an ovenproof serving dish and place in a warm oven. Remove some of the liquid from the pot and to it add a tablespoon of flour. Return to the pot and simmer for 5 minutes to thicken. Some good cooks add ⅓ cup sour cream. Pour around bulbs and serve. Serves 6.

Kohlrabi

Leafy Vegetables

Dolmas

Our attitudes towards greens—and leafy vegetables in particular—have changed enormously within the past generation. Meat and potatoes was the standard 30 years ago, and earlier cookbooks paid minimal attention to vegetables and salads.

Many of the vegetables we now take for granted and have no difficulty finding at the local supermarkets were barely known except by various ethnic groups. Until quite recently, bok choy was known as "mustard cabbage," or "mustard spinach" and called "an entirely new vegetable of Japanese origin." Swiss chard was known by the name "seakale beet," a strange name—but certainly no stranger than the name "Swiss" chard. That particular vegetable definitely did not originate in Switzerland.

Spinach was considered an accursed vegetable and eaten only because it was "good" for us. Then spinach came upon really hard times, and was treated like a poor relative in the leafy vegetable family due to its oxalic acid content and a poor press. But times continue to change, and now we eat spinach because we like it and don't seem to care at all about oxalic acid's interference with the absorption of calcium. After all, spinach contains good roughage, and spinach salads are, rightfully, very popular.

We eat a lot of leafy greens raw, which is the best way to enjoy the various textures and flavors. And I can't remember the last time I heard anyone call greens "rabbit food."

However, we seem determined to change some of the flavors that we profess to love. Belgian endive is the most frequent, and elegant, victim. Most of my cookbooks instruct me that before I may braise this lovely vegetable, I must first cook it in boiling water to cover for 7 or 8 minutes. To remove the "bitter" taste. Yet it seems to me that that delicate bitterness is exactly what we say we love about the oval, whitish heads. Why else do we eat endive raw most of the time? I never boil it first.

Our love of fresh greens has brought about important—and welcome—changes in cooking methods also. Undoubtedly increased knowledge of nutrition has had a great deal to do with both changes in selection and preparation. In the old days fresh greens were cooked for hours, and even salads were served preferably "wilted." In the South salad greens were frequently dressed several hours ahead and chilled so as to develop exactly that almost soggy texture and flavor that we now strive to avoid.

We know that tastes in food change. Not so long ago, we wouldn't eat vegetables unless they were downright mushy. We then "progressed" to the point where we were undercooking them to such a degree that they bit back when we bit into them. Now, however, I think that we have reached the point where we want them bright and full of color, but cooked. Tender/crisp is the term.

Of all foods, greens especially should not be overcooked as overcooking leaches out the vitamins and minerals. Many greens are valuable sources of these important nutrients. The most significant ones are as follows: beet tops; broccoli leaves; Chinese cabbage; kale; mustard greens; dark leafed lettuce; wild greens; New Zealand spinach; parsley; radish tops; Swiss chard; sorrel; turnip tops; watercress.

As you can see, I have listed a few items that most of us probably never think of using. Broccoli leaves for example, or radish tops. Always cook the broccoli leaves with the flowers and stems. As for radish tops, the radishes available in stores generally have leaves too large, bruised, and bitter to be used in the kitchen. But the tops of the radishes grown in your garden should be picked, washed and tossed into a salad or into a dish of greens to be cooked.

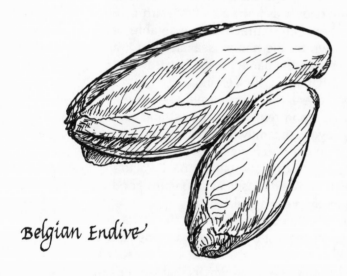

Belgian Endive

BELGIAN ENDIVE

What we popularly call Belgian endive is produced by a method of forcing, and is not a particular variety of endive. Any of the chicories can be cultivated with this forcing, which results in the slightly bitter, crisp, elegant vegetable so loved by discriminating cooks.

While other chicories are available year round, Belgian endive is available only from October through May. Most of our Belgian endive is still imported from Belgium, although it is the result of a process that can be mastered by any dedicated gardener.

Buy tight, oval heads free of blemishes. Avoid heads that are soft or wilted. Store in plastic bags in the coldest part of the refrigerator. Use within a week although under optimum conditions endive can be kept longer. I had occasion recently to buy a 10-pound box of them. I used most through the holidays, but there were still about a dozen unused endive that I kept in the box in which they were shipped, still wrapped in the paper they came in. The box was in the coldest part of a second refrigerator that was seldom opened. After 4 weeks those oval, whitish heads were just as crisp and tight as when I first bought them.

YIELD: There will be from 4 to 12 endives per pound. Generally allow 1 medium size endive per serving.

Belgian Endive with Prosciutto

Belgian Endive with Prosciutto

I serve this marvelous combination with a crusty hot bread and a nice soft cheese, a salad and nice white wine for luncheons. You can use any thinly sliced ham, but prosciutto is better.

6 Belgian endives, trimmed
¼ pound butter
6 ⅛-inch thick slices prosciutto
salt and pepper to taste
6 hard-cooked eggs
½ cup chopped parsley

Melt the butter in a skillet and sauté the endives in the butter very gently until the endives are *very* lightly colored and tender, about 25 minutes. This depends on the size of the endives. You can cover the skillet and let them stew gently in the butter. Shake the pan or turn endives frequently. They should be tender but not mushy. Remove from skillet and cool. Reserve pan liquids.

Brush a shallow casserole with butter. Wrap each endive in a piece of prosciutto and lay in the casserole. Pour the pan liquids over the endives. Salt and pepper lightly. Chop the hard-cooked eggs, add the chopped parsley, and strew this mixture over the endives. Bake at 400°F (205°C) for 10 minutes. Serve hot to 6.

Belgian Endive Tips and Ideas

Belgian endive is at its sophisticated best if the heads are simply split or quartered lengthwise and served with the open sides up. Dress with a lovely lemon vinaigrette. Eat with the fingers, if desired.

Belgian endive is perfect in salads, especially when combined with beets (*see page 138*). Don't forget to use the leaves as part of a vegetable tray with dips.

Braised Belgian Endive

I prefer this method instead of boiling and then braising.

6 to 12 Belgian endives
¼ cup butter
salt if desired
freshly ground black pepper
½ cup chicken broth or water

Trim off a quarter inch from the bottom of each endive. Remove any loose leaves. Melt the butter and cook the endive in the melted butter over low heat until just lightly browned on each side. Keep turning, but be careful so that the endives do not break up. Add salt and pepper if desired. Add the chicken broth or water and cover the pot with a lid. Let the endives stew gently in the butter and liquid until tender, about 25 to 30 minutes, depending on the size. They should be tender, but not mushy. Serves 6.

BOK CHOY

A member of the mustard family, bok choy is sometimes, and confusingly, called Chinese cabbage, which it is not. It is a Chinese mustard cabbage. It looks somewhat like a white and green Swiss chard. Buy crisp, fresh-looking heads and avoid limp, yellowing vegetables. Wrap in plastic wrap and keep, refrigerated, no longer than 4 or 5 days. Use in stir-frys, soups and stews. The leaves can be cooked as you would any other green. The stalks should be cut on the diagonal and cooked separately as they require longer cooking. I make a lovely, light soup with mushrooms, chicken slices and broth and bok choy stems. The heart of the vegetable can be used in salads.
YIELD: One pound will serve 2.

Bok Choy

GRAPE LEAVES

Used in a few Middle Eastern dishes, grape leaves have a delicacy of flavor that, to my mind at least, is far superior to the cabbage leaves that are usually used for stuffing. The rice-filled leaves (recipe follows) are usually used as an appetizer or first course. The meat-filled leaves are usually used as a main dish.

Unfortunately, the only grape leaves that are available to most Americans are packed in brine in glass jars. Fresh ones are much better. If you must use the brine-packed leaves, drain off the brine and rinse the leaves in cold water. If you have access to fresh grape leaves, clean them well and dip them in boiling water to blanch them and prepare them for use. The leaves freeze very well, a good point to keep in mind if you can get fresh ones.

When I am ready to freeze my year's supply of grape leaves, I pick them by the hundreds, the smaller ones for their greater delicacy of flavor and some larger ones to line the pot. I immediately place them in a sink full of cold water. This cleans and keeps them if I cannot get to them immediately. Any leaves left to sit at room temperature will dry out and be useless.

When ready to freeze, I arrange them in stacks of 25 each. That works well for me; you can freeze as many in a package as you like. I wrap each stack in plastic wrap and place several stacks in each freezer bag. Sometimes I roll the stacks and sometimes I leave them flat. I place them in the freezer and that's all there is to it.

When I want to use them, I simply remove however many stacks of grape leaves I think I will need. Each stack is unwrapped and placed in a pot of boiling water. This thaws the leaves and blanches them at the same time. I remove the leaves one by one and drain them.

Cold Stuffed Grape Leaves
(Dolmas)

These make an exquisite appetizer or a superb first course. They can also be served like an Italian antipasto, with slices of pimiento, twists of lemon and some pickled peppers. When you wish to serve the grape leaves, make them a day or even several days ahead. They will keep very well in plastic storage containers in the refrigerator. When ready to use, simply arrange as desired and let them sit at room temperature for an hour or 2 before serving.

30 to 36 grape leaves, drained and rinsed if bottled, blanched if fresh (*see above*)
¾ cup long-grain white rice
dry white wine or water
2 or 3 tomatoes, seeded and chopped
½ to ¾ cup finely chopped green onions, tops included
½ cup chopped parsley
2 tablespoons crushed dried mint or ¼ cup fresh mint
¼ teaspoon cinnamon
¼ teaspoon allspice
salt and pepper to taste
2 tomatoes, sliced
3 or 4 large cloves garlic
½ cup olive oil
½ cup fresh lemon juice
chicken broth or water

Prepare grape leaves as directed and set aside.

Place rice in a small pot and barely cover with the wine or water. Bring to a boil. Stir until liquid is absorbed, just a few minutes. You are blanching the rice, not cooking it. Set the rice aside. Combine the chopped tomatoes, green onions, parsley, mint, cinnamon and allspice. Add the rice and mix. Add salt and pepper to taste.

Take each grape leaf and cut off the stem end. Place a spoonful of the stuffing on the leaf. Fold the bottom over the filling, then the sides to the center and roll (see *illustration*). Line a pot with the tomato slices and any large or unusable grape leaves. Arrange the filled grape leaves over this, slipping in a clove of garlic every now and then.

Combine the olive oil with the lemon juice and pour over the grape leaves. Pour in chicken broth or water to cover the leaves. Then place a small plate over the leaves to hold them under the liquid. Any grape leaves that cook *above* the liquid will be a dark, dry, green. Place a cover over the pot and simmer until done, about 1½ to 2 hours. Add boiling chicken broth or water as needed. Cook the leaves gently so that they do not come apart. The plate helps in keeping the leaves together also. Cool in the pan and serve at room temperature. Decorate with wedges or slices of lemon.

Note. *When I was a child we used to fight over the grape leaves, tomatoes and garlic that were left in the pan. I still love them.*

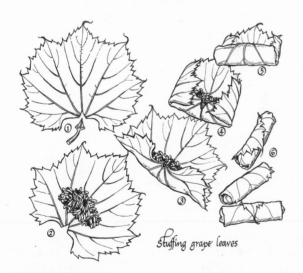

Stuffing grape leaves

Arabic Spices

My grandmother always made her own seasoning mixtures. For all Middle Eastern dishes which traditionally call for cinnamon or allspice she used the following: four teaspoons cinnamon combined with 2 teaspoons each of black pepper and white pepper and 1 teaspoon each of nutmeg, cloves and cardamom. If a recipe specified ¼ teaspoon each of cinnamon and allspice, she used ½ to ¾ teaspoon of Arabic Spices.

Swiss Chard

GREENS

These include spinach, chard, turnip, beet or mustard greens and sorrel. The term also includes collards and kale, which are discussed in The Entire Cabbage Family chapter. Although these greens are easily grown in the family garden and are best when picked while still quite small, most of us must buy them. When buying, choose leaves that are crisp and free of blemishes. Avoid yellowing leaves, or leaves that are limp. Wash greens in tepid water and spin dry in the salad spinner. Large chard leaves can be drained in a colander.

To store, trim washed and dried greens of their stems and some of the spine and place in a glass jar with a tight-fitting lid. Store in the coldest part of the refrigerator and use within 7 to 10 days. Roll large chard leaves, 6 or 7 to a roll, and store the same way, in a tightly sealed jar.

YIELD: A pound of any of the greens will generally serve 2.

Tips and Ideas on Using Greens

Young beet greens are a delicacy and make an excellent addition to the salad bowl, as does sorrel.

The leaves of any of the greens are good chopped and added to a hearty vegetable soup.

Use chard in place of cabbage leaves for stuffing. Trim off the stems and blanch the leaves until tender enough to roll.

To my mind sorrel is best in the salad bowl. It is also good mixed with other greens and cooked.

Spring Greens

Perhaps we enjoy most the memories of those dishes that can only be served occasionally. The Stuffed Baby Eggplant (*see page 83*) that I can prepare maybe two or three times during the summer; the turkey pie that is served the days after Thanksgiving and Christmas and at no other time; and these greens which grace the table just a few times in the spring.

Use any mixture of any of the following: beet or turnip greens; chard; spinach; sorrel; mustard greens or dandelion leaves. In the South they may include poke.

6 cups fresh greens (*see above*)
2 tablespoons butter, bacon fat or chicken fat
1 medium onion, minced
2 tablespoons lemon juice or vinegar
1 tablespoon brown sugar

Prepare leaves by cleaning and trimming. Cook in just the water that clings to the leaves, only until tender. Drain.

Melt the fat and in it sauté the onion until limp. Add the greens to the onion and stir together. Mix the lemon juice and sugar and pour over the greens. Stir together. Heat and serve to 3 or 4.

Southern Greens

Although in recent years we have become enamored of the quick cooking method of preparing vegetables, the long, slow cooking of these traditional greens lends them a particular flavor. Turnip greens are extremely delicious cooked this way, and you can mix in some kale, mustard greens, collards, poke or chard.

3 to 4 pounds mixed greens (*see above*)
¼ pound fatty ham
1 or 2 pods of red pepper
salt to taste if desired
freshly ground black pepper
1 tablespoon vinegar

Clean and trim greens. Place the meat in a large pot and add water to cover. Bring water to a boil. Add the greens and pepper pods and bring to the boil again. Reduce heat to low and simmer until greens are tender. Actually the greens will be tender before the flavor has developed. Simmer for 1½ to 2 hours. Then season to taste and add the vinegar. Serve the greens on a dish and slice the ham over it. Serves 4 to 6.

Southern Mustard Greens

Serve this with corn bread to dip into the "pot likker."

1 pound mustard greens
1 or 2 small fresh ham hocks
1 pound young turnip greens
green onions, minced

Combine mustard greens and ham hocks in a pot. Add water to cover. Cook until the meat is tender, 1 to 2 hours. When ready, shortly before serving, take the turnip greens and boil for 7 to 10 minutes or steam them (15 to 20 minutes) until barely tender. Add to the meat and mustard greens. Simmer a few minutes. Remove greens to a serving dish and cut the meat up over them. Sprinkle with minced green onions. Serves 4.

SPINACH

A cool weather vegetable, spinach is one of the easier plants to grow yourself. Most of the spinach we use, however, is bought. Choose leaves that are fresh and crisp. It doesn't matter if they are crinkled or smooth. Avoid wilted or yellowing leaves, or those that are straggly. Spinach is available all year. Wash spinach in cool water and pick over before using. Loose spinach may need 2 or 3 washings to remove all the sand. Snip off the stems and part of the spine.

Most books will tell you that fresh spinach should be used within 2 or 3 days. However, a friend taught me to keep it this way, and it works:

Wash and stem the spinach. Whirl it fairly dry in a salad spinner. Put the leaves in a glass jar. Put the lid on and store in the refrigerator. It will keep, beautifully, for 2 to 3 weeks. I have tried it with spinach just picked from the garden, and with store-bought spinach, and it works with either.

Spinach needs a minimal amount of cooking, in a minimal amount of liquid. Just use whatever moisture remains on the leaves after washing. Place in a pot with a lid and cook for 2 to 5 minutes, or until wilted and tender. If I am cooking the spinach with onions for example, I just add the spinach to the almost cooked onions. The steam from what is already cooking is enough moisture. Do not overcook.

YIELD: One pound of spinach will serve 2.

To Use Frozen Spinach

Spinach freezes quite well, although there is a definite difference in taste between the frozen and the fresh. However, any of the spinach recipes can be made with frozen spinach. Use a 10-ounce package of frozen chopped or whole leaf spinach for each pound of fresh. Swiss chard can be substituted for all or part of the spinach in any spinach recipe, also.

Garlicky Spinach

This is just about my favorite way of preparing spinach. The garlic does *not* dominate the dish. I served this once to a group of women and several of them asked for the recipe. When I gave them the recipe, one said, "But we don't like garlic; can I leave it out?"

3 pounds fresh spinach, well cleaned
2 medium white onions, minced
1 large *head* garlic, minced
¼ pound butter
dash of red pepper
¾ pound grated cheese (*I use a mixture of mozzarella and Cheddar cheese*)

Tear the spinach leaves into bite-sized pieces and set aside. Sauté the onions and garlic in the butter until limp. Add the spinach and red pepper and sauté for 4 or 5 minutes. Remove from heat and stir in the cheese. Pour into a well-greased shallow baking dish. Cover the top with some bread crumbs if desired. Bake in a 350°F (175°C) oven for 20 to 25 minutes. Serve to 6.

Note. *I frequently add some diced crisply fried bacon to the bread crumbs.*

Portuguese Spinach

The unusual addition of sardines makes this special indeed, and filling enough to be served as a luncheon dish.

2 to 3 pounds spinach, washed thoroughly and steamed until just tender
1 tin sardines in olive oil
½ cup bread crumbs
1 hard-cooked egg, chopped
juice of ½ lemon
3 tablespoons minced green onions
salt if desired
freshly ground black pepper to taste
butter

Cut steamed spinach leaves into smallish pieces, drain well, and place in a bowl. Drain and chop the sardines. Combine all ingredients except the butter with the spinach. Place in a buttered, shallow baking dish and dot with small pieces of butter. Bake in a 350°F (175°C) oven for 15 to 20 minutes. Serves 4 to 6.

Lebanese Spinach

The use of lemon juice adds a lovely, light flavor to this dish.

2 to 3 pounds spinach, washed thoroughly and torn into pieces
2 or 3 medium onions, minced
⅓ cup olive oil
juice of ½ lemon

Prepare spinach and set aside. Sauté onions in the oil until golden and soft. Add spinach and simmer for 10 minutes. Sprinkle with lemon juice. Serves 4 to 6.

Alba's Chard and Cheese Pie

This is very good, and just a little different.

BISCUIT SHELL

3 large eggs
½ cup butter, melted
¼ cup powdered skim milk
2 cups stirred and measured flour
1 teaspoon baking powder
1 teaspoon salt
½ teaspoon nutmeg

FILLING

1½ cups cooked chopped Swiss chard
½ to ⅔ cup juices drained from the chard
⅔ cup cottage cheese
2 large eggs, beaten
1 cup shredded mozzarella or Monterey Jack cheese
⅔ cup grated Parmesan cheese
1 medium onion, sliced and sautéed in 2 tablespoons butter
1 cup pitted ripe olives, sliced
½ teaspoon nutmeg
watercress and sliced ripe olives for garnish

In a large bowl, beat the eggs and add the melted butter. Stir together the powdered milk, flour, baking powder, salt and nutmeg. Add to the egg mixture. Mix very briefly to form a biscuit dough, mixing *just* until ingredients hold together. Too much mixing results in a tough dough. Press into a buttered pie tin, or an 11 by 7 by 1½-inch baking dish. Press the dough well up onto the sides. Set aside.

Prepare the chard as directed, draining well and reserving the juices. Combine the juices with the cottage cheese in a blender or food processor and purée. You should have about 1⅓ cups of purée. Combine with chard and remaining ingredients

and pour into the Biscuit Shell. Bake in a 350°F (175°C) oven for 30 minutes, or until custard is set. Garnish with watercress and sliced, pitted ripe olives.

Note. *You can substitute a 10-ounce package of frozen chopped spinach for the chard.*

Spinach

American Spinach Pie

2 9-inch prebaked Quiche Shells (*see page 168*)
3 10-ounce packages frozen chopped spinach
⅓ cup minced green onion
¼ cup butter
1 teaspoon freshly ground black pepper
pinch nutmeg
1 teaspoon salt if desired
6 large eggs
3 cups cottage cheese
1 cup sharp Cheddar cheese, grated
2 tablespoons butter in small pieces

Cook spinach as directed and squeeze completely dry. Sauté the onion in the butter. Add spinach and stir to evaporate any remaining water. Stir in seasonings. Beat together the eggs and cottage cheese. Add the spinach mixture to the egg mixture and combine thoroughly. Pour into Quiche Shells. Sprinkle the tops with the grated cheese and pieces of butter. Bake in a 350°F (175°C) oven for 30 minutes, or until custard is set.

Note. *This freezes well. Serve hot or cold. It, along with any of the other Spinach Pies, can be cut into small pieces to be served as an hors d'oeuvre, or in larger pieces to be served as a side dish.*

Italian Spinach Pie

There seem to be innumerable recipes for Spinach Pie, most of them simple variations on a basic theme. The Italians combine spinach, eggs, grated Parmesan and ricotta and bake it in a pie shell. The Greeks take the spinach and to it they add onions, a grated hard cheese such as Kaseri and a softer cheese such as feta, and of course plenty of eggs and parsley. They bake this between buttered layers of phyllo pastry.

1 8 or 9-inch prebaked Quiche Shell (*see page 168*)
2 pounds spinach, cleaned, torn into pieces and steamed until tender
½ cup grated Parmesan cheese
1½ to 2 pounds ricotta cheese
3 large eggs
½ teaspoon salt if desired
⅛ teaspoon freshly ground black pepper

Combine spinach with cheeses, eggs and seasonings. Mix well. Turn into Quiche Shell and bake in a 350°F (175°C) oven for 30 minutes, or until set in the center. Serve hot or cold. Serves 4 to 6 as a side dish.

Note. *Diced ham, prosciutto or crumbled cooked sausage meat can be added to the spinach. This pie freezes well.*

PHYLLO PASTRY

Phyllo pastry is a Middle Eastern pastry that is as versatile as puff pastry. Brand names are also spelled Filo, and Fillo, but the Greek spelling, phyllo, which means leaf, is the correct one. Most recipes which call for using phyllo use multiple layers to form a sturdy crust. When baked, these buttered layers of pastry become very flaky. If you live in a large city, you probably have access to fresh phyllo. If you live in a smaller community you will have to buy it frozen.

Frozen phyllo will keep for several months. If the edges become dry and flaky, they can be cut off

and discarded. It is best to thaw the phyllo in the refrigerator overnight. The important thing is to keep the pastry from drying out. Once it is thawed and you are ready to use it, unroll the pastry sheets carefully on a flat surface. Cover them with waxed paper, and over that place a damp towel. A damp towel touching the pastry will make it pasty.

Peel each sheet off carefully, keeping the unused ones covered. Work quickly. Brush each sheet with melted butter and then fit into the pan it will be baked in, or fill and fold according to the instructions in individual recipes.

If the sheets of pastry are too large for the pan you are using, just fold the edges in as best you can, and brush with melted butter to keep the sheets from drying out.

Greek Spinach Pie
(Spanakopita)

This is one of my personal all-time favorites, in part because so much can be done with the basic recipe. Traditionally this is made with spinach. However, I have used broccoli as well as Swiss chard with great success. The appetizer version is extremely popular as well as practical because the little triangles can be made when convenient and frozen, to be baked just before serving. The pies freeze well also, and I always keep several of the Beefy Spinach Pies in the freezer to be popped in the oven when unexpected company arrives.

2 10-ounce packages frozen chopped spinach or 2 or 3 pounds fresh spinach
1 large onion, minced
1 bunch green onions, chopped
½ cup parsley, minced
1 pound butter
½ cup grated Parmesan cheese
1 to 1½ cups grated Swiss cheese or crumbled feta cheese
4 to 6 large eggs
salt if desired
freshly ground black pepper
1 pound phyllo pastry

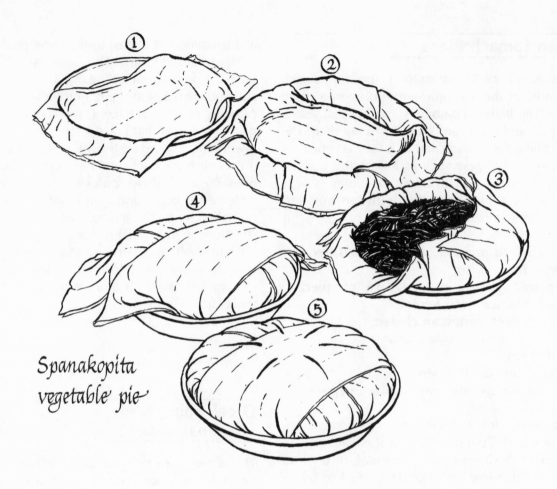

Spanakopita
vegetable pie

Thaw and drain the frozen spinach. If you are using fresh, chop the spinach but do not cook.

Sauté the onion and green onions in 4 tablespoons of the butter. When tender add the parsley and spinach. Cook and stir for 5 minutes. Drain off any excess liquid and cool mixture.

Chop finely, using quick on/off motions in your food processor, or a knife. Mixture should be chopped rather than puréed. Add the cheeses and the eggs and season to taste with salt, if desired, and pepper. At this point you can do a number of things with the filling. See the following variations.

Spinach Pie

This amount of filling will make 1 or 2 pies depending on the size. You will need 6 to 8 sheets of phyllo for each pie. Butter the pie tin liberally. Take a sheet of phyllo and fold it in half (see illustration) and place over the pie tin with the edges hanging over. Butter the phyllo. Take

another sheet and fold in half and place over the first. Continue as illustrated, buttering each folded sheet. You will have 3 or 4 sheets on the bottom, making 6 or 8 layers. Pour the filling into the pan and smooth it. Take the overhanging pieces of phyllo and fold them over the top. Butter lightly. Now take the remaining pieces of phyllo and arrange them over the top exactly as you did on the bottom, buttering each folded sheet. Use your fingers and tuck the overhanging pieces of phyllo around the sides, between the filling and the pie tin. Brush the top with melted butter and score it lightly into as many pieces of pie as you will be cutting. Bake in a 350°F to 375°F (175°C to 190°C) oven for about 30 minutes, or until top is a golden brown. Remove and cool for 5 minutes before cutting.

Note. To freeze, place unbaked pie in freezer until frozen solid. Wrap carefully. Return to freezer. When ready to use simply unwrap and pop the frozen pie into the oven. Turn the temperature

*control to 350°F (175°C) and bake for an hour. It
will take this long to thaw and heat the pie.
Remove when golden brown and serve as directed
above.*

Spinach Appetizers

Follow the preceding directions for using phyllo
pastry. Melt the remaining butter. Take 2 sheets of
phyllo and place on a flat surface. Brush quickly
with melted butter. Do not saturate, but brush the
entire surface. Remember to cover the unused
phyllo. Cut the phyllo into 6 or 8 strips. Cut with
the knife parallel to the surface of the phyllo so that
it doesn't gather on you.

Place a spoonful of filling at the bottom of each
strip (*see illustration*) and fold as illustrated. When
folded, place the triangles on a buttered baking
sheet and brush with melted butter. Continue until
all is used. Bake these in a 400°F (205°C) oven for
10 to 12 minutes, or until golden brown. Do not
overbake. Let set for 5 minutes and then serve hot.

Note. *To freeze, place on baking sheets close
together and brush with melted butter. Freeze unbaked. When frozen the little pies can be removed
from the baking sheets and stacked in plastic
storage containers. Keep frozen until used. I place
them in the oven when still frozen and bake as
directed above until golden brown.*

Spanakopita appetizers

Beefy Spinach Pies

For each 10-inch pie cook the following: 1 pound
ground beef cooked until done with a minced
onion and 2 cloves of minced garlic. Season to
taste with whatever you fancy. Just before meat is
done add 2 tomatoes, seeded and diced. Cool and
drain well. Prepare the pie tin with the phyllo
layers just as directed for the Spinach Pie and turn
the meat filling onto the bottom. Smooth the filling
and cover with the spinach filling. Smooth and
continue as directed for the Spinach Pie. Cook or
freeze as directed. These are very popular dinner
pies. All you need is a salad and some nice bread.

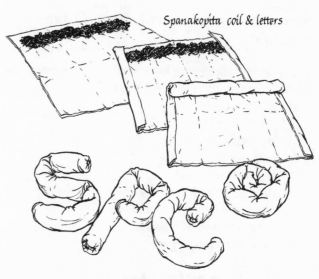

Spanakopita coil & letters

Spinach Coil or Letters

Follow the illustrations. Lay out 2 sheets of phyllo
and brush with melted butter. Lay a strip of filling
along the bottom edge of the pastry. Fold the sides
over the filling for about 1 inch. Then roll carefully. You will have a long strip of filled phyllo which
can then be shaped pretty much as desired. Coil it
around your finger to form a snail, or shape into
letters. Place on a buttered baking sheet and brush
with melted butter. Bake in a 350°F to 375°F
(175°C to 190°C) oven for about 20 minutes, or
until golden brown. Serve as a vegetable side dish.

Note. To freeze, place on buttered baking sheets and brush with melted butter. Cover baking sheets with plastic wrap and seal. Freeze. When ready to use remove plastic wrap and place baking sheets, with the frozen coil or letters on them, in the oven (see above for temperature) and bake for 30 to 40 minutes, or until golden brown. Serve as directed.

Broccoli Pie

Any of the preceding Spinach Pies can be made with chopped broccoli. Cook broccoli briefly, until just tender, before combining it with the other ingredients.

Spinach Timbales with Ripe Olive Sauce

This can be baked in a large mold or in several individual ones. It is a lovely side dish with roast pork or a baked ham.

> **½ cup minced onion**
> **1 clove garlic, minced**
> **¼ cup butter or oil**
> **1 cup fine bread crumbs**
> **½ cup grated Gruyère cheese**
> **½ teaspoon salt if desired**
> **⅛ teaspoon red pepper**
> **5 large eggs**
> **1 cup milk or half and half**
> **3 pounds (*about 4 bunches*) spinach, cleaned and trimmed**
> **Ripe Olive Sauce (*see below*)**

Sauté the onion and garlic in the butter or oil until transparent. Pour mixture into a bowl (including all the butter remaining in the skillet) and add ⅔ cup of the bread crumbs, the cheese, salt and red pepper. Beat in the eggs one at a time and then add the milk or half and half. Mix together and set aside.

Cook the spinach in just the water that clings to the leaves, only until wilted. Then drain thoroughly, pressing the leaves to express as much liquid as possible. You should have about 3 cups spinach. Now chop the spinach finely with a knife,

blender or food processor. Fold the spinach into the egg mixture and mix well. Pour into a well-buttered 1½-quart mold or soufflé dish, or into 8 ¾ to 1-cup individual well-buttered molds. I prefer the individual molds. Sprinkle with remaining bread crumbs. Place in a pan of hot water (*bain-marie*) and place in a 350°F (175°C) oven. Bake 35 to 40 minutes for the large mold, and about 20 minutes for the smaller molds. Test as for any custard. Stick a knife in the custard, between the edge and the center. If it comes out clean the custard is done. Remember that any custard continues cooking for a while after it is removed from the oven.

Run a knife around the edges to loosen custard from the mold. Unmold the large timbale on a serving dish. The individual ones I unmold onto thin toast rounds on individual serving plates. Drizzle with some of the sauce and serve the remainder in a separate sauce boat. Serves 8.

Ripe Olive Sauce

Make 1½ cups of a thin Bechamel Sauce (*see page 122*). To it add ¾ cup sliced ripe olives and then stir in 2 teaspoons lemon juice.

Spinach with Mozzarella

> **2 pounds (*about 3 bunches*) spinach, washed and trimmed**
> **1 onion, minced**
> **⅓ cup butter**
> **salt if desired**
> **freshly ground black pepper to taste**
> **1 cup grated mozzarella cheese**
> **1 cup grated Parmesan cheese**
> **1 hard-cooked egg, sieved**

Tear the spinach into pieces and set aside. Sauté the onion in the butter until golden. Add the spinach and stir and cook until spinach is limp and cooked. Remove from heat and add the seasonings and cheeses. Stir until cheese is melted. Transfer to a serving dish and top with the sieved egg. Serves 3 or 4.

Broccoli with Mozzarella

Take 2 pounds of broccoli flowers with some of the tender stem attached and blanch in boiling water with a clove of garlic until tender. Continue as with the above recipe, sautéing the broccoli with the onion for just a few minutes. You do not want to overcook the broccoli as overcooking makes it lose its color. Then add seasonings and cheeses and garnish with the hard-cooked egg.

Spinach Loaf

This is supposed to have been one of former First Lady Rosalynn Carter's favorite recipes. It is good, and just a little different.

> **3 or 4 slices bacon, cut into dice**
> **1 small onion, minced**
> **2 tablespoons butter**
> **3 tablespoons flour**
> **1 10-ounce package frozen chopped spinach, thawed**
> **⅓ cup milk**
> **5 large eggs**
> **¼ cup heavy cream**
> **½ teaspoon salt if desired**
> **½ teaspoon freshly ground black pepper**
> **½ teaspoon nutmeg**

Sauté bacon pieces until crisp. Remove, drain on paper towels and reserve. Sauté onion in the bacon fat. Add the butter to the bacon fat and onions and melt it. Then stir in the flour.

Squeeze the spinach to express as much of the liquid as possible, reserving the liquid in a measuring cup. To this spinach liquid add enough of the milk to measure a total of ¾ cup liquid. Stir into the flour mixture and continue stirring until the sauce thickens. Add the spinach and remove from the heat.

Combine the eggs with the cream and seasonings and whisk together. Add to spinach mixture and combine thoroughly.

Pour into a well-buttered 1½-quart casserole, soufflé mold or loaf pan and bake in a 375°F (190°C) oven for 50 to 60 minutes, or until loaf is done. Sprinkle the reserved bacon bits on top and serve immediately. Serves 4 to 6.

Variation

I like this way better: bake the loaf in a loaf pan for the required time; when done, turn off oven heat and let the loaf set in the cooling oven for 10 minutes. This helps to firm up the loaf so that it can be sliced. Unmold onto an oven-proof platter and slice into thickish slices. Place slices of your favorite cheese between the loaf slices. Sprinkle with the bacon bits. Return to the oven and bake just until the cheese *begins* to melt. Serve immediately.

Deep-fried Spinach Balls

I generally serve these plain, simply garnished with parsley sprigs and lemon wedges, but occasionally I serve them with a light Sauce Mornay (*see page 123*).

> **2 cups (2 *to 3 pounds*) cooked, chopped spinach, well-drained**
> **2 tablespoons melted butter**
> **salt if desired**
> **freshly ground black pepper**
> **1 large egg, lightly beaten**
> **1 cup fine bread crumbs**
> **2 tablespoons grated onion**
> **2 tablespoons grated Parmesan cheese**
> **¼ teaspoon nutmeg or allspice**
> **1 large egg**
> **¼ cup water**
> **more fine dry bread crumbs**

Combine the spinach with the melted butter, seasonings, beaten egg, 1 cup bread crumbs, onion, cheese and nutmeg or allspice. Mix well and let stand for 10 minutes. Then form into balls.

Combine the other egg with the water and whisk together. Roll the spinach balls in the fine dry bread crumbs, then dip into the egg-water mixture and then again in the bread crumbs. Fry in deep hot fat (375°F) (190°C) until a golden brown. Drain and serve hot. Serves 4.

Spinach with Anchovies

A lovely blend of flavors. Serve this with lamb.

> **2 pounds spinach** (*approximately 3
> bunches*), **washed and trimmed**
> **2 tablespoons butter**
> **2 tablespoons olive oil**
> **2 or 3 tablespoons minced anchovies**
> **grated Parmesan cheese**

Cook or steam the spinach in the water that clings to the leaves just until wilted. Remove and drain.

Melt the butter with the oil and add the anchovies. If you use salted anchovies you will probably wish to use a little less than if you use canned ones. Toss with the spinach and turn into a serving bowl. Sprinkle with some grated Parmesan. Serves 4.

Spinach and Artichoke Casserole

A hearty casserole, this is perfect because it can be made up ahead and baked at the last minute.

> **2 6-ounce jars marinated artichoke hearts**
> **2 cups cooked, chopped spinach (2 to 3
> pounds uncooked)**
> **1 8-ounce package cream cheese**
> **3 tablespoons softened butter**
> **⅓ cup milk or half and half**
> **⅓ cup grated Parmesan cheese**

Drain artichoke hearts, reserving the liquid to use in a salad dressing. Arrange the hearts in the bottom of a buttered baking dish. Cover with the spinach. Cream together the cream cheese, butter and milk. Beat until smooth and creamy. Pour over the spinach.

At this point, dish can be chilled for several hours or overnight, before baking. Bake in a 350°F (175°C) oven for 30 minutes. Sprinkle with Parmesan cheese and bake another 10 minutes. Serves 6.

Malfatti

Another great peasant dish, this is typically Italian.

> **2 cups ricotta cheese**
> **2 large eggs**
> **2 cups cooked, drained and gently pressed
> chopped spinach (2 to 3 pounds uncooked)**
> **1½ cups grated Parmesan cheese**
> **2 cloves garlic, crushed**
> **½ cup finely minced green onions**
> **2 teaspoons minced fresh basil or ¾ tea-
> spoon dried**
> **3 tablespoons flour**
> **¼ cup fine bread crumbs**
> **salt if desired**
> **freshly ground black pepper to taste**

Combine all ingredients and taste for seasonings. Chill for several hours. Then, with floured hands, pinch off tablespoon-size pieces of the mixture and form into small ovals about 1½ inches long. Place on a lightly floured surface while you continue.

Cook in boiling, salted water just until they rise to the surface. Remove with a slotted spoon and place on a serving platter. Dot with butter and sprinkle with more grated Parmesan cheese, or else cover with a light tomato sauce. Serve immediately to 6.

LETTUCE

While most lettuce is used for the salad bowl, it also lends itself well to cooking. Romaine lettuce is probably the most popular for some cooking purposes. Small heads of romaine lettuce are delightful when stuffed and braised or baked. Boston lettuce lends itself well to braising.

Buy whole heads with unblemished leaves. Wash thoroughly *before* storing. Core iceberg lettuce so that you can run water through the core to clean between the leaves. Spin dry in a salad spinner. Store in plastic containers, or wrap in paper towels. Fresh lettuce can be kept for up to 2 weeks in the refrigerator.

YIELD: A head of Boston or Bibb lettuce will serve 1 or 2 depending on size.

Braised Boston Lettuce

A delicate dish, worthy of your finest dinner party.

**3 heads Boston lettuce
1 tablespoon butter
4 slices bacon, diced
⅓ cup minced onion
⅓ cup chicken broth
½ teaspoon salt if desired
pinch freshly ground black pepper
2 tablespoons minced parsley**

Clean and trim the lettuce. Cut heads in half from top to bottom.

Arrange the lettuce halves in a well-buttered shallow baking dish. Sprinkle with the bacon, making certain that some is under the lettuce. Add the onion and pour the broth over. Season with salt and pepper. Cover the dish with a piece of aluminum foil and bake in a 350°F (175°C) oven for 1 hour. Remove dish from the oven and discard the foil. If there is too much liquid, pour it off into a small saucepan and boil it down quickly. When there are only a few spoonfuls left pour the sauce over the lettuce. Sprinkle with the parsley and serve. Serves 6.

Dutch Hot Lettuce and Potatoes

This is a filling, flavorful, one-dish meal if you serve it with some hot franks or sausages.

**2 large heads loose leaf lettuce
1 onion, minced
4 to 6 hard-cooked eggs, cut into quarters
8 to 10 slices bacon
4 medium potatoes, boiled until tender, peeled and sliced
2 tablespoons bacon fat
2 tablespoons cornstarch
⅓ cup cider or white wine vinegar
⅔ cup stock or water
2 teaspoons whole mustard or celery seed
salt and pepper**

Wash and dry the lettuce and tear into bite-sized pieces. Place in a large salad bowl. Sprinkle onion over the tops and then the hard-cooked egg quarters over that. Fry the bacon until crisp, drain, crumble and sprinkle that over the onion and eggs. Cut the potatoes into cubes and fry in the bacon fat until crisp and browned. Stir to prevent burning, but try not to crumble the potatoes.

While potatoes are frying prepare a sauce. Melt the 2 tablespoons bacon fat in another pan. Blend the cornstarch with the vinegar and stock and add to the bacon fat. Cook, stirring, until the sauce thickens and becomes clear.

When potatoes are done, turn them into the bowl over the lettuce, eggs, onion and bacon, adding any of the bacon fat that is left. Add the seeds and salt and pepper to taste. Pour the hot sauce over all and toss gently but thoroughly. Serve at once to 4 to 6.

Buttery Lettuce

A delicate dish, this is a summertime favorite.

**2 tablespoons butter
1 small clove garlic, crushed
6 cups shredded lettuce
salt if desired
freshly ground black pepper**

Heat the butter with the garlic until the garlic is golden. Remove if desired. Add the lettuce and stir it well. Cover the skillet and let cook, stirring occasionally, for about 3 or 4 minutes. Lettuce should be wilted, but not completely done in. Season to taste and serve immediately. Serves 4.

Creamed Lettuce

Make as above, only add 3 tablespoons heavy cream. Simmer rapidly until cream is reduced. Serves 4.

SORREL

This leafy green is also called sourgrass or dock. It looks somewhat like spinach, but with differently shaped leaves. The taste is lemony in the young leaves and more acid in the older leaves. It is easy to grow if it can't be bought in a local produce market. When buying, or picking, choose leaves that are free of blemishes and wilt. The leaves should be rinsed in tepid water and spun dry in a salad spinner. Store in glass jars as for spinach.

Sorrel is best combined with other greens for cooking, and is most often combined with spinach, which keeps its color when sorrel loses its color. It is excellent in soups, salads, or in bread stuffings for fish or poultry—especially for fish.

YIELD: One pound of fresh sorrel leaves will serve 2.

Roots and Tubers

Potato-Egg Pizza

These hardy and even homely vegetables, steeped in age-old traditions, are limited—though not by the imagination—to preparation in only a few different ways. Good cooks everywhere whip (mash, if you will) potatoes and then combine them with every conceivable other vegetable, either whipped themselves or cut into small pieces. The combinations are lightened with olive oil, butter, bacon fat or goose grease in combination with heavy cream, wine, or sour cream. In most cases the vegetables are folded together. Occasionally they are mounded side by side, especially to set a great color difference to esthetic advantage.

Potatoes, although extremely popular here and in Europe, are not often served in the Middle East nor in the Far East. There rice is the staple starch. Still, the potato is a new vegetable in all parts of the world except the Americas. In Peru, where it is a native, there are hundreds of varieties of the potato, in all shapes, sizes and colors. Also noteworthy: When first introduced to Europe, the potato, a member of the nightshade family, was widely considered as poisonous as the tomato was thought to be at that time.

The potato is one of the few vegetables for which an increase in size indicates an increase in quality. Carrots and potatoes store well and can be kept throughout a winter in a cool, dry *dark* place.

Turnips make one of the nicer pickled vegetables (recipes are in The Vegetable as Appetizer chapter), and are most frequently used in pickles in the Middle East and the Far East.

Beets probably are used for their color as much as for their flavor, and occasionally are used *just* for their color. Witness the red pickled eggs and the pickled vegetables in the Middle East.

In parts of France they use shredded turnips to make a "kraut" much like a German sauerkraut. And in the northern part of Italy shredded turnips are occasionally mixed with a fermented grape mash.

BEETS

When buying beets, always choose the smaller ones as they are more tender and flavorful. They should be smooth and firm. Avoid very large or spongy beets. Beets should always be cooked in their skins, unless you are grating them before cooking. The peel is easily rubbed off after cooking. If you are boiling the beets, add several tablespoons of vinegar or lemon juice to the water to stabilize the color. This isn't necessary if you are roasting the beets, by far the most flavorful method of cooking them. Store raw beets in plastic bags in the refrigerator for up to several weeks. Cooked beets should be used within 3 or 4 days, unless you have pickled or otherwise marinated them.
YIELD: 1 pound of cooked beets will serve 2 or 3 people.

Buttery Beets

2 pounds young beets, peeled and shredded
2 tablespoons olive oil
1 clove garlic, crushed
2 tablespoons lemon juice
salt and pepper to taste
¼ to ⅓ cup butter

Combine shredded beets with the oil, garlic, lemon juice and salt and pepper. Toss to coat well and then cook over medium heat for 15 to 20 minutes, or until just tender. If any more liquid is needed, use water or, preferably, chicken broth. Remove from heat as soon as tender and add the butter. Serve immediately. Serves 4 or 5.

Beet Hints and Ideas

Dress up hot or cold beets with some sour cream blended with a small amount of tarragon vinegar.

Burgundy Beets are good cold. Use small, cooked, peeled beets and marinate in a combination of Burgundy wine and a good basic vinaigrette. Drain off marinade when ready to use and serve cold. This marinade is reusable.

Add cooked, peeled beets, cut in small dice, to potato salad. Or, prepare potato salad according to your usual recipe and arrange alternate mounds of potato salad and pickled or marinated beets on a serving platter. Scatter the whole with chopped hard-cooked eggs.

Mashed Beets are good. Simply boil or bake 2 bunches young beets until tender. Skin the beets and bring to a boil again in a little water. Drain and whip with ⅓ cup melted butter, 1 teaspoon grated orange rind, a tablespoon of Burgundy and a tablespoon of orange or lemon juice. Mound on a serving plate and drizzle with a little more melted butter.

Beets with Horseradish

One favorite method of preparing beets, which you will find in almost every German, Polish or Russian cookbook, is to mix cooked, peeled beets with horseradish and sour cream. This is always served cold with boiled meats. One book suggests mixing 2 pounds of cooked, sliced beets with ½ cup horseradish and a tablespoon of sugar. This mixture is marinated for 3 or 4 days and served with cold meats.

Baked Beets

This simple method of cooking results in a remarkably sweet and tasty beet. They do, however, take a long time. Some recipes say to first rub the beets with oil, before baking. I don't. Wrap each beet in foil, place in a shallow baking pan and bake at 325°F (165°C) or 350°F (175°C) for about 2 hours for small beets. Large beets take 3 to 4 hours to bake. Let them cool slightly before peeling. Slice and serve with butter and salt and pepper to taste.

You can bake them unwrapped but the beets are not as moist and delicious.

Deep-fried Beets

Take fresh-cooked young beets and peel and slice them into fingers. Roll in seasoned flour and then dip into beaten egg and then into fine dry bread crumbs that have been mixed with a little red pepper. Chill for 30 minutes to set the crust. Then deep fry at 375°F (190°C) until golden brown and done. These will surprise you.

CARROTS

The bright orange carrots that we grow in our gardens and buy in the markets are descended from a purple carrot that was grown in Afghanistan as early as the 7th century A.D. Although they traveled through the Middle Eastern countries and then into Europe, carrots did not become popular until the 19th century.

Available throughout the year commercially, the best carrots are still the ones that you grow. We like to eat the tiny, freshly picked carrots raw, or gently poached and then marinated. Older carrots are ideal for any slow-cooking or braising treatment.

Choose firm, well-shaped carrots, preferably with the greens still attached. Gardeners store their supply of carrots in sand, but you should store commercial carrots in plastic bags in the refrigerator, where they will keep for a month.
YIELD: 1 pound will serve 3 to 4.

My Favorite Carrots

I like small carrots this way, so that they can be served whole. I cook them until *just* done, in simmering chicken broth, then drain them and cook gently in sweet butter with a sprinkle of sugar until they take on a glazed look.

Buttery Grated Carrots

This simple method for preparing carrots is also one of the best.

2 pounds carrots
2 tablespoons olive oil
1 clove garlic, crushed
2 tablespoons water
salt if desired
freshly ground black pepper to taste
¼ to ⅓ cup butter

Clean carrots. To pare them or not is your decision. I don't unless they are really scrungy looking. Grate carrots in long shreds. Toss with the oil, garlic, water, salt and a little pepper. You can add more later if you wish. Cook, covered, over medium heat until tender, about 12 minutes. Stir occasionally. When done to your liking, remove from stove and turn into a serving dish. Add butter and toss. Taste for seasoning. Add more salt and pepper if needed. Serves 4 or 5.

Carrot Tips and Ideas

Slice a pound of carrots diagonally and parboil for 5 minutes. Finish cooking with 1 tablespoon soy sauce and a teaspoon of sugar in ½ cup chicken broth. Very tasty and quick.

Shred 2 cups of raw carrots and toss with ¼ cup lemon juice, 2 tablespoons sugar and a pinch of salt and pepper. Serve in lettuce cups as a salad.

For more flavor, cook carrots with a bay leaf, a clove of garlic and a pinch of sugar.

If you just steam or boil your carrots, serve them dressed with an herb butter of some kind. Chives, chervil or basil are especially nice for this purpose.

Oven Carrots

This simple method of preparing carrots preserves the flavor in such a way that they actually taste a little like sweet potatoes. Prepare carrots this way when you are already using the oven for another part of the meal. Depending on size, allow 1 or 2 carrots per serving.

Scrub carrots. Leave them whole. Lay them in a shallow baking dish and dot lightly with butter. Sprinkle with brown sugar or drizzle with maple syrup. Cover the dish with foil and bake in a 350°F (175°C) oven for 1 hour, or until tender and done.

Creamed Carrots

These carrots are "creamed" with cream cheese. This is a currently popular recipe.

6 medium carrots, scraped
1 cup commercial sour cream
1 3-ounce package cream cheese
1 or 2 minced green onions
salt and pepper to taste

Slice the carrots diagonally and blanch in boiling water or chicken broth until tender. The length of time depends upon how thin or thick the slices are. Drain. Blend together the sour cream, cream cheese, green onions and salt and pepper to taste. Add to the carrots and fold together. Turn into a 1-quart buttered shallow baking dish. Bake in a 350° (175°C) oven for 10 minutes, or until just heated through. Serves 4 or 5.

Baked Carrots

This recipe is perfect for the busy cook. Another baked vegetable dish that tends to itself.

2 pounds carrots
1 onion, minced
1 clove garlic, crushed
¼ cup hot water or chicken broth
3 tablespoons lemon juice or dry white wine
salt and pepper to taste
⅓ cup melted butter

Clean carrots and pare them or not as you desire. Cut into thin diagonal slices. Place in a buttered shallow baking dish with remaining ingredients. Cover with foil and bake in a 350°F (175°C) oven for 1 hour, or until tender. Serves 4 or 5.

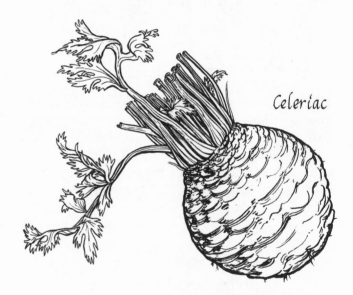

Celeriac

CELERIAC

This is also called celery root, knob celery and turnip-rooted celery. Celeriac is cultivated for its root. The leaves are tough and tasteless. Some cooks insist that celery root tastes just like celery. I disagree. To me celery is all crunch with little flavor, while celeriac combines the two in a thoroughly delightful way. Celeriac has always been a much more popular vegetable in Europe than here.

Celeriac is usually cooked before being eaten, even in salads, although I have always liked the taste and texture of the uncooked root. Peel before using. The white flesh will darken, so have a bowl of cold water to which you have added the juice of a lemon ready. Drop the celeriac in this. It is easiest to cook the root whole in boiling water for 20 to 30 minutes, depending on the size. You can also quarter it or slice it. Cook it just until barely tender as it turns mushy when overcooked.

Celeriac is available from September through April. Buy firm roots without any soft spots as these indicate internal decay. Do not wash until ready to cook and serve. Buy smaller roots as the large ones tend to be woody. Store, wrapped in plastic, in the refrigerator and use within 2 weeks.

YIELD: 1 pound will serve 2 or 3.

Celeriac Tips and Ideas

The Europeans combine mashed celeriac with whipped potatoes, butter, cream and seasonings. Some cooks use 2 cups celeriac to 1 cup potatoes, and others do exactly the opposite. Which proportions you use depends of course, on which flavor you wish to dominate.

Celeriac is also good cooked, sliced and dressed with any good vinaigrette, preferably one with mustard in it, and heaped in tomato cups.

Add diced celeriac to stews and soups.

Jerusalem Artichokes

JERUSALEM ARTICHOKES (SUNCHOKES)

The name Jerusalem artichoke comes from the Italian *girasole*, meaning sunflower. The Jerusalem artichoke is a potato-like tuber and a member of the sunflower family. The flesh is white and crisp and wonderful in salads. The peel is very thin and may be tinged with brown, yellow or purple.

Available from October through March, you should buy firm chokes that are smooth and evenly sized, heavy for their size. Avoid any that are wrinkled, soft or spongy. They can be wrapped in plastic and stored in the refrigerator for up to several weeks. If you have a bumper crop, the best way to store them is in sand as you store carrots or potatoes.

YIELD: 1½ pounds of Jerusalem artichokes will serve 4 or 5.

Jerusalem Artichokes Tips and Ideas

We prefer the little chokes raw. Just scrub well. The peel is very thin and does not need to be removed. Slice and add to salads. They blend especially well with shrimp, and I always dice or cut them into strips and add to shrimp salads.

When cooking, be careful not to overcook. No vegetable benefits by overcooking, and chokes suffer more than many.

When serving raw, peel and cut into water to which you have added the juice of a lemon. Chokes will darken on standing.

Deep-fried Jerusalem Artichokes

Scrub the chokes and cut into slices or fingers. Dip into seasoned flour, then in beaten egg and then in fine, dry bread crumbs. Let stand for 20 to 30 minutes, then deep fry at 375°F (190°C) until golden brown. Serve hot, sprinkled with salt if desired.

JICAMA

Much used in Mexican cooking, this tuber is a member of the morning glory family. It is just now being increasingly offered in American markets, and is well worth trying. It is crisp and sweet, with a flavor that is a cross between a water chestnut and a potato. It does not darken on standing and stays crisp even after cooking.

It is a large, turnip-shaped root, with skin like that of a potato. When you buy, look for firm, smooth jicama. The size is not as important as it is with some vegetables. At least I have not found the smaller ones to be any sweeter or crisper than the larger ones, and jicama can grow to a foot across. Avoid wrinkled or spongy jicama, or those with hard, woody spots. It will keep in the refrigerator for several weeks. If you buy a large one and use only part of it, just wrap the remainder in plastic wrap.

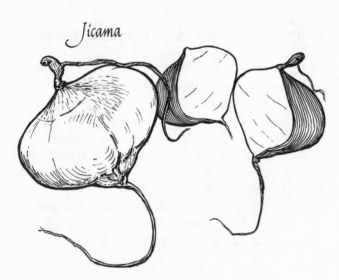

Jicama

Jicama Tips and Ideas

Cut up jicama and use in Oriental dishes when you can't find water chestnuts.

Add to any salad, even fruit salads.

Serve as the Mexicans do; peel and cut into fingers, serve with some lemon or lime to squeeze over and a tablespoon of salt mixed with a teaspoon of chili powder for dipping.

I always use jicama, peeled and cut into fingers, as part of a vegetable tray with a dip.

Jicama Salad

Peel a medium sized jicama and cut into thin fingers. Place in a refrigerator container and cover

with a mixture of ⅓ to ½ cup olive oil, 1 minced clove garlic and chopped fresh coriander (cilantro) to taste. Chill thoroughly and serve, drained, on lettuce leaves.

ONIONS

Like potatoes, there are many varieties of onions, ranging from the mild chive to the pungent garlic. In between, we have white, yellow or red flat onions, boiling onions, Italian red, yellow or white globe onions, leeks and shallots. I don't know about you, but I would sooner try cooking without pots and pans than I would without onions and garlic.

I have never been especially interested in the medicinal qualities of the onion family, but it is interesting to note that it has recently been suggested by the medical profession that onions and garlic help to prevent colds. Our grandmothers, of course, believed this, and used onion syrup for colds, onion soup as a sedative, and the heart of the onion, or a clove of garlic, warmed, was inserted in the ear for earaches.

One kind or another is available year round. Globe or boiling onions can be stored in a cool, dry place (*never the refrigerator*) for up to 6 months. Bermuda onions and pickling onions will keep just a few weeks. Shallots will store, again in a cool, dry place, for up to 4 months, as will garlic.

Onions Clementine

These are excellent with any kind of meat or poultry.

1 20-ounce package frozen tiny onions
¼ pound butter
2 teaspoons sugar
1 tablespoon tarragon vinegar

Thaw the onions and set aside.

Combine remaining ingredients in a small saucepan and bring to a boil. Let the butter just begin to brown and then reduce the heat. Add the onions, cover the pan and simmer together for 30 minutes, stirring occasionally. This will serve 4 to 6.

Onion Tips and Ideas

Take the tiny pickling onions, either fresh or frozen (not canned), and cook them in chicken broth until barely tender. Drain and cover with a good vinaigrette. Serve as a side dish with other marinated vegetables. These will keep in the refrigerator for several weeks.

Place large raw onions, left in their skins, in a baking pan in a 350°F (175°C) oven for 2 hours. Serve whole with butter and salt. The peels will slip right off.

Green peas and tiny onions are a time-honored combination. To cream them, simply add a cup of heavy cream and reduce it quickly.

Cook tiny onions in a strong meat or chicken broth until just barely done. You don't want them too soft. Then drain and pan fry in good olive oil with cracked black pepper.

Grilled Onions with Herbs

This herbed dish is perfect with steak, or with roast chicken or beef. In the summertime I use a collection of herbs from my garden.

4 large onions, cut in ½-inch round slices
4 tablespoons butter or olive oil
salt and pepper to taste
½ teaspoon dried marjoram
pinch of dried thyme

Prepare onions and set aside. Warm the butter or olive oil and add the seasonings and herbs. Let set for 20 to 30 minutes and then strain. Lay the onions in the melted butter or oil and sauté gently on one side until golden. Turn and sauté on the other side. Cover and simmer until done, about 15 minutes. Serves 6.

Note. *Another way to prepare this dish is to lay the sliced onions in a baking dish and drench with melted butter or bacon fat to which ½ teaspoon dried marjoram and a pinch of thyme has been added. Cover the dish with foil and bake in a 350°F (175°C) oven for 25 to 30 minutes, or until tender. Brown under the broiler.*

Puffed Deep-fried Onions

Marvelous deep-fried, crisp onions, these are nice for entertaining because the initial part can be done ahead. The last minute deep frying takes little time. Allow 1 whole onion per serving for true onion lovers, half an onion if there is a large menu.

Peel large onions and cut into ¼ to ½-inch slices. Separate rings. Place in a bowl and cover with milk or half and half. Chill for several hours, preferably overnight. Remove rings from milk. Dip in seasoned flour, then in the milk and then back into the flour.

Fry in deep fat at 375°F (190°C) until just barely golden. Remove from fat and drain. Set aside. This can be done several hours ahead of the final frying time. When ready to serve, reheat deep fat to 400°F (205°C) and fry the onion rings again until crisp, puffy and brown. Drain and serve. The best dipping sauce to serve these with is a seafood cocktail sauce made with tomato and horseradish.

Note. *An excellent batter for deep-fried onion rings is made as follows: Combine 2 cups flour with ¼ cup pancake mix, 2 or 3 large eggs, ½ cup cornstarch and 1 or 2 teaspoons baking powder. Add just enough water to make a batter. Chill the onion rings first in ice water then dip in flour before dipping into the batter. Deep fry at 400°F (205°C).*

Sautéed Green Onions

Green onions (scallions) are generally confined to use in salads and with dips. But cooked this way, they are delicious. I serve them at room temperature as part of a buffet.

6 green onions per guest
4 cloves garlic, crushed
olive oil
lemon juice
coarse salt

Cut off the bottoms and tops of the green onions, leaving just 1½ inches of green. Clean and dry.

Sauté the garlic in some olive oil very gently, just until it is golden. Add a layer of green onions and simmer gently until they are cooked on one side and just barely begin to take on some color. Test one. They should be cooked but not completely limp. Remove from pan and arrange in 1 layer on a serving plate. Sprinkle with lemon juice and a little salt. Cool to room temperature before serving.

Note. To bake just the cloves, use garlic heads with large cloves. Allow several cloves per person. Heat 2 tablespoons each butter and olive oil in a small, shallow baking dish. Add peeled cloves and stir to make certain they are coated with the oil/butter mixture. Add salt and pepper if desired. Bake in a 350°F (175°C) oven for 30 minutes, basting occasionally. They must be soft. Serve with bread or crackers.

Slow-cooked Onions

These onions are marvelous. The slow cooking converts the harsh pungency to a mellow sweetness. This same conversion takes place when garlic is cooked slowly, and is worth exploring. These onions can be added to other vegetables, or served by themselves. They are marvelous with hamburgers.

Peel and slice into rings 4 large onions. Separate the rings. Heat 3 tablespoons olive oil in a large skillet. Add the onions and cook over gentle heat, covered, for 30 to 35 minutes, or until very limp and just barely golden. Cook longer if necessary. Add salt and pepper if desired, or add a tablespoon of tarragon vinegar.

Roast Garlic

Cooking garlic slowly results in a dish that is excellent as a first course, with a crusty bread on which to spread the creamy buttons. The heads of garlic can also be set around a roast and baked at 325°F (165°C) for an hour or longer and then served with the roast. The flavor is much more mellow than garlic butter, and is excellent with baked potatoes and many vegetables.

Simply place 8 whole *heads* of garlic in a baking dish and add salt and pepper if desired. Add a little butter and olive oil. As with baked potatoes, the garlic heads will bake at any temperature. The temperature just determines the baking time. But don't bake them at over 350°F (175°C). Allow 1 head per person.

Chinese Pickled Garlic

We love this, and so do almost all of the men I know. Meant to be served as a relish along with many other Chinese dishes, I serve this in a decidedly non-Oriental manner, with cheese and dark bread.

2 to 3 cups whole, unpeeled garlic cloves
1 cup soy sauce
1 cup dry white wine
1 cup white or rice wine vinegar
⅓ cup light brown sugar
2 tablespoons Oriental sesame oil
1 or 2 tablespoons Hot Chili Oil (see page 141)
1 cup whole water chestnuts (optional)

This is best made during that time of year when you can find the large heads of garlic, with those beautiful large cloves. Remove cloves from the whole head, but do not peel. Discard the brittle outer shell. Measure and set aside.

Combine the soy sauce, wine, vinegar, sugar and oils. Turn into a saucepan and add the garlic cloves. Set over medium-low heat and cook, stirring occasionally, until mixture comes to a boil. Let boil for 1 minute and then remove from heat. Stir in the water chestnuts if you use them. Let cool somewhat and then turn into a jar. Cap and let stand at room temperature for 3 days. After that, keep refrigerated.

The original recipe said that the garlic would be ready to eat after 10 to 14 days. However, we start eating it almost immediately. Refrigerated, this will keep indefinitely.

PARSNIPS

With their sweet, nutlike flavor, you would think that parsnips would be much more popular than they are. They are excellent cooked and served on their own, as well as when added to soups and stews. Available all year, the peak seasons are fall and winter. Store parsnips in plastic storage bags in the refrigerator. They will keep for up to 4 weeks. YIELD: 1 pound will serve 3.

Old-fashioned Parsnip Cakes

2 cups mashed cooked parsnips
1 teaspoon salt if desired
freshly ground black pepper to taste
½ teaspoon sugar
1 teaspoon paprika
1 teaspoon lemon juice
1 large egg
½ cup or more of fine dry bread crumbs
flour as needed

Combine parsnips with seasonings, lemon juice and egg. Add bread crumbs until you have a mixture just firm enough to form into patties. Roll patties in flour or in more bread crumbs. Fry in bacon drippings, or in butter, until golden brown on each side. Serve hot with pork or ham, or even with lamb. Makes 4 to 5 servings.

Parsnip Tips and Ideas

Cook parsnips with an equal amount of sweet potatoes. While they are cooking, make a medium cream sauce. When vegetables are done, drain and turn into a serving dish. Add cream sauce and serve.

Cook parsnips with a clove of garlic and then mash. Season with salt and pepper and 1 or 2 tablespoons of butter. Chill and then add 1 large egg to each 2 cups. Form into balls and dip in beaten egg and then roll in fine dry bread crumbs. Deep fry until golden.

Fully grown parsnips are good when peeled and cooked until tender, then halved lengthwise, dredged in flour and fried in butter until golden. The young parsnips can be cooked and fried whole.

Cook parsnips until nearly tender. Add to roast beef, pork or lamb the last 30 to 40 minutes of roasting time, basting frequently.

One friend steams sliced parsnips until tender, then tosses them with vinaigrette and serves the parsnips cold.

Boil or steam equal amounts of parsnips and carrots until tender. Cool them and then shred. Sauté until golden ¼ as much minced onion as you have parsnips and carrots. Chop as much ham as you have minced onion and set aside. Add the parsnips and carrot mixture to the sautéed onions and toss to mix. Stir in the ham and heat thoroughly.

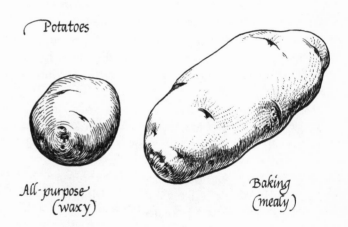

Potatoes

All-purpose (waxy)

Baking (mealy)

POTATOES

The perfect accompaniment to meat. The potato is a member of the nightshade family and a relative to the tomato and eggplant. A native of Peru, potatoes are now grown in most areas of the world, and in the United States potatoes are harvested and marketed every month of the year.

Although there are a great many varieties of potatoes grown in the United States, for most of us potatoes can be put into one of three groups. *New potatoes*, harvested before they are mature, are thin skinned and tender and cook quickly. They make a fine salad and are excellent prepared in the simplest of ways. They do not store well and should be used within 10 days of purchasing. *Baking potatoes* are long and oval in shape, mealy in texture and light and fluffy when baked. They do not boil well, falling apart easily, and thus do not make good salad. The most popular baking potatoes are the Idaho, the Long Island Russet and the Maine potato. The *all-purpose potato* comes in both round and long types, and is somewhat waxier in texture. These can be boiled, fried and occasionally baked.

To store at home, if you grow your own, store covered with sand. When buying, avoid potatoes with green sunburn damage, blemishes, any decay, or those that have sprouted. Potatoes should be stored in a cool, dry place. Do not store in the refrigerator. The best temperature is from 45° to 50°F (10°C). Lower temperatures cause the starch to turn to sugar, giving the potatoes a sweet taste. If this happens, you can restore some of the flavor by storing the potatoes for a week or two at 70°to 80°F (20° to 25°C). Avoid prolonged storage at temperatures above 50°F (10°C) however, as warmer temperatures will cause sprouting and withering.

Many of the nutrients are stored directly under the skin, making it a good idea to cook the potatoes with their skins on whenever possible. Scrub and wash thoroughly before cooking.
YIELD: 1½ to 2 pounds potatoes will serve 4 to 6. One pound of cooked potatoes will yield approximately 2 cups mashed potatoes.

Potato Tips and Ideas

I leave the peel on the potato in more and more dishes, including French fries and hash browns.

Our favorite hash browns are made as follows. Cut as many potatoes as you wish (allow 1 per person), scrubbed but unpeeled, in small dice. Mince 1 or 2 onions and 1 or 2 cloves of garlic. Turn into a skillet with from ¼ to ½ cup butter, depending on how many potatoes you are using. Sprinkle with salt and pepper. Cook slowly, turning the potatoes when browned and crisp. With raw

potatoes, it will take about 45 minutes to cook them slowly until browned, crisp and tender. Delicious.

Whip potatoes in your usual manner, using heavy cream, and whatever seasoning you prefer. Turn onto an ovenproof platter and spoon into a large, peaked mound. Sprinkle with grated Parmesan cheese and brown under the broiler. Make a crater in the center and fill with melted butter. Serve.

Potato Pudding

This is perfect with any kind of roast. One of our favorite potato dishes.

**4 large potatoes, scrubbed and grated (*peel
  first if you wish a white dish*)**
1 small onion, minced
2 tablespoons butter
2 large eggs, beaten
½ cup hot cream
¼ cup melted butter
½ teaspoon salt if desired
¼ teaspoon freshly ground black pepper

Prepare potatoes. Sauté onion in the 2 tablespoons butter until limp. Add all ingredients to the potatoes and stir very well. Pour into a well-buttered baking dish. Dot top with a little more butter if desired. Bake at 350°F (175°C) for 1 hour and 20 to 30 minutes. Serves 4 or 5.

Overbaked Potatoes

James Beard first developed the idea of overbaking potatoes, to eat on diets. The potatoes come out dry, crunchy and delicious. This is the way I do them, but they are not diet food, unfortunately, because they are great for munching. Bake Idaho bakers at 400°F (205°C) for 2 hours. Remove from oven, cut into wedges, arrange on a serving plate and drizzle with a good vinaigrette. Serve with a small pitcher of vinaigrette for those who wish more.

Barbecue Potato Casserole

This simple dish is great at any season of the year. In the summertime, heat the casserole on the outdoor grill. In the winter, pop it in the oven. Don't use baking potatoes for this dish, as they tend to fall apart more readily when boiled.

 4 cups diced hot cooked potatoes
 ¼ cup dry white wine
 2 tablespoons olive oil
 1 tablespoon white wine vinegar
 ½ teaspoon salt if desired
 1 teaspoon Dijon mustard
 ¼ teaspoon freshly ground black pepper
 ¼ teaspoon basil
 1 bunch green onions, minced
 ½ cup commercial sour cream
 ⅓ cup mayonnaise

Combine all ingredients except the potatoes. Stir together. Then add potatoes and stir gently. Let stand for 1 hour and then heat on a grill or bake in a 350°F (175°C) oven for 30 minutes. Serves 4 to 6.

Baked Potato Wedges

This is a nice dish just to munch on. It should be rather sharply flavored.

 3 or 4 baking potatoes, scrubbed and cut
   into wedges
 ⅓ cup butter
 1 teaspoon paprika
 1 teaspoon seasoning salt
 2 tablespoons bread crumbs
 dash each: onion powder, nutmeg, thyme,
   garlic powder
 ⅓ cup grated Cheddar cheese
 ⅓ cup grated Parmesan cheese

Prepare potatoes and melt the butter. Combine remaining ingredients and stir well to mix. Dip the cut wedges of the potato first in the melted butter and then in the seasoning mixture. Place in a shallow baking pan. Drizzle with a little more melted butter if desired. Bake in a 425°F (220°C)

oven for 30 to 35 minutes, or until potatoes test done when pierced with a fork. Remove to a serving plate. Serve with cold beer.

Gnocchi
(Gnocchi di Patate)

A basic potato dumpling, gnocchi is very similar to the French potato croquettes, except that the gnocchi is boiled and served with a sauce, and the croquette is deep fried and served plain. Some cooks do not add eggs to the gnocchi, while others use more flour. I serve this with Pesto (see page 127), mixing the Pesto with a little of the cooking water, or with a tomato sauce.

 1½ pounds potatoes
 1 or 2 cloves garlic
 1½ cups flour
 2 large eggs
 1 teaspoon salt if desired
 freshly ground black pepper to taste if
   desired

Boil potatoes with the garlic until done. Do not overcook or the potatoes will absorb water making the use of more flour necessary. Drain and whip, leaving the garlic in. Whip until smooth and then add remaining ingredients, working in thoroughly.
 Turn dough out onto a very lightly floured surface and knead gently 10 to 12 times. Shape into a loaf and set aside.

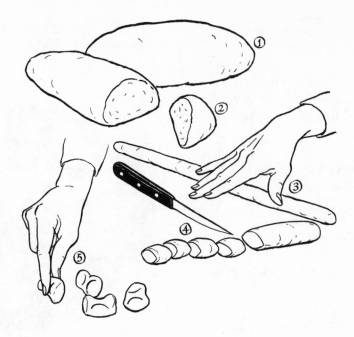

Break off pieces of dough from the loaf and roll each piece into a rope about ½ inch thick. Cut into 1 to 1½-inch lengths. Roll each piece lightly to give it a slightly bowed appearance. (*See illustration.*) Set gnocchi aside.

When all are shaped they can be either cooked or frozen. My friend Alba lays them on a cookie sheet, freezes them, then transfers them to freezer containers and stores. Thaw for 20 minutes, no longer, before cooking. They will not be completely thawed in 20 minutes, but thawed enough.

To cook, simply drop about ⅓ of the gnocchi at a time into gently boiling, salted water. They will sink to the bottom and then, after a minute, will bob to the top. Continue cooking for another 5 minutes. Remove with a slotted spoon and turn into a serving dish and stir gently with a little butter to keep them from sticking together. Cook another ⅓ of the gnocchi. Continue until all are cooked. The gnocchi can be kept warm in a 150°F (65°C) oven for up to several hours. Keep covered so that they don't dry out.

To serve, simply toss very gently with Pesto or place a layer of gnocchi on a serving platter and top with tomato sauce. Add another layer of gnocchi and another layer of sauce. Top with plenty of grated Parmesan, Romano or Pecorino cheese and serve immediately.

These little dumplings are also good when added to soup.

Potatoes au Gratin

This type of potato dish originated in the mountain areas of eastern France.

1 or 2 cloves garlic, crushed
3 tablespoons butter
5 medium new potatoes
salt if desired
freshly ground black pepper
1 cup minced green onions
2 cups shredded Jarlsberg or Gruyère
cheese
1½ cups milk or beef broth or half and half

Mix together the garlic and butter. Use a little of it to butter a 2-quart shallow baking dish. Cut the potatoes, peeled or unpeeled as desired, into thin slices. Now layer the potatoes, onions and cheese in the dish, sprinkling each layer with salt and pepper. The top layer should be cheese. Pour the milk or broth over the layers and dot with the remaining butter. Bake, uncovered, in a 350°F (175°C) oven for 1½ hours, or until tender. Serves 6 to 8.

Barbecued New Potatoes

Take small new potatoes and blanch them for 10 minutes. Then grill them, brushing with garlic butter or with a good vinaigrette, until browned and done. Delicious.

Potato Casserole

This is an excellent and easy dish, marvelous for a buffet or a holiday dinner.

    6 medium potatoes
    1 or 2 cloves garlic
    3 cups cottage cheese, drained
    ¾ cup sour cream
    salt if desired
    freshly ground black pepper to taste
    ½ cup minced green onions

Peel the potatoes and cut them into pieces. Cook in boiling water with the garlic, until tender. Mash, leaving the garlic in with the potatoes, without using any butter or cream. Just beat until smooth. Then add remaining ingredients, mixing all together thoroughly. Turn into a well-buttered 2-quart casserole. Brush top with melted butter. Bake in a 350°F (175°C) oven for 40 minutes, or until golden brown on top and hot throughout. If desired, you can sprinkle the top with ½ cup sliced, blanched almonds the last 15 minutes. Serves 8.

Perfect Boiled Potatoes

Small, new potatoes are best prepared this way. Cook them in boiling, salted water with 1 or 2 cloves of garlic, just until tender. Drain and shake over low heat to dry thoroughly. Then turn into a hot serving bowl and douse with melted butter to which you have added some chopped chives, basil or parsley.

Potato-Egg Pizza

Deliciously different, this sounds rather plebian, but can actually be an opulent dish. Nice for a luncheon or a light supper. One of my students told me that when her husband worked the graveyard shift the morning meal was a real problem. He wanted dinner and she and the children wanted breakfast. This dish satisfied all of them, and she served it at least once a week. Use any kind of sausage you want, or franks.

    ½ cup olive oil or other good oil
    3 or 4 cups well-seasoned leftover whipped
        potatoes
    1 large onion, minced
    2 cloves garlic, minced
    2 cups fresh mushrooms, sliced if large
    1 green pepper, seeded and sliced (*optional*)
    ½ to ¾ pound cooked sausage, sliced
    6 medium eggs
    6 slices firm, fresh tomato
    ⅓ cup grated Parmesan cheese
    1 cup grated Monterey Jack or mozzarella
        cheese

Use some of the oil to thoroughly grease a 15-inch round pizza pan. You can also use a 10 by 15 by 1-inch jelly-roll pan. Spread whipped potatoes evenly in the prepared pan. Make 6 indentations for the eggs, but do not drop them into the indentations yet.

Bake the potato crust in a 400°F (205°C) oven for 30 to 40 minutes, or until it is crisp on the bottom. You should be able to lift it off the bottom with a spatula.

While the potato crust is cooking, sauté the onion, garlic, mushrooms and green pepper in the remaining oil. Cook gently until soft. Combine with cooked sausage and mix well.

When the crust is done, spread it with the sautéed mixture, leaving the indentations clear. Break an egg into each indentation. Arrange tomato slices over the sautéed mixture also, but arrange them towards the center, not between the eggs. Sprinkle with the grated cheeses and then return to the oven for another 15 to 20 minutes, or until eggs are set and the cheese is melted. Cut into wedges to serve. Serves 6.

Note. *Obviously a recipe like this can be adjusted up or down according to need. Just use a smaller pan and less of everything. The baking time will be the same. The crust can be as thick or thin as you*

*like it, and the topping is as flexible as your im-
agination. I always use the eggs and the cheeses,
and I especially like tomato slices on it, also.*

Twice-fried Potatoes
(Pommes Frites)

These are the perfect fried potatoes. They can be
made ahead and finished when ready to use. Baking potatoes are used because they have less
moisture in them. With this method the fried
potatoes stay crisp. This double frying method
works equally well with zucchini or eggplant.

Use medium sized baking potatoes, allowing 1
per person. Peel and then slice vertically into
¼-inch thick slices. Now slice them horizontally ¼
inch thick, making fingers. If you are not going to
cook the potatoes immediately, keep them in ice
water.

Heat the oil or lard for deep frying to 400°F
(205°C). If the potato fingers have been soaking in
ice water, drain them and pat dry with paper
towels. The potatoes must be dry. Drop a handful
at a time—do not overload the fat as this will cause
the temperature to drop and the potatoes will absorb the grease and become greasy—into the hot
fat and fry just until they are a pale golden color.
Remove potatoes from the fat and drain on paper
towels. They can then be stored in the refrigerator
or at room temperature until ready to finish cooking.

When ready to finish cooking the potatoes, heat
the fat again to 400°F (205°C). Drop the precooked
potatoes into the hot fat and fry until they are a
deep golden color. You do not want to scorch or
burn them, but they must be a deep color to stay
crisp. Drain on paper towels and salt or not to
taste. Serve immediately.

Italian Oven Roast Potatoes

One of the simplest of potato recipes, these are
especially good with barbecues, or with any kind
of oven roast.

2 pounds baking potatoes, peeled if desired
   and cut into small dice
3 medium onions, minced
½ cup olive oil or melted butter
1 teaspoon seasoning salt, if desired
2 cloves garlic, minced
¼ to ½ teaspoon freshly ground black
   pepper

Combine all ingredients and toss lightly so that the
oil, or melted butter, and seasonings are evenly
distributed. Turn into a shallow baking pan and
bake in a 325°F (165°C) oven, uncovered, for 2
hours or longer, until potatoes are a golden brown
and soft. Stir occasionally. Serves 8.

Variation

Turnips can be roasted the same way. And a combination of turnips and potatoes is very good.

Roquefort Potatoes

These are bubbly and delicious. Good company
fare.

SAUCE

5 tablespoons butter
5 tablespoons flour
2 cups half and half
¾ cup chicken broth
5 tablespoons grated Parmesan cheese
½ teaspoon salt if desired

REMAINING INGREDIENTS

2 pounds potatoes, cooked, peeled and cut
   in small dice
¾ to 1 cup crumbled Roquefort cheese
¼ to ⅓ cup melted butter
paprika

Prepare the Sauce first. Melt the butter in a small
saucepan. Add the flour and stir and cook until it is
foamy. This will take approximately 2 minutes.
Gradually add the half and half and the chicken

broth. Cook, stirring with a whisk, until sauce is thick and smooth. Add remaining sauce ingredients and stir. Remove from heat and reserve. The sauce can be made earlier in the day if desired.

When ready to bake, butter 6 individual ramekins and set aside.

Fold the sauce into the potatoes and turn mixture into the ramekins. Sprinkle each with 2 tablespoons of the crumbled Roquefort and 2 teaspoons of the melted butter. Sprinkle with paprika and bake in a 425°F (220°C) oven for 10 to 12 minutes, or until bubbly. Serve immediately. Serves 6.

Potato-Cheese Pie

This recipe was suggested to me by an Italian friend, who then proceeded to make it for a luncheon. Filling and delicious, I serve it with a very light soup, some hot sausages, a green salad and icy cold beer. It's also nice with roast beef or chicken.

       3 pounds potatoes, scrubbed
       2 cloves garlic, left whole
       ⅓ cup butter or olive oil
       ⅓ cup half and half
       ½ cup grated Parmesan cheese
       ⅓ to ½ cup minced green onions
       2 large eggs
       salt if desired
       freshly ground black pepper to taste
       a dash of red pepper if desired
       1 to 1½ cups grated mozzarella cheese
       2 tablespoons fine dry bread crumbs
       2 tablespoons grated Parmesan cheese

Boil the potatoes and garlic until tender. Peel the potatoes and mash them with the garlic. Add the butter, half and half, Parmesan cheese, green onions, eggs, salt and peppers. Whip as for whipped potatoes.

Butter a 9 or 10-inch pie tin and arrange half of the potatoes in the tin. Cover with the grated mozzarella, using as much as you think necessary. I usually use the full 1½ cups. Press it in very lightly and then cover with remaining potato mixture.

Smooth the top. Sprinkle with the bread crumbs and Parmesan cheese and dot with a little more butter if desired. Bake in a 375°F (190°C) oven until the top is browned and crusty, about 30 to 40 minutes. Serves 6 generously.

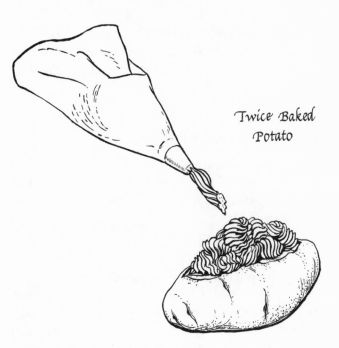

Twice Baked Potato

Twice Baked Potatoes

All you have to do to make Twice Baked Potatoes is to take baking potatoes, clean them well and place in the oven. If you bake them at 400°F (205°C) they will bake faster than if you bake them at 325°F (165°C), but you can bake them at either temperature, or any in between. Bake until done, cut a lid off the top and scoop out the inside. Whip the insides with butter, cream and seasonings and whatever else you fancy—shredded cheese, crisp bacon bits, etc.—and pile back into the shells. Sprinkle with paprika and reheat in the oven. These freeze very well, before reheating, and thus are a practical as well as a delicious item.

When I make Twice Baked Potatoes, I make a lot of them, generally about 25 or 30. The shells are placed on baking sheets while I whip the insides. I generally season them pretty highly and almost always add some finely minced green onions and grated cheese. I use a large pastry bag (see *illustration*) and fill it with the whipped potatoes and pipe them back into the shells. They look lovely, and I can do it twice as fast as it would take using two spoons. I place a tiny piece of butter in the center of each and sprinkle with paprika. I place the filled baking sheets in the freezer to freeze and then bag the potatoes. When we want to use them, I just place however many I need in a 350°F (175°C) oven (*without thawing*) and bake for 1 hour.

You might like any of the following variations. The variations can be used with Whipped Potatoes also.

Garlic Mashed Potatoes

Make as above except: in place of butter use olive oil; in place of any parsley or green onion use minced garlic; and in place of milk use sour cream.

Ricotta Potato Mounds

Whip the potatoes until light adding seasonings as desired. For 3 or 4 large potatoes whip in 2 cups ricotta cheese, 2 tablespoons parsley and enough milk to make the mixture light. Pile back into potato shells and sprinkle with grated Parmesan cheese before reheating in the oven.

Italian Style Potatoes

This is my favorite! For each 4 large baked potatoes, whip in the following: ⅓ cup butter, ½ pound ricotta cheese, ½ pound grated mozzarella cheese, 1 large egg, ⅓ cup milk or cream, 1 table-spoon minced parsley and salt and pepper to taste. Pipe back into potato shells and top with a thin strip of mozzarella and some paprika. Reheat in oven.

Potatoes Vinaigrette

Too good and too simple to leave out. This is marvelous as a side dish, especially with summer barbecues.

Remove a strip of peel around the center of as many small red potatoes as you wish to cook.

Cook, in salted boiling water until just done. Do not overcook. Drain thoroughly and, while hot, drench with Anchovy Vinaigrette (*see page 160*) or other variation of the Basic Vinaigrette if Anchovy doesn't appeal to you. Let stand for 20 minutes before serving. The potatoes absorb the vinaigrette and are delicious.

Whipped Potatoes

It is difficult to give an exact recipe for whipped, or mashed, potatoes. But I can tell you that however you make them they will be better if you cut the peeled potatoes into uniform pieces, place them in cold water and add several cloves of garlic (whip them with the potatoes), or a bay leaf or two, and cook until your fork tells you they are done. Remove from the heat and drain immediately.

This recipe is adapted from Helen Evans Brown's *West Coast Cook Book*.

5 pounds hot, cooked potatoes (*see above*)
1 cup cream
¾ cup butter
salt if desired
freshly ground black pepper to taste
3 egg yolks, optional
½ cup parsley, chopped

Whip the potatoes, adding the cream and butter, which have first been heated together. Salt if desired and add pepper to taste. When done, take a little of the hot mixture and whip it into the yolks and then add these to the rest of the whipped potatoes. Fold the parsley in. Turn into a heated bowl and dot with butter. Serve to 6 to 8 people.

RADISHES

There are more kinds of radishes than the average cook dreams of. There are red round ones, and long white ones, and little pinks trimmed in white, and long black radishes. One or more for each season of the year. There is some kind of radish available year round, although the peak season for the round red kind that we usually buy in the market is from May through July.

The best way to keep radishes is to clean them just as soon as you pick or buy them. If you have picked them from the garden, the leaves will be nice in any stir-fried dish, or added to salads or soups, or just cooked with other greens. If you buy the radishes, throw the tops away. Store the cleaned radishes, with a bit of the top left on, in a bowl of cold water in the refrigerator. Change the water every other day. The radishes will keep this way for 7 to 10 days.

YIELD: Allow 4 to 6 radishes per serving.

Oriental Radish Salad

This is more of a side dish than a salad.

12 nice fat radishes
¾ teaspoon salt
¾ teaspoon sugar
2 teaspoons soy sauce
1 teaspoon brown sugar
¼ teaspoon Oriental sesame oil (*optional*)
¼ teaspoon Hot Chili Oil (*see page 141*)

Place the radishes on a wood surface and hit each with the flat side of a cleaver to *lightly* crush them. Place in a bowl and add the salt and the ¾ teaspoon sugar. Let stand for an hour. The salt will draw out the excess liquid from the radishes. Then rinse and drain. Press the radishes lightly to express any more liquid.

Combine remaining ingredients and pour over the radishes. Toss together and let stand at room temperature for 1 hour, stirring occasionally. Serve with any Oriental meal.

Radish Tips and Ideas

Grate radishes (using the food processor is easiest) and add to a mixture of soft butter and whipped cream cheese. Serve as a spread with dark bread.

Serve a bowl of radishes with sweet butter and salt. Cut a piece off the top and spread the radish

with a bit of sweet butter and sprinkle with the salt for a taste treat.

Slice radishes fairly thin and cover with a good vinaigrette. Chill, then drain and serve as a side dish.

Creamed Radishes

Steam 2 pounds of cleaned, trimmed radishes for 15 minutes, or until tender. Turn into a serving dish and cover with a Bechamel Sauce (*see page 122*) to which you have added some chopped hard-cooked eggs. During asparagus season, add some cooked asparagus tips.

RUTABAGAS

Often called the "yellow turnip," the rutabaga is a different vegetable, and the two should not be confused. Available year round, the peak season is from July through April. All root vegetables, when bought, should be firm and free of blemishes. Store in plastic storage bags in the refrigerator, where they will keep for a month.

YIELD: 1 pound will serve 2 or 3.

Rutabaga Casserole

This often-neglected vegetable is very nutritious, and especially good in this casserole dish.

1 medium sized rutabaga
1 cup Bechamel Sauce (*see page 122*)
salt and pepper to taste
1 cup grated Cheddar cheese

Peel and dice the rutabaga. Cover it with water and cook until tender, about 20 minutes. Then drain well. The water can be saved for use in soups and stews.

Turn rutabaga into a shallow casserole and pour the white sauce over it. Sprinkle with cheese and bake in a 350°F (175°C) oven for 10 minutes, or until cheese has melted. Serves 4.

Potatoes and Rutabagas

This vegetable purée is simply another dish that combines whipped potatoes with another vegetable, to the benefit of both. What you need is a total of 8 cups diced vegetable in whatever proportions you desire.

8 cups peeled diced potatoes and rutabagas (*see above*)
1 teaspoon salt if desired
2 teaspoons sugar
freshly ground black pepper to taste
1 cup grated Cheddar cheese
⅓ cup minced green onion
minced parsley or chives

Cook potatoes and rutabagas in boiling water, or steam them, until tender. Then drain and whip well, adding the seasonings, sugar, cheese and onion. Beat until fluffy. Turn into a serving bowl and sprinkle with parsley or chives. Serves 6.

SALSIFY

Also called Oyster Plant and Vegetable Oyster because it is said that this root tastes somewhat like oysters. I have never thought so. In early America salsify was called "John-go-to-bed-at-noon" because its flowers close at noon.

Salsify discolors when cut, so it is necessary, upon peeling and slicing, to place the pieces in cold water to which you have added some lemon juice. When buying, avoid over-large roots, as these are often woody. Wrap in plastic and store in the refrigerator.
YIELD: 1 pound will serve 3 or 4.

Salsify Tips and Ideas

Serve it, cut in small fingers, as part of a vegetable tray with dips.

Cook first and dress with a good vinaigrette. Serve cold.

Cooked salsify is good dipped in a batter and deep fried.

Salsify Oysters

Boil or steam the peeled roots until tender. Drain well and then mash. Beat an egg into each 2 cups of the mashed salsify and season to taste with salt and pepper and just a hint of red pepper. Now add just enough flour to make the mixture firm enough to mold into patties. Roll in fine dry bread crumbs and fry.

SWEET POTATOES AND YAMS

A member of the morning glory family, sweet potatoes are not a true potato. The name potato is a corruption of the West Indian name "batata." Native to the Americas, sweet potatoes have never caught on in Europe.

Yams belong to a different family altogether, and are deeper in color and sweeter than sweet potatoes, as well as being more moist. For culinary purposes however, the two are interchangeable.

While there is an enormous range in size, shape and color with either, the smaller to medium sized sweet potatoes and yams are best. When buying, avoid over-large sweets and yams as well as any that are cracked.

Generally available throughout the year, they are most common from September through March.

Store in a cool, dry place where they will keep for 3 to 4 weeks. Do not refrigerate.
YIELD: 1 small to medium per person, or ⅓ to ½ pound per person.

Sweet Potato-Banana Casserole

This is nice with ham, and not as sweet as some.

1 pound sweet potatoes
1 large banana, cut into thick slices
¼ cup orange juice
salt if desired
¼ teaspoon cinnamon
dash of nutmeg

Cook sweet potatoes in boiling water until nearly done. Peel and cut into thick slices. Place in a well-buttered shallow baking dish. Cover with the banana slices and then pour on the orange juice. Sprinkle with salt, cinnamon and a dash of nutmeg. Cover and bake in a 350°F (175°C) oven for 30 minutes. Serves 4 to 5.

Sweet Potato Casserole

½ to ¾ pound pork sausage or Italian
   sausage
1 small onion, minced
1 large egg
⅓ cup half and half
3 cups leftover whipped sweet potatoes
salt if desired
2 or 3 tablespoons butter
¼ cup brown sugar
2 or 3 tablespoons cream

Remove sausage from casings and brown in a skillet with the onion. Pour off fat. Beat sausage mixture with the egg, half and half and sweet potatoes. Season with salt if desired. Turn into a shallow, buttered 1-quart baking dish. Smooth surface if desired.

Now blend the butter with the brown sugar and cream. Heat until hot and then pour over the potatoes. Bake in a 350°F (175°C) oven for 30 minutes, or until hot. Serves 4 or 5.

Sweet Potato Croquettes

The chopped pecans take this above the ordinary.

2 cups whipped sweet potatoes
2 eggs
¼ cup hot cream
¾ cup minced pecans or walnuts
pinch of salt
1 beaten egg
fine dry bread crumbs or cracker crumbs

Combine the potatoes, 2 eggs, cream, nuts and salt. Mix together thoroughly. Shape into fat, round patties. Dip lightly in beaten egg and then in crumbs. Let stand for a while to firm up, then pan fry in butter, or deep fry in hot fat. Serves 4.

Lemony Mashed Sweet Potatoes

If you don't care for lemon juice, you can use orange juice in this recipe.

½ cup half and half
¼ cup butter
5 hot cooked sweet potatoes
salt and pepper to taste
1 tablespoon grated lemon rind
1½ or 2 tablespoons lemon juice

Heat the half and half with the butter. Peel and whip the sweet potatoes, adding the cream and butter, until light and fluffy. Season with salt and pepper and the lemon rind and juice. Reheat if necessary. Mound in a serving bowl and drizzle with more melted butter. Serves 4 to 6.

Sweet Potato Hints and Ideas

There is no denying that sweet potatoes blend very well with many fruits.

Add a ripe banana or 2 when whipping sweet potatoes.

Or whip with some orange juice and pile into orange shells. Broil until browned and then drizzle with a little butter and serve.

TURNIPS

The turnip is among the most maligned of vegetables, possibly because it has always been associated, in literature and in history, with poverty. Can you think of any book or story in which any wealthy and/or beautiful individual ate turnips? Or cabbage for that matter, although I don't think that even the lowly cabbage is as maligned as the turnip. Yet the turnip is a lovely vegetable, with a good, crisp bite and clean flavor when eaten raw, and a comforting sturdiness in the flavor of the cooked.

If you raise turnips in the garden, pick some while still small enough to cook and serve whole. Cook the greens separately and serve the turnips, dressed with melted butter to which you have added some fresh basil, mounded in a ring of cooked greens.

Available all year, the peak season for turnips is from October through March. Buy smooth, firm-fleshed roots. Avoid spongy or over-large turnips as they get pithy and bitter with age.

YIELD: 1 pound will serve 2 or 3.

Sweet Spiced Turnips

Just a little sweet and spicy, this combination appeals to many who claim not to like turnips.

    2 pounds turnips
    1 teaspoon salt if desired
    ¼ cup chicken stock
    1 teaspoon sugar
    ⅛ teaspoon freshly ground black pepper
    ⅛ teaspoon nutmeg
    2 tablespoons butter
    2 tablespoons brown sugar

Peel turnips and cut into quarters. Turn into a skillet with a tight-fitting lid and add 1 inch of water. Salt if desired. Bring to a boil, reduce heat to simmer and cook gently for about 3 minutes. Then drain, discarding the water.

Add chicken stock, sugar, pepper and nutmeg. Cover and cook over medium heat for 6 or 7 minutes, or until tender. Remove lid and cook a few minutes longer to completely evaporate any remaining liquid. Add the butter and brown sugar and cook over medium heat, without the lid, for 3 or 4 minutes, or long enough to give a lightly glazed look. Serves 5 or 6.

Scalloped Turnips

Turnips can be quite surprising when scalloped. Scrub nice round ones and peel or not as desired. Cut into thin slices and layer in a shallow baking dish with grated cheese and dots of butter. Pour a meat gravy over the whole and sprinkle with bread crumbs mixed with grated Parmesan cheese. Dot with butter and bake in a 350°F (175°C) oven until turnips are tender, 45 minutes.

The Squashes

Stuffed Zucchini

Squash is yet another vegetable that belongs to the Americas. It is thought by some to be the most ancient vegetable grown by man. Others think that beans are. Regardless of which merits the title, squash is certainly the easiest to grow. Who has not been inundated by the prolific zucchini? I was told recently of a man who planted 15 hills of zucchini in his back-yard garden. He refused to take the advice of more experienced gardeners. Any of us who has ever spent our summers cooking our way through one or two hills knows what happened.

Most of the summer squashes are fairly interchangeable in recipes, although not quite as much so as the winter squashes. For that reason I have included only a few zucchini recipes, and only those I felt might be a little different. Zucchini, called *courgettes* in France and England, and also known as vegetable marrow, is the most popular of the squashes, and with every summer harvest magazines provide a crop of articles filled with more and more zucchini recipes, from pickles to cakes, breads and even a "zucchini pineapple."

Chayote is an interesting member of the squash family, although in some books it is called a fruit. It is excellent when sliced raw and eaten as is or added to salads. And it takes to a marinade quite well. Chayote is also called mirliton, vegetable pear, or mango squash. The large, flat seed can be eaten also, and I do not even remove it when cutting the squash. With very young chayote, I just scrub the skins; when older and larger, I peel them. As an appetizer, cut the chayote into wedges and serve with lemon and salt as you would jicama.

The recipes in this section deal with those squashes that we are most apt to be buying or growing. I have omitted the more exotic varieties.

Zucchini

Yellow Straightneck

Scallop

Yellow Crookneck

Summer Squashes

SUMMER SQUASHES

Zucchini is the most common of the summer squashes, in part because of its growth habits. Learn to pick zucchini when it is small. Zucchini is at its best when no larger than 5 or 6 inches in length. It is pure delight when it is picked when finger size, blanched whole until barely tender, and then covered with a good vinaigrette and chilled. These are lovely on an hors d'oeuvre tray. Tiny crookneck squash can be treated the same way.

Yet I still know people who pride themselves on their giant zucchinis. One lady I know grew them so large that the skin was so thick that she thought she could store them as you would store winter squash. Of course they rotted. Even if they had not rotted, the flavor of summer squash, however much we may love it, lacks the richness of the winter varieties. Summer squash simply must be eaten fresh.

The pattypan and crookneck squashes are generally picked when too large also. Crookneck and zucchini picked when so small that the blossom is still attached can be sautéed, blossom and all, gently in butter with a touch of garlic and some herbs. Serve hot and allow 4 or 5 per serving.

The pattypan (also known as cymling or scalloped squash) is best picked small enough so that it can be cooked whole also.

Pattypan squash is good either steamed or boiled until tender and then well drained, with as much water pressed out as possible. Then mash and reheat with plenty of butter and salt and pepper to taste.

To buy, look for firm, unblemished squash. Store in the refrigerator and use within 4 or 5 days.

Zucchini can be successfully frozen, but only for use in casseroles or cooked dishes. I simply slice or grate the zucchini and then freeze it, a recipe's worth to a container or freezer bag. When thawed, be sure to drain thoroughly before using.

Don't forget to try zucchini, cut in lengthwise strips and sautéed gently in oil, in place of eggplant in either Eggplant Parmigiana or the Layered Moussaka.

Zucchini Niçoise

This is a nice way with zucchini.

3 tablespoons olive oil
1 onion, minced
2 cloves garlic, crushed

3 medium zucchini, thinly sliced
1 cup whole ripe olives, pitted
¼ cup minced pimiento
3 medium tomatoes, or 5 or 6 fresh Italian
   plum tomatoes, seeded and chopped
¼ cup tomato paste
2 tablespoons chopped parsley
2 tablespoons fresh basil, or 1 teaspoon
   dried
salt and pepper to taste

Heat the oil in a large skillet with a cover. Sauté the onion and garlic until limp. Add remaining ingredients and bring to a boil. Reduce heat, cover the skillet and simmer gently until the zucchini is cooked and tender, about 25 minutes. This type of dish can always simmer a little longer to give all of the flavors a chance to blend and mellow. Serves 5 or 6.

*hollowing zucchini
with the zucchini corer~*

Stuffed Zucchini
(Koosa Mahshi)

In Lebanese, ''koosa'' means squash, and ''mahshi'' means stuffed. A good Lebanese cook leaves as thin a shell as possible on the zucchini, and uses small zucchini—small enough so that 2 or 3 or even more are required for a serving. I generally use the 5 or 6-inch long zucchini and allow approximately 1½ per serving. In my family the pulp of the zucchini was always used to line the pot with, along with garlic and tomatoes, etc. There is a recipe however, called *Mnazlit Koosa*, which calls for sautéing the pulp in olive oil with some minced onion and diced tomatoes and salt and pepper to taste. This mixture is simmered for 15 minutes, or until tender, and 2 eggs are then stirred into the mixture until set.

FILLING

1 pound lean lamb, ground
½ cup long-grain rice, blanched in boiling
   water or wine for 4 minutes
2 fresh tomatoes, seeded and diced
6 green onions, minced
1 teaspoon salt and pepper to taste
¼ cup pine nuts
½ teaspoon cinnamon

REMAINING INGREDIENTS

12 zucchini, 5 or 6 inches long
6 cloves garlic, whole
3 large tomatoes, seeded and diced
1 teaspoon salt or more

Combine Filling ingredients, mixing together thoroughly. Hollow the zucchini as directed in the illustration, holding on to the zucchini firmly around the middle. The purpose is to hollow the squash without puncturing the shell. Leave as thin a shell as possible.

Now fill the zucchini with the Filling, leaving about 1 inch space at the hollow end for the filling to expand. Place the pulp of the zucchini over the bottom of a saucepan large enough to hold all of the zucchini. Add the whole cloves of garlic and the tomatoes. Arrange the zucchini over this, layering them until all are in the pot. Add water or chicken broth to barely cover. Add the salt. Cover and bring to a boil. Reduce heat and let simmer until the zucchini is tender and the filling cooked, 45 minutes to 1 hour. Arrange on a serving platter and garnish with lemon and olives. Serves 8.

Zucchini Pizza

This simple recipe is not only delicious, but an excellent way of using up some of that extra zucchini. I have served this to people who didn't even like vegetables, and they loved this. As with all recipes of this type, the topping is extremely flexible. Make the crust as directed, but for the Topping, be creative. I have used fresh Italian plum tomatoes which I chopped up in the food processor mixed with sliced olives and cheese for the

Topping. Delicious! I have on occasion used cooked Italian sausage in with the sauce, or under it, spread over the crust.

CRUST

3 cups grated raw zucchini, well drained and pressed
2 or 3 large eggs
1 to 1½ cups grated mozzarella or Monterey Jack cheese
3 slices bacon, diced and cooked until crisp

FILLING

1 to 1½ cups Basic Tomato Sauce (*see page 126*)
1 cup grated mozzarella or Monterey Jack cheese
½ cup grated Parmesan cheese
1 teaspoon oregano

Use a 10-inch pie tin that is well greased. Combine the crust ingredients and mix well. Press into the pie tin. Bake in a 400°F (205°C) oven for 15 minutes. The crust will "set." Remove from oven and spread with filling ingredients. Bake for another 20 to 25 minutes. Let stand for 10 minutes before cutting and serving.

Zucchini-Cheese Pie

This pie is an interesting variation of *Spanakopita*, and one that zucchini lovers will adore. The pie freezes very well.

16 sheets phyllo pastry
¼ pound butter, melted
6 cups grated zucchini, drained
1 cup green onions, minced
¼ cup each: olive oil, butter
½ pound feta cheese, crumbled
1 cup ricotta cheese
1 cup grated Parmesan cheese
1 cup grated Swiss cheese or Kasseri
⅓ cup minced parsley
5 large eggs, beaten

Brush a 9 by 13-inch baking pan with melted butter. Line the pan with 8 sheets of phyllo, brushing every other sheet with melted butter. The edges of the pastry can be left hanging over the sides of the pan to be folded over later, or they can be folded over the bottom. It won't matter to the finished dish, except that in the one case you will have sides of phyllo and in the other you won't.

To make the filling, sauté the drained zucchini (press it lightly while in the colander to express as much liquid as possible) and the onions in the oil and butter until almost dry. Turn into a mixing bowl and cool slightly. Then add remaining ingredients and mix together thoroughly. Turn this into the phyllo-lined baking pan. Cover with the remaining 8 sheets of phyllo, again brushing every other layer with melted butter. Tuck the edges in, brush the top with more melted butter and score with a knife into squares. You do not need to cut all the way through, just through the top layers so that the finished pie will be easy to cut. Bake in a 350°F (175°C) oven for 45 minutes, or until golden brown. Serve warm or at room temperature. Serves 8 to 10.

Tomato-Zucchini Pie

This is simple enough for the children in the family to prepare. It tastes something like pizza.

CRUST

2 cups grated raw potatoes
1 small onion, minced
1 large egg, beaten
¼ cup flour

FILLING

2½ to 3 cups grated Cheddar and/or Monterey Jack cheese
2 cups *very thinly* sliced zucchini
3 large tomatoes, thinly sliced
1 teaspoon dried basil
1 teaspoon dried oregano
2 cloves garlic, crushed
salt and pepper
1 small onion, minced

Make the Crust as follows: Squeeze as much liquid as possible out of the potatoes and then mix with the onion, egg and flour. Press into a well-greased 10-inch pie pan and bake in a 350°F (175°C) oven for 30 minutes, or until browned and done. Remove from oven and cool slightly.

Place half of the grated cheese over the bottom of the Crust. Cover with the zucchini (which must be cut into very thin slices or else it will not cook properly), and then the tomatoes. Mix remaining ingredients with the remaining cheese and press all over the tomatoes, making an even covering. Return to the oven and bake for another 45 minutes, or until the cheese is browned and bubbly and the zucchini is done. This will serve at least 6.

Zucchini Loaf

This is an excellent way to use some of that extra zucchini from the garden. This can be used as an hors d'oeuvre or as a side dish at dinner. It also makes a nice snack.

    4 cups grated zucchini
    1 teaspoon salt
    ⅓ cup minced green onion
    5 large eggs, beaten
    1 teaspoon basil
    ½ cup Herb-seasoned Bread Crumbs (*see page 95*)
    2 tablespoons oil
    ½ cup grated Parmesan cheese

Cook the grated zucchini in boiling water or chicken broth to cover, for 3 to 4 minutes or until just barely tender. Drain thoroughly, pressing to remove excess water. Set aside until cooled.

Combine all ingredients, including the cooled zucchini, mixing thoroughly. Turn into a greased 8-inch loaf pan. Cover if desired with another ¼ cup each of bread crumbs and grated Parmesan cheese. Bake in a 350°F (175°C) oven for approximately 1 hour 15 minutes, or until done. Serve cold, cut into slices. It tastes like pizza!

Note. *If you have only 3 or 3½ cups grated zucchini, simply cut the eggs to 4, leaving the remain-*

ing ingredients the same. If you have 5 cups of zucchini, leave the recipe as is. If it seems dry, add another egg.

Summer Squash

For this old-timer, you can use either the pattypan or the crookneck squash.

    2 pounds squash
    ½ cup butter
    1 onion, minced
    salt and pepper to taste
    some sweet basil
    1 cup heavy cream

Wash and remove the ends from the squash. If the squash is old, peel it; otherwise leave the peel on. Coarsely dice. Melt the butter and add the squash and the onion and cook until limp and lightly browned. Add the salt, pepper, sweet basil and cream. Bring to a simmer, cover and simmer over low heat until the squash is tender, about 7 or 8 minutes. Serves 6.

Crookneck Squash and Corn

    1 pound small crookneck squash, thinly sliced
    4 or 5 ears of corn
    salt and pepper
    some sweet basil
    ¼ cup butter

Steam the squash until just barely tender. Cook the corn for 5 minutes and then cut the kernels off of the cobs. Combine squash and corn in a casserole and sprinkle with the salt and pepper and basil. Dot with the butter and bake in a 350°F (175°C) oven just until hot. Do not overcook. Serves 5 or 6.

Stuffed Pattypan Squash

You can get quite creative with these.

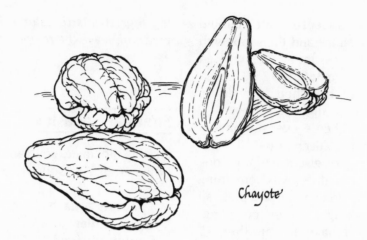

Chayote

12 medium pattypan squashes
1 can (*about 2 cups*) cream-style corn
¼ cup butter
salt and pepper to taste
1 cup grated Cheddar cheese

Steam the squashes, whole, until just tender. Drain and cut a slice from the top of each. Scoop out the insides leaving a nice shell. Turn the insides into a skillet and cook until thick. Add the corn and butter and season to taste. Cook some more until nice and thick. Stir half of the cheese into the filling. Fill the squash shells and place on a baking sheet. Sprinkle with the remaining cheese. Bake in a 350°F (175°C) oven just until hot and bubbling. Serves 12.

Note. *These can be prepared ahead of time and baked at the last minute.*

Onion-filled Pattypan Squash

Make as above, using for the filling some tiny onions that have been cooked until tender in chicken broth. Add the onions to a rich cream sauce and fill the squash. Top with some grated cheese and bake as above.

Variation

Make as in the first recipe, only cook up a minced onion and a little garlic with the squash pulp. Add some chopped ham or some crisp cooked bacon to the filling. Season with a little tarragon or basil and add just enough soft bread crumbs to make enough filling for all of the shells. Bake as above.

Chayote with Shrimp

I generally prefer large shrimp, cut in pieces, for a dish like this. You can use small or medium shrimp if you prefer, and leave whole.

3 medium sized chayotes
1 medium onion, minced
2 to 3 tablespoons olive oil
1½ pounds fresh raw shrimp, peeled and deveined
salt and pepper
2 tablespoons minced chives
½ cup buttered bread crumbs

Cut the chayotes in half and remove the seeds. Boil the chayotes in lightly salted water until very tender, about 40 to 45 minutes. Drain and cool. Remove skin and cut the flesh into dice.

Sauté the onion in the olive oil until limp. Add the shrimp, either whole or cut into pieces depending on the size of the shrimp and personal preference. Cook gently *just* until barely pink. Remember that the shrimp will continue cooking after being removed from the heat, and also that they will cook further in the oven. Season with salt and pepper to taste and stir in the chives. Add the chayote and turn into a shallow, buttered baking dish. Sprinkle the crumbs over the top.

Bake in a 350°F (175°C) oven for 20 to 25 minutes, or until the crumbs are lightly browned. Serves 4 or 5.

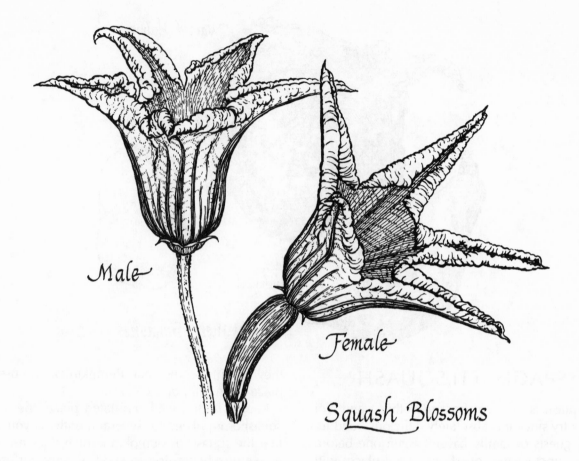

Male

Female

Squash Blossoms

SQUASH BLOSSOMS

Squash blossoms have been eaten by the Italians for centuries. The blossoms of any squash, either summer or winter, or even pumpkin blossoms, can be used. They can be dipped into a beer batter and deep fried. Unopened squash blossoms can be picked and sautéed briefly in butter with just a sprinkle of salt and pepper. And don't forget their enormous appeal as a garnish for soups or salads. The blossoms are extremely perishable, so either pick them as close to cooking time as possible, or if you must pick them ahead of time simply keep them in cold water until you are ready to use them. They close in the heat of the day.

Stuffed Squash Blossoms

You can make this recipe first, and then experiment with ideas of your own for stuffing the fragile blossoms.

20 squash blossoms

FILLING

½ pound lean ground lamb
1 cup cooked rice
3 green onions, minced
1 large egg
salt and pepper to taste
¼ teaspoon or more of cinnamon

REMAINING INGREDIENTS

1 cup chicken broth
¼ cup butter

Wash the blossoms and gently remove the stamens. Keep in cold water. Mix the Filling ingredients thoroughly. Use to fill the blossoms. Fold the ends of the flowers gently over the filling. Lay filled blossoms over the bottom of a buttered casserole. Pour over the chicken broth and dot each with butter. Bake in a 350°F (175°C) oven for 20 minutes, or until done. Serves 4.

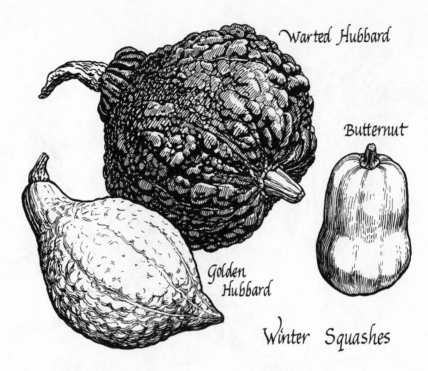

Warted Hubbard

Butternut

Golden Hubbard

Winter Squashes

SPAGHETTI SQUASH

This squash is different from the others, and well worth a try since it is absolutely delicious—and fun if your guests or family haven't eaten one before. Merely puncture the squash in several places with a skewer and cook it in boiling water to cover for 30 minutes. Remove from the water and place on a serving platter. Cut the squash in half, lengthwise. Remove and discard the seeds. Many books say that the strands come tumbling out. Well, not in my experience. You have to use a fork. I scrape from the ends towards the middle. *Then* you get those lovely spaghetti-like strands of squash. Dress with melted butter, cheese and some crisp cooked bacon, or with whatever sauce or dressing you would prefer. The squash is delicious no matter what you put on it.

WINTER SQUASHES

There are many varieties of winter squash; acorn, butternut, Hubbard and turban are probably the most popular. The various varieties are interchangeable in recipes. Which variety you use depends entirely on which flavor you prefer since

they all differ somewhat. Pumpkin can be used in place of squash, or vice versa.

Kept in a dry, well-ventilated place, the winter squashes will keep for several months. If you think that the squash or pumpkin (which does not keep as well) is beginning to spoil, simply cut off the bad part and cook the rest. Use in a recipe, or cook, then purée and freeze the purée.

To cook, cut the squash or pumpkin in half and scoop out the seeds, discarding the strings. The seeds are excellent when roasted and salted. They make a nourishing as well as a delicious snack. The squash is now ready to cook. You can bake it or steam it. When not following a specific recipe, I like to turn the squash or pumpkin upside down on a baking sheet and bake it at 350°F (175°C) until a toothpick or cake tester punctures the skin and flesh easily. The time varies according to the size of the pieces. The flesh is easily scooped out of the skin and puréed for use in other recipes. Pumpkin pie made with fresh pumpkin, cooked and puréed, tastes completely different from that made with canned pumpkin.

Apple and Acorn Bake

This is a lovely dish to accompany Thanksgiving or Christmas dinner, which is usually when I serve it.

6 acorn squashes
¼ cup butter
salt to taste
2 medium sized green apples
2 medium sized oranges
⅓ cup brown sugar or maple syrup

Cut the squashes in half lengthwise and remove seeds. Butter the insides and sprinkle with salt. Peel, core and slice the apples thinly. Peel and section the oranges. Arrange apple and orange slices on the squash, sprinkle with the sugar, or pour on the syrup, and dot with the butter. Bake in a 375°F (190°C) oven for about 1 hour, or until squash is tender. Serves at least 6.

Acorn Squash with Rum

Split small acorn squash, allowing ½ per person. Remove seeds. Score deeply and sprinkle each half with a little salt and pepper, a teaspoon of brown sugar, a tablespoon of melted butter and a teaspoon of rum. Place in a baking pan, cover and bake in a 350°F (175°C) oven until nearly tender, about 35 to 45 minutes. Remove cover, sprinkle each half with some chopped nuts and baste with a little more butter and rum. Continue baking, uncovered, until nuts are browned and the squash is tender, about another 20 minutes.

Stuffed Acorn Squash

This method is delightful. Serve to hearty eaters.

Split 4 acorn squash down the middle and remove the seeds. For this dish you will need to allow a whole squash per person since half of the shells will be discarded. Place the halves, cut side down, in a shallow baking pan and bake in a 350°F (175°C) oven until tender, about 50 minutes to an hour. Remove from oven and scoop out the pulp. Save 4 of the best shells. Beat into the mashed pulp 1 tablespoon butter, 1 tablespoon half and half or heavy cream, a pinch of nutmeg, salt and pepper and brown sugar to taste. Heap back into the 4 good shells and place back on a

baking sheet. Brown in a 400°F oven or in the broiler.

These can be made several hours ahead and reheated when ready to serve. If you need another serving or 2, add some hot applesauce or hot mashed pumpkin to the squash mixture and use more of the shells.

Acorn Squash with Oysters

One old book that I treasure mentions baking or steaming halves of acorn squash until tender, and then scooping out the pulp. This is mashed and mixed with chopped broiled oysters before being piled back into the shells.

South Pacific Squash and Coconut

This dish, a sort of vegetable stew, is lovely with any kind of pork dish, or with baked ham. Don't be afraid to try it; the combination of flavors is different and delightful.

2 pounds Hubbard squash or other winter
   squash
1 fresh coconut
½ cup roasted peanuts
1 teaspoon sugar
2 to 3 tablespoons soy sauce
1 tablespoon white wine vinegar

Peel the squash, first discarding the seeds and strings. Dice the squash meat in chunks. Coarsely grate the coconut and add to the squash along with the peanuts. Turn into a pot and add just enough water to come to the top of the squash. Cover and simmer slowly until the squash is tender. Add remaining ingredients to taste. This will serve 4 to 6.

Squash or Pumpkin Ring

This delicious ring mold will certainly be a hit at your next buffet. I always fill the center with creamed mushrooms mixed with the tiny whole onions that you buy frozen. However, you can use whatever vegetable or combination of vegetables pleases you, keeping in mind that there should be a difference in colors as well as textures.

3 pounds pumpkin or winter squash
¼ cup melted butter
¼ cup half and half
3 large eggs, beaten
¼ cup fresh bread crumbs
¼ cup minced onion
salt and pepper to taste

Remove seeds and strings from the pumpkin. Peel. Cut into dice and cover with boiling water. Cook until just tender, about 20 minutes. Drain well and purée or at least mash well. Add remaining ingredients and mix well. Pack into a buttered 1-quart ring mold. Set in a pan of hot water (*bain-marie*) and bake in a 350°F (175°C) oven until firm, about 45 minutes. Remove from oven and let set for 5 minutes before turning out onto a serving

dish. Fill the center as above or with the vegetable of your choice. Serves 4 to 6.

Mashed Winter Squash

You can use any of the winter squashes or pumpkin in this recipe.

2 or 3 pounds winter squash
¼ cup butter
½ teaspoon nutmeg
salt and pepper to taste
⅓ to ⅔ cup sour cream
2 or 3 tablespoons honey

Cut squash in half and remove seeds and strings. Peel and cut into dice. Steam or boil until tender. Mash as smooth or as lumpy as you wish, seasoning with the butter, nutmeg and salt and pepper. Beat in enough sour cream to make mixture fluffy and sweeten with the honey. Pile into a serving dish and serve to 4 to 6. This can be made ahead and just reheated in the oven for 8 to 10 minutes.

The Vegetable Fruits

I'll bet that I know 100 ways of preparing eggplant. Also, I know many people who don't like it, or think that they don't, because the only eggplant they have ever eaten has been improperly prepared. Eggplant used to be a joke with some of my guests. One would ask what a particular dish was and in response I would suggest that they taste it before I tell them. Then someone else would pipe up, "That means it has eggplant in it."

Extremely popular throughout the Mediterranean area, eggplant is called "the poor man's meat." Many people think that because it tastes so rich, it must contain a lot of protein and vitamins. Actually, eggplant is relatively low in nutrients. Its rich flavor comes from the oil it absorbs in cooking, and from the fact that it is usually cooked with tomatoes and other ingredients in a blend that becomes rich. Properly prepared, eggplant is always delicious.

Tomatoes and peppers of course, are used in practically everything, in all imaginable ways. Even green tomatoes are good, made into pickles or relishes or sliced and fried, or made into a pie, either sweet or savory.

Green peppers are just that—green, meaning unripe. The red pepper is the ripe pepper. I have had students who actually did not know that, possibly because of the short growing season here in Idaho.

Cucumbers and okra are vegetable fruits also. And if you have never picked a small cucumber (cukes are edible at any stage of growth, the smaller the better), washed it and eaten it immediately, then you have never eaten a really good cucumber. Commercial ones are usually waxed, generally soft and seedy, not even a shadow of the real thing. Now, however, we can buy one particular type of good cucumber. Individually wrapped in plastic, long and narrow, this seedless cucumber goes by an assortment of names. European—Oriental—Armenian—all refer to the same variety and it is a crisp, good cucumber.

CUCUMBERS

Cucumbers are available all year in varying degrees of edibility. Their peak season is from May through August. At the end of the season I buy a bushel of the tiny last pickings. I put some up as *cornichons*, some as my Arabic Pickles (*see page 106*). Many get eaten fresh; they are so deliciously crisp.

When buying cucumbers, choose those that are firm, well shaped and brightly colored. Large cucumbers, excepting the seedless kind, should be halved lengthwise and seeded (*see Salads chapter for illustration*). Some people peel the cucumbers carefully and thoroughly, while others just score them with a fork. The seedless kind do not need to be peeled. Store them in the refrigerator and use within a week for best flavor.

Sautéed Cucumbers

I was surprised the first time a friend of mine cut cucumbers into thin slices, dipped the slices in flour and fried them in butter until crispy brown, to serve with breakfast. This is another way to sauté cucumbers. Serve as a side dish with lunch or dinner.

> 1 green onion, minced
> 3 tablespoons butter
> 3 cucumbers, cut into ½-inch slices
> salt and pepper to taste
> some chopped dill

Sauté the green onion in the butter until limp. Add the sliced cucumbers and salt and pepper to taste. Cook, turning the cucumbers frequently, for 5 minutes, or until tender. Sprinkle with chopped dill and serve.

Mushroom-stuffed Cucumbers

These are excellent and a true surprise if you have never tasted them before.

DUXELLES

> 2 tablespoons butter
> 2 or 3 green onions, minced
> ½ pound mushrooms, minced
> salt and pepper

> 2 medium tomatoes, seeded and chopped
> 3 or 4 cucumbers
> 1 large egg
> ⅓ to ½ cup bread crumbs
> salt and pepper

SAUCE

> 2 cups heavy cream
> 1 tablespoon minced chives
> 1 tablespoon minced parsley
> salt and pepper to taste

To make the Duxelles heat the butter and in it cook the green onions until soft. Add mushrooms, a very small amount of salt and a good sprinkling of pepper. Cook over high heat, stirring constantly, until all moisture has evaporated, leaving just the sizzling butter. Remove from heat and reserve.

Dice the tomatoes and place in a strainer. Sprinkle with 1 teaspoon salt and let drain.

Peel cucumbers lengthwise in strips, leaving some peel. Cut cucumbers into 4 or 5-inch lengths and halve each lengthwise. Seed with a teaspoon. Blanch the cucumbers in boiling salted water for 4 minutes, drain and rinse under cold water to stop the cooking. Drain again.

Butter a shallow baking dish. Toss the tomatoes with the Duxelles and stir in the egg and bread crumbs. Add salt and pepper to taste. Pack into the cucumber shells and place filled shells in the baking dish. Bake in a 375°F (190°C) for 10 minutes.

While the cucumbers are baking, make the Sauce as follows: Boil the cream over high heat until reduced to 1 cup. This will take at least 5 to 7 minutes and maybe a little longer. Stay with it so that the cream does not boil over. Stir in the herbs and season to taste with salt and pepper if desired. The sauce is deliciously rich and creamy and you might not feel the need of adding salt and pepper. To serve, spoon a little of the sauce onto serving plates and place 1 or 2 stuffed cucumber shells on top. Drizzle with a little more sauce. Serves 6.

Icy Cold Sweet and Sour Cucumbers

People of all nations slice and marinate cucumbers as a cold side dish. This is from Flora Chang's *Creative Chinese Cooking Made Easy.*

> **2 cucumbers, peeled, cut lengthwise and seeded (***I do not seed the European cuke***)**
> **½ teaspoon salt**
> **2 tablespoons vinegar**
> **4 tablespoons sugar (***I use 2 tablespoons***)**
> **1 teaspoon sesame seeds**
> **½ teaspoon Oriental sesame oil**

Slice cucumbers diagonally into thin slices and sprinkle with the salt. Let stand for 30 minutes, then drain. Combine the cucumbers with the vinegar and sugar and chill for at least 2 hours. At serving time sprinkle with the sesame seeds and oil. Serve as a side dish or appetizer.

Note. These will keep, covered in the refrigerator, for up to 2 weeks. You can substitute carrots, cabbage, or daikon radishes, all thinly sliced, for the cucumbers.

EGGPLANT

Friends have always laughed at my addiction to eggplant. And certainly there are enough eggplant recipes throughout this book to indicate a more

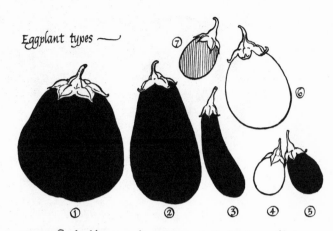

Eggplant types —

①&② *standard large purple;* ③ *Japanese;* ④ *miniature white;* ⑤ *immature purple;* ⑥ *standard white;* & ⑦ *miniature golden.*

than passing interest on my part. My friendly neighborhood produce manager calls me the "eggplant lady," and when he gets in some extra large, extra lovely specimens he saves them for me. I also grow my own so that I can have the tiny ones, as well as different varieties.

The eggplant, called *aubergine* by the French and British, probably originated in India or China, although it is the Mediterranean peoples who have done the most to make it popular.

Eggplant is edible at any stage, although the extra large ones occasionally have too many seeds. Available all year, the peak season is through August and September. Buy those that are firm and smooth. If the eggplant is soft in spots, it is probably brownish on the inside. Eggplants should have a bright, glossy color and be heavy for their size, whatever their size. A bowl of eggplants makes a lovely centerpiece. To store, however, keep them in the refrigerator and use within 2 or 3 days.

To Prepare Eggplant

Before using eggplant, it should first be salted and drained. The only time you do not do this is if you are roasting it whole. Slice it or cut it in half, depending on how you are going to use it. Salt it and place in a colander to drain for 20 to 30

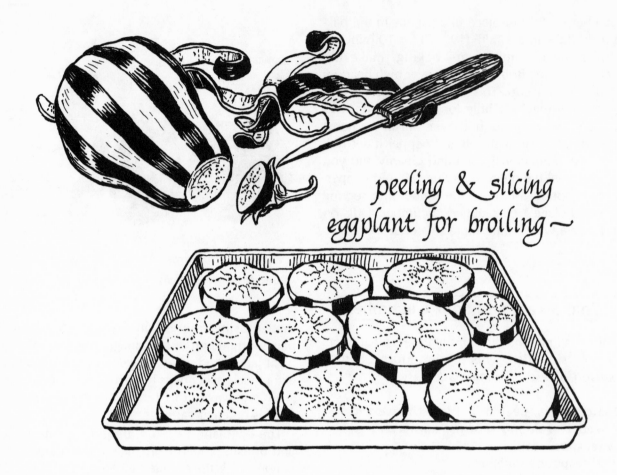

*peeling & slicing
eggplant for broiling~*

minutes. Then rinse and dry. The eggplant should absorb less oil in the cooking when this is done.

Noted for its ability to absorb oil in the frying and then release it while baking, eggplant takes some careful preparation. I rarely fry it, except for making Caponata and Eggplant Parmigiana. A better method is to place the eggplant on an oiled baking sheet and brush each slice with a little oil. Broil until lightly browned, then turn the slices over and brush again with a little oil and broil again until lightly browned. With this method you can at least control the amount of oil that is used.

You can peel eggplant or not, depending on the size of the eggplant and on the use to which it will be put. Larger eggplants generally have a tougher skin and must be peeled. Small eggplants and long, thin ones have a thinner, more tender skin and need not be peeled. I always peel when I make Moussaka or Eggplant Parmigiana.

YIELD: One medium sized eggplant, about 1½ pounds, will serve 4, depending on how it is prepared.

Deep-fried Eggplant Sandwiches

Unfortunately this is not for dieters.

> **2 medium eggplants**
> **salt**
> **flour**
> **olive oil**
> **2 egg yolks**
> **¼ cup grated Parmesan cheese**
> **8 ounces mozzarella cheese, cut into thin
>   slices**
> **2 whole eggs, beaten**
> **fine dry bread crumbs**

Slice eggplant in ¼-inch thick slices and salt and drain as directed in To Prepare Eggplant (*see above*). Then dredge the slices in flour and fry in oil until brown on each side, or broil as directed in To Prepare.

Beat the egg yolks with the grated Parmesan cheese and spread a little of this mixture on ½ of the slices. Cover each of these with a thin slice of mozzarella cut to fit. Cover with another slice of eggplant and press lightly to form a sandwich. Roll each sandwich in flour, then in the beaten eggs and finally in the bread crumbs. Deep fry in hot oil until browned and crisp. Drain well and serve hot. Serves 4 to 6.

Eggplant Sandwiches

This is an alternative to deep frying eggplant sandwiches. These can be served as a side dish with a light meal, or you can cut them carefully into quarters and serve as an appetizer. They are delicious.

> **2 medium eggplants**
> **salt**
> **8 ounces mozzarella cheese, cut into thin slices**
> **½ pound boiled or baked ham, sliced thin**
> **flour for dredging**
> **2 eggs, beaten**
> **½ cup grated Parmesan cheese**
> **½ cup fine dry bread crumbs**
> **olive oil or salad oil**

Peel the eggplant and cut into ¼-inch slices. Salt and drain. Rinse and dry. Place a slice of cheese on half of the eggplant slices. Add a slice of ham. Cover with the remaining eggplant slices and trim if necessary so that they are even all around. Coat with flour and then dip in beaten egg and then in a mixture of the bread crumbs and Parmesan cheese. (Add a tablespoon of onion powder to the crumb mixture, if desired.) Fry gently in oil until browned and cooked on one side then turn over to brown and cook the other side. Serves 4 to 6.

Note. *You can substitute thin slices of tomato for the sliced ham.*

Grilled Eggplant

Cut small eggplants in half lengthwise and brush with a really garlicky olive oil. Place on the bar-becue, cut side down, and grill until browned and slightly burned. Then turn over and grill lightly just until the eggplant feels soft all over. Serve hot as is or sprinkle with a vinaigrette and serve either hot or at room temperature.

Eggplant Parmigiana

A basic Italian dish, this can be complex or simple. But it is always delicious and a dish that is easy to get addicted to. You can substitute your favorite tomato sauce for the Basic Tomato Sauce or use a simple tomato purée. Add Italian sausage or other meat to the sauce to make a light main dish.

> **2 medium eggplants, peeled and sliced in half lengthwise and salted**
> **flour**
> **olive oil**
> **2 cups Basic Tomato Sauce (*see page 126*)**
> **½ pound sliced mozzarella cheese**
> **½ cup grated Parmesan cheese**

Let the salted eggplant drain for 30 minutes, then rinse off the salt and dry the eggplant. Cut the eggplant into lengthwise slices about ½ inch thick. Dredge with flour and brown on each side in hot oil. Drain on paper towels. (See below for variations on this step of preparation.)

Place a single layer of the eggplant in a buttered baking dish. Cover with ⅓ of the sauce and ⅓ of each of the cheeses. Continue layering until you have used all of the ingredients, ending with cheese and sauce on top. Bake in a 350°F (175°C) oven for about 30 minutes. Serves 6.

Note. *One Italian friend of mine slices and salts the eggplant then dips it in a batter made with the following: 1 cup flour, 1 teaspoon baking powder, 1 teaspoon salt, 2 eggs and ½ cup milk. She then fries the slices in hot oil. Another friend dips the slices first in flour, then in beaten egg and lastly in fine, dry bread crumbs before frying.*

This dish freezes well. Freeze before baking, thaw, and proceed as above.

Moussaka

This Greek dish freezes well (I freeze it without the Yogurt Sauce, adding that just at baking time). It can be made with long, thin slices of zucchini or potato instead of the eggplant. Substitute 2 pounds of zucchini, sliced lengthwise and fried, for the eggplant, or an equal amount of sliced, cooked potatoes. Either is traditional, although not as well known. For party purposes the Moussaka can be made a day ahead, (except for the Yogurt Sauce) covered and refrigerated. Add Yogurt Sauce when ready to bake. It is a perfect party dish for 10 or 12 people.

3 large, firm eggplants

SAUCE

2 pounds ground lamb
2 large onions, minced
3 cloves garlic, crushed
½ cup olive oil
1 teaspoon cinnamon
⅓ cup minced parsley
1 8-ounce can tomato sauce
¾ cup dry red wine
salt and pepper

YOGURT SAUCE

4 large eggs
3 cups plain yogurt
¾ cup grated Parmesan cheese
salt and pepper to taste

Peel eggplants in strips, leaving an inch of peel between strips. Cut into ½-inch slices and salt and drain as directed in To Prepare Egglant (*see page 79*). Make the Sauce. Sauté the lamb, onions and garlic in ¼ cup of the olive oil, stirring to break up the meat. Add the cinnamon, parsley, tomato sauce and wine and simmer for 30 minutes to blend flavors. Add salt and pepper to taste.

When the eggplant is ready, broil it as directed in To Prepare, broiling each side.

Make the Yogurt Sauce by combining ingredients and whisking together until smooth and blended.

This recipe will fill two 9 by 13-inch shallow baking dishes. Oil each dish with the remaining ¼ cup oil and cover the bottom of each with a layer of broiled eggplant. Sprinkle each with some grated Parmesan cheese and then spread with the Sauce. Cover each with another layer of eggplant and sprinkle again with some cheese. Cover with the Yogurt Sauce and sprinkle with some more Parmesan cheese. Bake in a 350°F (175°C) oven for 50 minutes to an hour. Cut into squares to serve, first allowing the pans to set at room temperature for 15 minutes. Serves 10 to 12.

Assembling a
Molded Moussaka —

Molded Moussaka

This version of moussaka is a lovely company dish, and is not as difficult to prepare as it appears.

2 1-pound eggplants
⅓ cup olive oil
2 onions, minced
3 cloves garlic, crushed
1½ pounds ground lamb
½ to 1 teaspoon cinnamon
salt and pepper to taste
1 large tomato, seeded and chopped
½ cup plain yogurt
3 tablespoons lemon juice

Prepare eggplants by removing the stems and cutting the fruit lengthwise into quarters. Remove pulp, leaving a shell about ¼ inch thick. Chop the pulp, place it in a colander and sprinkle lightly with salt. Let drain for 20 minutes.

Molded Moussaka

Rub skins with oil and arrange, cut side down, on a lightly oiled baking sheet. Bake, uncovered, in a 450°F (230°C) oven for 35 to 40 minutes. The skins should be quite soft. Loosen from the pan and cool slightly. Then arrange the shells, skin side down, crosswise in an oiled 6-cup ring mold. Set aside.

Heat the ⅓ cup olive oil in a skillet and in it sauté the onion, the eggplant pulp which has been rinsed and patted dry, the garlic and ground lamb. Cook over medium heat, stirring frequently, until the eggplant is tender. Then stir in the cinnamon, salt and pepper and tomato. Continue cooking until the juices have cooked away, and the mixture is somewhat dry. Then stir in the yogurt and the lemon juice. Cook, stirring, until bubbly. If mixture seems too moist at this point, stir in 2 tablespoons of flour. Taste for seasoning and adjust if necessary.

Turn into the ring mold, over the skins, carefully, so as to not move the skins. Fold the ends of the shells (skins) over the filling. Place ring mold on a rimmed baking sheet and bake in a 400°F (205°C) oven for approximately 45 minutes, or until hot in the center. Remove from oven and let stand for 5 minutes. Then place a serving dish upside down over the mold. Hold dish and mold securely and invert. Shake to loosen the moussaka from the mold, and then remove the mold. Serve either hot or at room temperature, with a small bowl of yogurt in the center of the mold. Garnish with lemon twists and fresh mint. Serves 8.

Stuffed Eggplant

Stuffed eggplant, whether small or large, has always been a favorite dish of mine. Two or three times each summer I manage to obtain enough of the small ones for a dinner party. I try to use some of the white ones and some of the purple for the visual appeal, which is quite striking.

For the small eggplant I cut a lid off of the stem end and scoop out the pulp. The pulp is reserved for the bottom of the pot. Salt the eggplants and drain for 30 minutes. Rinse and dry. Continue as for Stuffed Zucchini (*see page 69*), pinning the lid over the stuffing with a toothpick. When cooked, arrange on a serving platter. Depending on size, you would allow 1 or 2 per serving.

The Italians make almost the same dish, only they use a mixture of chopped plum tomatoes, bread crumbs, grated Parmesan cheese and some garlic, and add basil, parsley, salt and pepper to taste. Again, the eggplants are cooked in a pot over the chopped-up pulp and some onion and garlic. A combination of tomato purée and wine is used to cook the eggplant in. You can also use chicken broth, either combined with the tomato or with the wine.

How eggplant is stuffed depends on its size. The small ones, of course, are stuffed whole, except for the long eggplants which are cut lengthwise. Larger eggplants are cut in half lengthwise, or even in quarters, making thick wedge-shaped pieces. (See illustration.) The eggplants are salted and drained for 30 minutes, and then rinsed and dried. A deep slit is cut into the eggplant, and at this point they are usually browned in oil before being stuffed. See the following recipe for a traditional stuffing.

Cook small eggplants on top of the stove, nestled in their own pulp with whole cloves of garlic, some onion and sliced tomato.

Arrange larger eggplants in a shallow baking dish, pour over tomato purée or a homemade tomato sauce (see *Basic Tomato Sauce, page 126*) and bake in a 375°F (190°C) oven for about 45 minutes, or until the eggplant is soft. These are good either hot or at room temperature.

Stuffing for Eggplant

1 onion, minced
1 pound ground lamb
⅓ cup olive oil
1 or 2 cloves garlic, crushed
¼ cup pine nuts
½ teaspoon cinnamon
salt and pepper to taste

Sauté onion and ground lamb in the olive oil until the lamb is cooked and the onion limp. Add the garlic, pine nuts, cinnamon, salt and pepper and cook for another 10 minutes, stirring. This will fill 5 or 6 medium eggplants, or a dozen small whole ones.

Note. *The Lebanese cook will frequently add some chopped fresh tomato and a cup of cooked rice to the filling.*

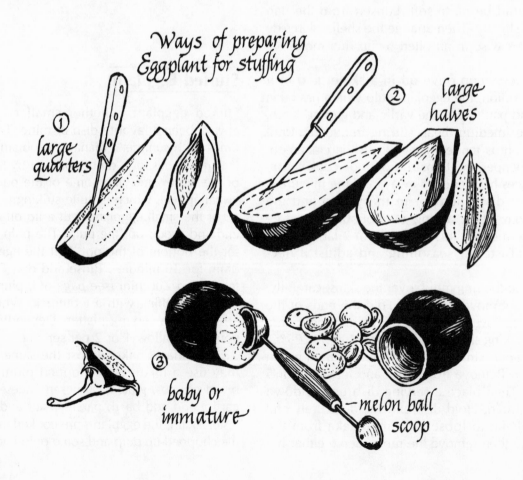

Ways of preparing
Eggplant for stuffing

① large quarters

② large halves

③ baby or immature

melon ball scoop

Eggplant with Pesto

**1 large eggplant, washed and left unpeeled,
cut into 1-inch cubes
oil as needed
1 cup Pesto (*see page 127*)**

Salt the cubes of eggplant and let drain for at least
20 minutes. Then rinse and dry. Sauté the cubes of
eggplant in oil, turning frequently until golden
brown all over. Drain and place in a shallow baking pan and bake in a 350°F (175°C) oven for 20
minutes, or until eggplant is tender. Cool.

When ready to serve, toss the eggplant cubes
with the Pesto very gently, so as to not break up
the cubes. Serve at room temperature. Serves 4 to
6.

Fried Baby Eggplant

This year, for the first time in my life, I actually had
a surplus of baby eggplants. They are just too
choice an item to cut up and use in some dish
where size doesn't matter. So I cut them in half
lengthwise and sprinkled them with salt and let
them drain. Then I rinsed and dried them. I dusted
them with flour, dipped them in beaten egg and
then in bread crumbs and grated Parmesan cheese
and fried them slowly in olive oil. They need to be
fried slowly so that they will cook through. When
well browned and almost done, I turned them over
to fry gently on the skin side for awhile. Piled high
on a platter, crusty side up, they looked as
delicious as they tasted, and they were even good
when cold.

OKRA

A fruit and pod vegetable, okra has a natural
thickening agent and is used to thicken creole
dishes and gumbos. Okra is a vegetable that you
either love or hate. At least I have never met a person who was neutral about it. Okra is popular in
the southern United States, and in the Middle
Eastern countries where it is called "bamia."

To buy, choose medium sized pods either
smooth or ridged, and use within 3 or 4 days.

When cooked, serve immediately. When preparing, do not bruise or break the pods, or they will
become slimy. Cutting is all right. In the south,
okra is available all year. In the north it is available
from April through November.
YIELD: One pound will serve 4.

Okra Hints and Ideas

My stepfather, C.J. Bennett, tells me that his
mother used to slice the okra and "smother-fry" it
in just a little oil, with potatoes and tomatoes.

The okra can be split in half lengthwise, or cut
into horizontal slices, rolled in cornmeal and deep
fried.

It is also very good steamed just until tender and
served with Hollandaise or melted butter.

I steam the okra just until tender and then cover
it with a vinaigrette. It will keep for weeks in the
refrigerator.

Middle Eastern Okra
(Bamia Stew)

Traditionally Middle Eastern, many cooks season
this with coriander.

**1 pound small fresh okra
¼ cup olive oil
½ pound tiny frozen onions, or ½ cup
minced green onions
2 cloves garlic, crushed
½ pound fresh tomatoes, chopped, or 1
8-ounce can tomato purée
salt and pepper to taste
½ cup water or chicken broth
½ lemon**

Wash the okra and cut off the hard stem. Dry. Heat
the oil in a saucepan and sauté the onions and the
garlic until softened. Add okra and fry until lightly
browned. Add tomatoes and season with salt and
pepper. Add water or chicken broth. Cover and
simmer for 30 minutes. Add the juice of ½ lemon
and cook another 10 minutes. Serve hot or lukewarm; the latter is the traditional way. Serves 4.

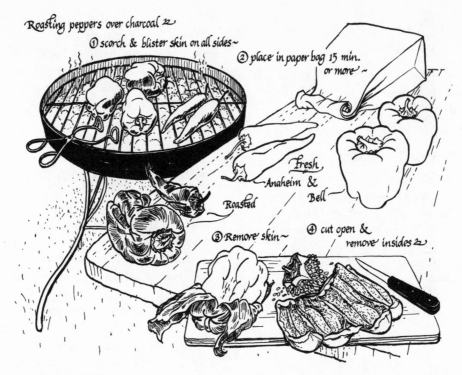

Roasting peppers over charcoal
① scorch & blister skin on all sides~
② place in paper bag 15 min. or more~
Fresh
Anaheim &
Bell
Roasted
③ Remove skin~
④ cut open & remove insides

PEPPERS

There are so many types of peppers, both sweet and hot varieties, that we will deal only with those few found commonly in the market. When buying peppers, buy only those that are firm and well shaped, with thick, brightly colored flesh, whatever that color may be: green, red or yellow. Peppers are best kept, like tomatoes, at a temperature of about 50°F. Lacking that, keep them in the refrigerator and use within a week. Green peppers are available all year. Red peppers are usually available in the markets only during August and September.

Peppers freeze well if chopped first. Whole or sliced peppers do not freeze satisfactorily. Just chop in small dice and freeze on baking sheets. When frozen, bag the chopped peppers in whatever quantity you wish. The amount of peppers you wish to use can just be shaken out.

YIELD: Allow 1 pepper per person, unless you are preparing the peppers with quantities of other vegetables.

Roasted Peeled Peppers

Around the Mediterranean bell peppers, either red or green, are frequently roasted and peeled before use. The Italians cut the roasted peeled peppers in quarters and use them in sandwiches as well as diced in salads, and cut in strips and marinated in oil with garlic and anchovies as part of an antipasto tray. The Basques use them in their Piperade and the Spanish in Paella. The Moroccans dice the peeled peppers and use them in salads.

The roasted, peeled red pepper is the pimiento that we buy in small jars to use in potato and macaroni salads. As you can see the popular bell pepper assumes a completely different character when roasted and peeled. The crispness is gone, but in its place is a rich softness.

The process is simple, although not quite as simple as the instructions in some books and magazines would have you believe. I read in one magazine that all you have to do is place the pepper in a 400°F oven for 10 to 12 minutes and the skin will peel off. *Not so.* What you will have is a half-cooked pepper that isn't going to do anything. Other authorities will tell you how to properly char the peppers, but then they insist that the peppers must be peeled immediately, while still hot. *Again, not so.*

Use your broiler or charcoal grill, or the burners on a gas stove.

The peppers must be roasted until the skin is uniformly blistered and charred. Turn them frequently. Large peppers which are rounded and have no convolutions are easiest to roast. The ripe red pepper will char more quickly and you should be careful that it doesn't burn. The peel of the peppers must be blackened, but you must catch it right before the flesh burns.

Place the charred peppers in a paper or plastic bag and seal. The peppers will steam in their own heat for at least 15 or 20 minutes, at the end of which time the skin will peel right off. However, I have on occasion left the peppers in the bag for several hours at the end of which time they still peeled easily. Peel them under running water, or with a bowl of water nearby in which to dip the peppers so that all of the charred pieces are washed off. Then cut the peppers in half lengthwise and remove the stem and seeds.

Place the peppers in a jar or refrigerator container with some of their own juices and cover with oil to which you have added a clove of garlic. The peppers will keep, refrigerated, for at least a week.

To Freeze Roast Peppers

Roast and peel peppers as directed above. After seeding simply lay the peppers in ½-pint jars with a clove of garlic and some of their own juices. They do not need to be covered with liquid. Seal and freeze. Thaw before using.

Peppers with Anchovies

Roast, peel and seed the peppers as directed. Lay the peppers in a container with several cloves of garlic and several flat fillets of anchovies. Cover with some of the juices and a good olive oil. Keep refrigerated. These are especially good on an antipasto tray.

In Denmark the roasted peeled peppers are marinated in a delicious mixture of olive oil, wine vinegar and Dijon mustard.

Roasted California Green Chilis

California green chilis, or Anaheims, as they are also called, are simple to roast and peel. Do it yourself to save half the cost of the canned green chilis and to produce a flavor and texture which is

remarkably better. Simply roast and peel them as directed for Roasted Peeled Peppers (*See above.*). However, the green chilis peel more easily *after* they have been frozen. I simply put 8 hot roasted peppers into a plastic bag and let them steam. Then I squeeze the air out of the bag and seal it. I've kept them frozen for up to 8 months. To use simply thaw and the peel comes right off. These chilis are marvelous in dips, casseroles, sauces and of course are a necessary ingredient in Chilis Rellenos. Use a few for a mild flavor. Use a lot and they become increasingly hotter and spicier.

Chilis Rellenos 1

This is of Mexican origin. You can use either the canned Anaheim chilis, or the fresh which have been roasted and peeled (*see above*). The fresh are, of course, much better. I deep fry these so that they will stay reasonably round. You can pan fry them if you wish.

**12 large California green chilis, roasted and
 peeled
strips of Monterey Jack cheese
Batter** (*see below*)
oil for deep frying

Leave the stems on the chilis for appearance's sake. Open a small slit just below the stem and remove seeds with your fingers. Insert strips of cheese into the chilis, using care not to split them. If you do split a few, just continue as directed and, when deep frying, hold the split ones together with tongs until the batter has firmed. They won't look as good, but they will still taste good. Place the filled peppers on paper towels to drain. Make the Batter and dip the stuffed chilis into the Batter and then into hot fat. Fry until golden. Drain and serve hot with a side dish of red or green chili *salsa*, which you can find in your Mexican food department. Or see Salsa Verde (*page 126*).

Batter For Chilis Rellenos

The blue cornmeal is not blue, but rather a grayish color. It doesn't look as nice as the yellow, but it seems to fry up crisper.

1 cup flour
1 teaspoon baking powder
pinch of salt
¾ cup blue or yellow cornmeal
1 cup milk
2 eggs, beaten

Combine dry and liquid ingredients. Add more milk if necessary. Batter should be smooth and should cling to the chilis.

Chilis Rellenos 2

In this dish, a popover batter puffs above the cheese-filled chilis. This is nice with breakfast, or with barbecues.

1 7-ounce can green chili sauce or fresh
   Salsa Verde *(see page 126)*
8 California green chilis, roasted and
   peeled
8 finger strips of Monterey Jack cheese
2 large eggs
½ cup milk
1 small clove garlic, crushed
½ cup flour
pinch salt
¹/₈ teaspoon cumin
¹/₈ teaspoon oregano

Butter an 8-inch square shallow baking dish. Spoon the green chili salsa into the dish. Prepare chilis by removing the stems and stuffing each with a strip of cheese. Arrange in the dish over the salsa. Set aside.

Combine the eggs, milk, garlic, flour, salt, cumin and oregano and blend or process until smooth. Pour over the chilis. Bake in a 400°F (205°C) oven for 15 to 20 minutes, or until puffy and lightly browned. Cut into squares to serve. Serves 4.

Red and Green Pepper Sauce with Pasta

This is a little different for those who have not yet been exposed to a cold vegetable sauce over hot pasta. The contrast in temperature, texture and flavors is excellent.

1 large green pepper
1 large red pepper
2 California green chilis, roasted and
   peeled, diced
1 bunch green onions, thinly sliced
2 cloves garlic, crushed
1 tablespoon fresh basil, or 1 teaspoon
   dried basil
½ teaspoon salt
freshly ground black pepper to taste
1 tablespoon red wine vinegar
¼ cup olive oil
2 or 3 ripe tomatoes, peeled, seeded and
   chopped
½ cup grated Parmesan cheese
12 ounces linguine or other pasta

Remove stems, cores and seeds from the peppers. Cut into fine strips, or shred in a food processor. Turn into a mixing bowl and add the green chilis, the green onions, garlic, basil, salt, pepper, vinegar and olive oil. Chill for at least several hours, or overnight, stirring occasionally. Remove from refrigerator several hours before using, to allow the sauce to come to room temperature. Add the tomatoes and cheese just before using.

Cook the linguine just until al dente. Drain quickly, but *do not rinse*. Turn into a serving bowl or platter and mix with the sauce quickly and thoroughly. Serve with more cheese. Serves 4.

Italian Peppers
(Peperonata)

This is a lovely side dish with almost anything, and looks as lovely as it tastes.

5 or 6 peppers (*a mixture of red, green and
   yellow if possible*)
1 onion, minced
⅓ cup olive oil

2 cups chopped plum tomatoes
½ teaspoon salt
2 or 3 cloves garlic, crushed
1 tablespoon fresh basil, or 1 teaspoon dried
⅓ cup dry white wine

Remove stews, cores and seeds from the peppers. Cut them into narrow strips.

Sauté the onion in the oil just until limp. Add the peppers and sauté briskly for about 15 minutes. Add the tomatoes, salt, garlic and basil and cook for 15 to 20 minutes, or until vegetables are cooked. Add wine and cook for another 5 minutes. The tomatoes should have reduced to a thick mixture. Serves 4 to 6.

TOMATOES

The best tomatoes, of course, are those we pick, fully ripe, and eat out of hand, still warm from the sun. Next best are vine-ripened tomatoes from the vegetable market.

The tomato is a member of the nightshade family, along with the potato, peppers and eggplant. And tobacco. It originated in Peru and from there found its way to Europe, where it was grown as an ornamental, considered to be too poisonous to eat. The Italians, however, began using it as food several hundred years ago. The French followed suit, but it was not eaten in this country until the latter half of the 19th century.

Tomatoes are available year round, but peak during the spring and summer months. When buying tomatoes, buy those that are firm and red. Avoid pink or green-tinged tomatoes, and those that are soft or bruised. Most people store tomatoes in the refrigerator. However, they are best kept at room temperature, except on the hottest days.

My favorite variety for all-around use is the Italian plum tomato. Pear-shaped, and either red or yellow, the plum tomato is thick-fleshed and pulpy, with little liquid and few seeds. It has a rich flavor and is easily chopped and used in sauces or in salads, or sliced and served sprinkled with olive oil and basil.

The large beefsteak tomatoes are lovely just sliced and served alongside a salad.

Tomato Hints and Ideas

Cherry tomatoes can be marinated in a vinaigrette for several hours and served as a side dish. First poke some holes in each with a toothpick, so that the flavor penetrates.

Cherry tomatoes are also nice when stuffed. Scoop out the seeds and some of pulp with a melon baller and drain the tomatoes. Use a pastry tube to fill them with some flavorful cream cheese mixture, or with a smoked salmon and cream cheese mixture.

Take medium tomatoes and cut them in half horizontally. Combine ½ cup homemade mayonnaise with ½ cup sour cream and ½ teaspoon curry powder. Spread on the tomato halves and bake in a 350°F (175°C) oven for 25 minutes, or until soft.

Cherry tomatoes are good when sautéed in garlic and butter just until the skins pop, about 7 or 8 minutes. Serve hot.

Don't forget how nice green tomatoes are when sliced and dredged in cornmeal or flour and lightly fried in butter.

I frequently add wedges of green tomato to my Arabic Pickles (*see page 106*).

To Freeze Tomatoes

Tomatoes freeze very successfully, for cooking purposes. One friend packs them either whole or halved in containers. When thawed, they look and feel like canned tomatoes, but taste as if freshly picked. Use them as you would any canned tomato.

Another way to freeze tomatoes is as a basic sauce. First, chop fresh tomatoes in the food processor. Note that I said *chop* them. Do *not* purée them. Turn them into a large pot with some minced onion and crushed garlic and a bay leaf or 2, some sweet basil and salt and pepper. (The amounts of course, depend on how many tomatoes I am using, however, I generally do this in quantity.) Simmer mixture gently until it is reduced by half. Then turn it into containers and freeze it (be sure to allow an inch of head space). To use, thaw some of the sauce and thin with red wine, or chicken or beef broth.

Italian Tomatoes

A friend shared this with me and we love them.

3 tablespoons minced parsley
3 tablespoons minced fresh basil
1 tablespoon minced fresh chives
½ teaspoon salt if desired
½ cup soft fresh bread crumbs
3 tablespoons olive oil
1 bunch green onions, minced
1 large clove garlic, crushed
6 large ripe tomatoes, sliced
some grated Parmesan cheese

Mix the herbs with the salt and bread crumbs. Set aside. Heat the oil in a large skillet. Add the onions and garlic and cook, stirring, until limp but not browned. Spread onion mixture in a shallow baking dish. Top with the sliced tomatoes. Sprinkle with the bread crumb mixture and drizzle with a little more olive oil and the cheese. Bake in a 350°F (175°C) oven for 25 minutes, or until the tomatoes are tender and the crumbs lightly browned. Serves 6.

Baked Green Tomatoes

1 teaspoon salt
½ teaspoon freshly ground black pepper
2 tablespoons minced fresh chives
2 tablespoons minced fresh basil
½ cup each: fresh bread crumbs and grated Parmesan cheese
8 medium sized green tomatoes, cut into thick slices
¼ cup butter
¼ cup grated Parmesan cheese

Combine the salt and pepper, herbs and the ½ cup each of bread crumbs and grated cheese. Set aside.

Layer the green tomatoes in a greased 9 by 13-inch baking dish, sprinkling each layer with some of the herb mixture. Dot the top with the butter and sprinkle with the ¼ cup cheese. Bake in a 350°F (175°C) oven for 1 hour. Serve hot. Serves 6 to 8.

Pennsylvania Dutch Tomatoes

These are delicious.

6 large, firm, ripe tomatoes
flour
¼ pound butter
some brown sugar
½ teaspoon salt if desired
freshly ground black pepper
1½ cups heavy cream

Cut each tomato into thick slices, first discarding the little stem end. Dredge in flour. Melt the butter and when it is hot, add as many tomato slices as will fit. Fry until brown. Then place ½ teaspoon brown sugar on each slice and turn the slices. Sprinkle with a little salt and black pepper and a little more brown sugar if desired. When the second side is browned, turn the slices again, so as to carmelize the sugar. Continue, until all of the tomato slices are cooked, keeping some cooked slices warm in the oven if your skillet isn't large enough to fit them all. Do not overcook. The tomato slices should not cook to mush. Return all slices to the skillet and pour on the cream. Cook a few minutes longer and serve to 6.

Tomato Cases

Remove stems if they are still attached. Place each tomato stem end down, as the tomato sits solidly on this end. Cut a slice off the base (opposite end) and reserve. Use a spoon to scoop out the seeds and pulp, leaving a good sustaining shell. Invert the shells to drain for about 20 minutes before filling.

Following are recipes using Tomato Cases, uncooked and cooked.

Cold Stuffed Tomatoes

Tomatoes make marvelous containers for almost anything, and stuffed tomatoes are practical in the summertime, either as side dishes or as appetizers.

Prepare Tomato Cases (*see above*) and fill with any of the following.

1. Your favorite tuna, crab or shrimp salad.
2. A zippy macaroni or potato salad. If using potato salad, cut the potatoes rather small.
3. One of the better magazines recently showed tomatoes stuffed with vermicelli that had been cooked and then mixed with Pesto (*see Sauces*) and grated Parmesan cheese. I have made it several times, and each time the combination has been a big hit with my guests and students. The pale green filling contrasts beautifully with the bright red of the tomato.
4. A cold rice salad mixed with a good vinaigrette and plenty of fresh vegetables.
5. Make a shrimp salad with small cooked shrimp, sliced black olives, feta cheese and minced green onion. Dress with a good vinaigrette and fill the tomatoes. Garnish with mint.

Stuffed Tomatoes

Hot Stuffed Tomatoes

6 large tomatoes
⅓ cup butter
1 onion, minced
1 cup long-grain white rice
2 or 3 large mushrooms, minced
1 cup dry white wine
2 cups chicken broth
¼ cup grated Parmesan cheese
olive oil

Prepare Tomato Cases as directed (*See above*). Reserve pulp.

Cook the reserved pulp with 1 tablespoon of the butter until reduced to a moderately thick paste. Purée and set aside.

Heat remaining butter and in it sauté the onion until limp. Add the rice, stirring to coat with the butter. Then add the mushrooms. Stir and cook for several minutes until rice begins to turn opaque. Then add the wine and chicken broth. Cover and let cook until rice is done, about 20 minutes. The liquid should have been absorbed. Stir in the cheese and remaining butter.

Fill tomato shells with the rice and coat the tops with the reserved tomato paste. Sprinkle with a little olive oil. Arrange on a shallow baking dish and bake in a 400°F (205°C) oven for 20 minutes, or until shells are tender. Do not overcook. Serves 6.

Baked Stuffed Tomatoes

In the Middle East these are traditionally served cold. You can serve them either hot or cold.

12 medium tomatoes
½ cup olive oil
1 onion, minced
1 clove garlic, crushed
⅓ cup pine nuts
1 cup long-grain white rice
1 teaspoon salt if desired
1¾ cups water
¾ cup dry white wine
2 tablespoons minced parsley
mint leaves for garnish

Prepare the tomatoes for stuffing, reserving the pulp (*see Tomato Cases, above*). Turn the pulp into a saucepan with some salt and pepper. Simmer until soft and then press through a sieve. If you are certain that there are no seeds in the pulp, it can be puréed in the food processor.

Heat ¼ cup of the oil. Sauté the onion and garlic until limp. Add pine nuts and cook another 3 or 4 minutes, stirring. Stir in the rice, salt, water, wine and parsley and simmer until liquid is absorbed and rice is tender. Fill the tomatoes. Combine the tomato pulp with an equal quantity of white wine and turn into a shallow baking dish. Add tomatoes, topping them with the lids. Drizzle with the remaining ¼ cup olive oil and bake in a 350°F (175°C) oven for 25 to 30 minutes. Serves 6.

Middle Eastern Stuffed Tomatoes

A combination of stuffed vegetables is often served in the Middle East. Stuffed green peppers and tomatoes are a lovely combination.

6 medium tomatoes
6 medium peppers

FILLING

½ cup long-grain rice
1 pound lean lamb, ground
2 fresh tomatoes, seeded and diced
6 green onions, minced
1 teaspoon salt, if desired
pepper to taste
¼ cup pine nuts
½ teaspoon cinnamon

Prepare the tomatoes for stuffing (*see Tomato Cases*), reserving the pulp. Cut the lids off the peppers and remove seeds and cores. Save all the lids.

To make the filling cook the rice, drain, and reserve. Sauté the ground lamb in a small amount of oil, stirring to break up lumps, until it loses color. Combine rice, lamb, and remaining filling ingredients.

Stuff the vegetables with the filling, allowing room for expansion. Combine the tomato pulp with an equal amount of white wine and pour into a shallow baking dish. Arrange the stuffed peppers and tomatoes over this in a single layer. Drizzle with a little oil and replace the lids. Bake, uncovered, in a 350°F (175°C) oven for 45 minutes to an hour, or until peppers are done. If you wish the tomatoes to retain their shape better, add them to the baking dish about 20 minutes after the peppers, as the peppers take longer to bake than do the tomatoes. Serves 6 to 8.

Spinach-stuffed Tomatoes

Prepare 8 Tomato Cases. (*See above.*). Cook 2 10-ounce packages frozen chopped spinach and drain well. Combine spinach, 2 tablespoons fresh basil, and ¼ cup grated Parmesan cheese (or some crumbled Roquefort), and fill the tomatoes. Take 8 nice mushrooms and push 1 down into the filling of each tomato. Dot with a little butter and place in a shallow baking pan. Bake in a 400°F (205°C) oven for 20 to 25 minutes. Serve immediately to 8.

The Mavericks

The mavericks in this chapter are simply those vegetables which didn't seem to fit into any of the other vegetable categories. Celery and asparagus are stalks. Globe artichokes are the fleshy, leafy buds of a perfectly beautiful plant. Mushrooms are a fungus; they have had entire books devoted just to them.

To appreciate mushrooms at their best you should taste some wild mushrooms. Morels are my particular favorite. When I receive morels from mushroom-hunting friends, I slice them and sauté them gently in butter with a hint of garlic and some good white wine. I serve them with chilled white wine and a crusty bread to soak up all of the lovely, delicious sauce.

ARTICHOKES

Anyone who has ever traveled the California coastal towns where artichokes are the main commercial crop can testify to the beauty of the plant, with its feathery, silver green foliage and the purple-blue flower heads of the unpicked artichokes.

There is no such thing as a "green" artichoke. A larger size, for example, does not mean that the ar-

tichoke is riper than the smaller ones. The small artichokes that one finds for sale in areas around the commercial growers are not "babies." The size of the artichoke is determined by where on the plant it grows. The largest artichoke on a plant grows right on the tip. Those a little farther down will be the next largest. The farther down the plant an artichoke grows, the smaller will be its size.

Buy artichokes with tight, compact heads. You can safely buy artichokes with bruised outer leaves

as these can be discarded. Avoid artichokes with leaves that have opened, or those whose leaves have curled on the side or are turning brown. To store the artichokes wrap them, without washing, in clear plastic wrap and refrigerate for up to 2 weeks.

To prepare artichokes, first remove and discard any bruised leaves. Cut an inch off of the top of the artichoke. Cut off the stem end to make a flat base for the artichoke to sit on. Now trim each leaf with a scissors. Since artichokes will darken on standing, drop them into acidulated water (*add 1 tablespoon lemon juice to 1 quart water*) until ready to use.

Either boil or steam artichokes. Boil in salted water with ⅓ cup lemon juice or white wine vinegar, 2 tablespoons olive oil, 2 bay leaves and 3 cloves garlic. Rest a plate on the artichokes to keep them submerged. They will take about 20 to 30 minutes, depending on size.

Or stand them upright in a deep saucepan. Poke a whole clove of garlic into the center of each artichoke and drizzle them with a little olive oil, about 2 or 3 tablespoons for the entire pot. Add salted boiling water to come about 2 inches up the chokes. Sprinkle with ⅓ cup lemon juice. Cover and cook gently for about 20 to 25 minutes, or until they are done. Larger chokes will take longer.

To steam, place the artichokes, either whole or halved lengthwise, in a steamer and steam for the same amount of time, or until tender.

Artichoke Hints and Ideas

Serve any of the cooked artichokes with a dipping sauce. Use mayonnaise, or Hollandaise Sauce (*see page 124*), or melted butter blended with a touch of garlic and some lemon juice.

You can deep fry small artichokes. Parboil them, cut in halves or quarters. Dip in flour, then in beaten egg and bread crumbs and deep fry. Serve hot.

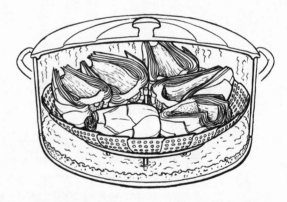

Don't forget that the canned artichoke bottoms can be stuffed with any cold mixture to serve as an hors d'oeuvre.

Canned artichoke hearts are worth keeping on the shelf to use in salads or other cooked dishes, and of course in marinades. The frozen chokes are also good.

Make up a dozen tart shells. Cream together an 8-ounce package cream cheese with 1 egg, 2 dashes Worcestershire sauce, a dash Tabasco, 2 tablespoons melted butter and a 14-ounce can artichoke hearts, drained and chopped. Turn into the tart shells and bake in a 350°F (175°C) oven for 25 to 30 minutes.

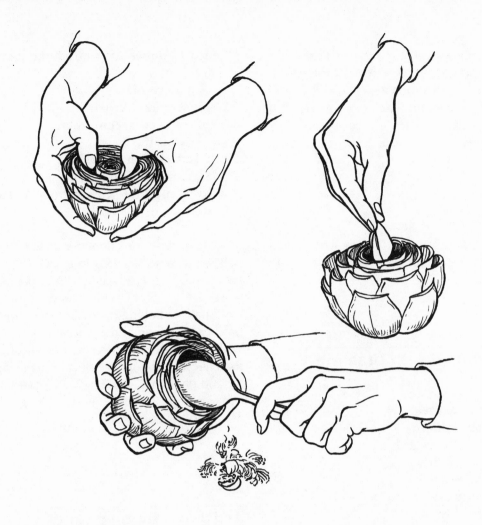

Stuffed Artichokes Italian Style

This is a dramatic dish. Prepare and cook the artichokes as previously directed, only cook them just 15 minutes. Do not overcook. Remove from the water and drain upside down. Cool. To make a hollow for the stuffing, gently pull out the center leaves and, with a teaspoon, scrape out and remove the fuzzy inner choke.

8 medium artichokes, prepared as directed above
5 cups Herb-seasoned Bread Crumbs (see below)
4 hard-cooked eggs, chopped
8 anchovy fillets, minced
salt and pepper to taste
¼ cup olive oil

5 cups Basic Tomato Sauce (see page 126)
1 cup grated Parmesan cheese

Combine bread crumbs, egg, anchovies, salt and pepper. Mix well and stuff the filling in the center cavity of the artichokes and then fill between the leaves, using a teaspoon to stuff the filling in. Place the filled chokes in a greased shallow baking dish. Drizzle with the olive oil. Pour half of the Tomato Sauce around the chokes and the rest over them. Sprinkle with the cheese. Cover the dish with foil and bake in a 350°F (175°C) oven for 25 to 30 minutes. Remove foil for the last few minutes. Chokes are done when the heart can be pierced easily. Serves 8.

Herb-seasoned Bread Crumbs

Combine all of the following: 6 cups fine dry bread crumbs, ¼ cup minced dried parsley, 3 tablespoons onion powder, 1 cup grated Parmesan cheese, 1 teaspoon garlic powder, 1 tablespoon dried oregano, 1 tablespoon dried basil, 2 tea-spoons salt and 1 teaspoon black pepper. Keep in the refrigerator. This is the same mix that you buy packaged for several dollars a pound.

Artichoke Caviar

Drain artichoke bottoms and fill each with a nice egg salad. Sprinkle the tops with caviar and serve as an hors d'oeuvre.

Artichokes Stuffed with Crab Meat

**10 artichokes
1 cup cooked crab meat
3 green onions, minced
1 teaspoon Dijon mustard
salt and pepper to taste
mayonnaise to moisten
some very thinly sliced celery
20 pitted black olives
20 thin small carrot sticks**

Prepare artichokes as directed in the introduction. Cook completely, then remove from water and drain upside down. Cool and remove inner leaves and the fuzzy choke. Set aside.

Combine the crab meat, green onions, mustard, salt and pepper, mayonnaise and celery. Mix well and stuff into the centers of the artichokes. Insert a carrot stick into each olive. Serve the artichokes, cold, on individual plates garnished with the carrot sticks and olives and some shredded lettuce if desired.

Artichokes al Forno

This is Italian. You can substitute sliced zucchini or eggplant for the artichokes. The eggplant should be salted and drained before rinsing, drying and sau-téing in oil.

**1 or 2 14-ounce cans artichoke hearts, well
   drained
⅓ cup olive oil
2 cloves garlic, crushed
1 cup minced green onions
1 teaspoon basil
salt and pepper if desired
6 large eggs, beaten
⅓ to ½ cup grated Parmesan cheese
butter**

Drain and rinse the canned artichoke hearts. Cut in half lengthwise. Sauté gently in the olive oil with the garlic. You are sautéing to enhance the flavor, since the artichokes are already cooked. Remove to a shallow baking dish. Sauté the onion with the basil gently, then add to the artichokes and season with salt and pepper to taste. Beat the eggs with the cheese and pour over the chokes. Dot with butter and bake in a 350°F (175°C) oven until set, approximately 25 minutes. Check at 20 minutes. Serve hot or cold to 6.

Artichoke Dipping Sauce

Yet another dipping sauce for plain boiled or steamed artichokes is made as follows: Combine 2 tablespoons each: Oriental sesame oil (or corn or peanut oil) and white wine vinegar with 1 table-spoon minced fresh coriander, 1 tablespoon lemon juice, 1 small clove garlic, crushed, a teaspoon minced green onion and a dash of freshly ground black pepper.

Artichokes with Mushrooms

For this I like to use large mushrooms and leave them whole, or cut in halves or quarters if extreme-ly large.

**1 pound large mushrooms
⅓ cup butter
2 14-ounce cans artichoke hearts,
   well drained**

salt and pepper to taste
pinch of thyme
½ cup dry sherry

Prepare mushrooms by snapping out the stems and wiping the mushrooms clean. Reserve mushroom stems for another use. Sauté the mushrooms in the butter until just tender. Add the drained artichokes, the seasonings and the wine. Cook over high heat to reduce the sauce. This will take about 2 or 3 minutes. Serve immediately to 6.

ASPARAGUS

Asparagus is an early spring vegetable. When buying, look for stalks that are a nice green, brittle, and with tips that are well formed and tight. If the tips are spread, that means the stalks are overmature.

To store, wrap unwashed in plastic bags, or in a refrigerator container. Use as soon as possible. Allow about ½ pound per person.

Asparagus Hints and Ideas

Asparagus is good hot, cold or in between. If you are going to serve it raw, in a salad, first blanch the tips for exactly 1 minute. It livens the flavor.

Add the raw, blanched tips to pasta salads or green salads. Or serve with a dip as part of a vegetable tray.

Serve the whole stalks as a first course, simply dressed with Hollandaise or melted butter with a touch of lemon juice.

Cut 2 pounds asparagus diagonally into 2-inch lengths. Blanch for 3 minutes in boiling water. Chill in the following sauce for at least 30 minutes: Combine ½ cup soy sauce, ¼ cup white wine vinegar, ½ teaspoon sugar and 1 teaspoon toasted sesame seeds.

Serve cooked asparagus with dill-seasoned sour cream. The asparagus may be either hot or cold.

Sprinkle hot cooked asparagus with grated Parmesan cheese and drizzle with browned butter.

Dress with a good vinaigrette and chill for 24 hours before serving.

The Perfect Way to Cook Asparagus

You may already cook asparagus this way. But most people I've seen struggle to cook it standing upright in the pot. Simply snap the stems and either discard the bottoms or save to use in stocks. Lay the asparagus in a skillet no more than 2 layers deep. Cover with boiling salted water and cook for 7 to 8 minutes only, unless the asparagus is extremely chunky in which case it *may* take a minute longer. The asparagus should be tender/crisp and bright green. It works perfectly every time.

Crepes with Asparagus

Make your favorite crepes, about 6 inches in diameter, allowing 1 per serving. Cook asparagus as directed above (*The Perfect Way to Cook Asparagus*). Use 2 or 3 spears, wrapped in prosciutto, as the filling for each crepe. Lay filled crepes in a shallow baking pan and heat in a moderate oven for 10 to 15 minutes. Before serving sprinkle with chopped hard-cooked egg and drizzle with Hollandaise Sauce (*see page 124*).

CELERY

We tend to take celery for granted as we do carrots and potatoes, only more so. We rarely prepare celery by itself, but relegate it to the back steps where its only function, it seems, is to complement other vegetables by adding flavor and texture. Prepared by itself, as in the recipes and ideas that follow, celery is delicious.

When buying, choose heads with crisp stalks and bright leaves. Avoid celery that is flaccid or bruised. Celery will keep, in a plastic bag, for up to 2 weeks in the refrigerator.

Celery Tips and Ideas

Clean the celery and trim top and bottom to make about 6-inch lengths. Cut into halves or quarters lengthwise and cook until just done in chicken broth or beef stock. Serve dressed with a Mornay, Bearnaise or Hollandaise sauce.

And don't forget how nice celery is when the stalks are stuffed with a cream cheese mixture. I like to mix softened cream cheese with red caviar. Almost any cream cheese mixture is good.

Braised Celery in Wine

This is a lovely use for the celery hearts that are sold packaged.

**3 medium heads celery, or the whole celery
   hearts**
⅓ cup butter
1 cup chicken broth
½ cup dry white wine
**sliced almonds, sautéed in butter until
   golden, optional**

Wash the celery and cut stalks lengthwise from top to bottom. Sauté in the butter until golden green, turning when necessary. Add the chicken broth and wine and cover and simmer until celery is crisp/tender. Remove to a hot serving dish and keep warm. Reduce the sauce until it has a glazed appearance and pour over the celery. Garnish with the almonds and strips of pimiento. Serves 8.

Celery Victor

This is for your finest dinner party.

2 large bunches celery
1 quart chicken broth
¾ cup olive oil
⅓ cup Sauterne
1 tablespoon lemon juice
1 teaspoon salt if desired
freshly ground black pepper to taste
¼ teaspoon paprika
¼ teaspoon Worcestershire sauce
1 tablespoon grated onion
16 anchovy fillets

Trim the root and leaf ends of the celery to make bunches about 6 inches long. Cut lengthwise into quarters. If necessary remove some of the outer stalks so that you have a nice trim bundle. Wash and dry.

Cook the celery in the chicken broth for 20 minutes, or until just tender. Let the celery cool in the broth and then drain. Arrange in a large, shallow dish. Combine the oil, wine, lemon juice, salt, pepper, paprika, Worcestershire and onion and whisk together. Pour over celery wedges and chill overnight if possible, or at least for several hours.

To serve, line individual salad dishes with chopped lettuce. Lay a celery wedge over each and crisscross with anchovy fillets, 2 on each. Drizzle with some of the marinade and serve to 8.

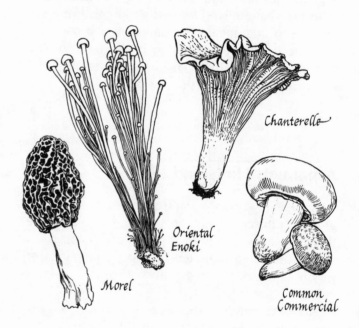

Chanterelle

Oriental
Enoki

Morel

Common
Commercial

MUSHROOMS

Not truly a vegetable, but rather a curious plant with no roots, stems or leaves. There are over 3000 species of edible mushrooms but it still is not safe to pick any wild ones unless you are expert at it.

You need not buy the large, perfect, expensive mushrooms if all you will be doing with them is chopping them to sauté or add to some other dish. For that purpose, you can buy small mushrooms or those that are browner and have open caps. These are simply more mature and have a more definite flavor. They are fine for most cooking purposes. Avoid mushrooms that are slimy, bruised, or shriveled. If you are planning to stuff the mushrooms, where appearances count, then you want perfect mushrooms that are large, with closed caps.

I frequently buy the bargain-basket mushrooms, if they look good enough, chop them and simmer gently in butter with minced onion, garlic and some herbs. When cooked, I package them in small containers and freeze. They are perfect for mushroom flavor.

Mushrooms should be refrigerated and used quickly. Do not wash them. Just wipe with a damp towel.

The Enoki mushroom, which is sold in some specialty markets, grows in leggy stemmed clusters. It has a small, tight cap and is sometimes called Velvet Stem or Snow Puff. It has a mild flavor that is excellent in salads and clear soups or added to a stir-fry just before removing from the stove.

As for dried mushrooms, you can dry your own quite successfully. However, none of the home-dried can equal the Italian *Boletus*, which I soak and use in Italian tomato sauce, or the Oriental *Shiitaki*. I can't resist sharing one idea for Shiitaki that is Japanese in origin, but which I serve with all Oriental meals. Select 10 large Shiitaki and soak in 2 cups warm water to cover for 20 minutes. Then remove from the water, reserving both the liquid and the mushrooms. Remove and discard the stems and cut the mushrooms into wedges. Pour off 1½ cups of the soaking liquid into a saucepan and add 1½ teaspoons of sugar. Bring to a boil and boil gently for 5 minutes. Actually that would be a nice simmer. Then add 1 tablespoon soy sauce and simmer for another 5 minutes. One minute before removing from the stove add 1 tablespoon Mirin (a sweet rice cooking wine—if unavailable, use sweet sherry). Add Shiitaki and let stand for 15 minutes before serving, to allow the mushrooms to soak up as much liquid as possible. Serve as a side dish.

YIELD: One pound will serve 4. One pound sliced cooked mushrooms equals an 8-ounce can of mushrooms. Two ounces of dried mushrooms, soaked in 1½ cups lukewarm water, equals 1⅓ cups chopped with liquid. There are 20 to 24 medium sized mushrooms in a pound. Twelve to 14 very large mushrooms make a pound.

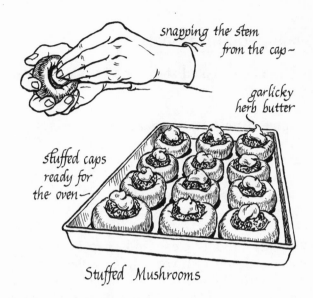

snapping the stem from the cap~

garlicky herb butter

stuffed caps ready for the oven~

Stuffed Mushrooms

Stuffed Mushrooms

The extra large mushroom caps (those that weigh in at 12 to 14 to the pound) are very nice when stuffed. Wipe them with a damp cloth. Snap the stems out and save for use chopped. Drop mushroom caps into acidulated water (1 tablespoon lemon juice to 1 quart water) for several minutes. Remove from water and stuff with any of the following:

1. For 1 pound of mushrooms use a tablespoon of minced green onion mixed with ½ cup minced salami and ½ cup smoked cheese spread with a tablespoon of catsup. Sprinkle stuffed mushrooms with bread crumbs. To bake, see below.

2. Melt ¼ cup butter and in it sauté 4 minced cloves of garlic, ⅓ cup minced onion, ⅓ cup each minced green pepper and red pepper or pimiento. Add ⅓ cup fine, dry bread crumbs, 1 beaten egg, salt and pepper, some basil and oregano. Taste for seasoning.

3. Italians like to cook up some Italian sausage and mix it with bread crumbs, minced garlic and grated Parmesan cheese.

4. Stuff with creamed crab meat well laced with dry sherry.

TO BAKE: Bake on a well-greased baking sheet in a 350°F (175°C) oven for 25 to 30 minutes. Serve hot.

TO FREEZE: Except for the creamed crab, any of these freeze well. Freeze unbaked on a baking pan. Wrap securely. Thaw in the refrigerator overnight and bake as directed above.

Scalloped Mushrooms

This can be prepared ahead and baked at the last minute.

1 pound fresh mushrooms
½ cup melted butter
2 cups soft bread crumbs
¼ cup grated Parmesan cheese
salt and pepper if desired
⅓ cup dry white wine

Wipe mushrooms clean and snap off stems if desired. For this dish you can leave the stems on and just trim bottoms of each. Slice mushrooms and place ⅓ of them in a buttered 1½-quart casserole. Cover with ⅓ of the bread crumbs and 2 tablespoons of the cheese. Drizzle with ⅓ of the butter. Continue layering until ingredients are used. Add salt and pepper if desired and add the wine. Bake in a 325°F (165°C) oven for approximately 30 minutes. Mushrooms should be tender and the tops lightly browned. Serves 6 to 8.

Red Wine and Mushrooms

These are delicious served either as an appetizer—speared on short bamboo sticks—or as a vegetable side dish with roasts.

1 pound fresh mushrooms
1 cup Chianti or Burgundy or Zinfandel
2 tablespoons minced parsley
2 tablespoons minced green onions
2 cloves garlic, crushed
¼ cup butter
salt and pepper as desired

Wipe mushrooms clean and snap off the stems. Save stems for another use. Turn all of the ingredients into a skillet, bring to a boil, then reduce heat to a simmer and simmer for 7 or 8 minutes, or until mushrooms are tender. Serves 4 to 6.

Mushroom Hints and Ideas

Marinate whole or sliced mushrooms in a mixture of equal parts teriyaki sauce and dry sherry for an hour. Drain and sauté in butter and some of the marinating mixture. Add salt and pepper if desired. Turn mushrooms into a serving bowl, reduce remaining marinade over high heat, and pour over mushrooms to serve.

A friend of mine sautés sliced mushrooms in butter with a dash or two of vermouth.

Sauté whole or sliced mushrooms in butter and add some heavy cream. Cook over high heat until cream is slightly reduced and thickened. Add salt and pepper if desired and serve as a side dish or over noodles or rice.

Pickled Mushrooms and Onions

A friend gave me a jar of these with the recipe.

⅓ cup red wine vinegar
½ cup olive oil
1 small red onion, thinly sliced and separated into rings
1 teaspoon seasoning salt
2 tablespoons parsley
1 teaspoon prepared mustard
1 tablespoon brown sugar
2 pounds button mushrooms, wiped clean and stems removed

Combine all ingredients and bring to a boil. Reduce heat immediately and let simmer for 5 minutes. Pour into a bowl and cool. Then cover and chill in the refrigerator overnight, stirring occasionally. Drain and serve with toothpicks.

The Vegetable as Appetizer

Vegetable Bouquet

Vegetables shine as stars of any course of a meal. When it comes to appetizers however, many cooks still set out crackers with dip and perhaps a few types of crisp, raw vegetables along with the crackers. Many good cooks don't realize that there is a vast array of interesting vegetable dishes that serve beautifully as appetizers. Spanakopita and Caponata (see Index) are two. A vegetable quiche (see The Quiche and The Egg chapter) makes a lovely appetizer as do any of the marinated vegetables in the Salads chapter.

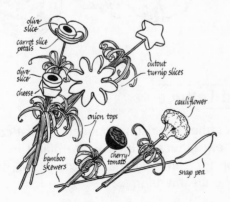

Edible Centerpiece

This makes a striking centerpiece and is extremely adaptable. Cover a round loaf of bread with parsley to serve as a leafy, green base in which to stick the picks. You can also use an eggplant, a cauliflower, or a cabbage; or make individual vegetable bouquets with small picks in oranges, small grapefruit, or apples.

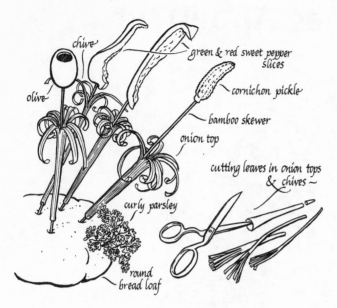

The accompanying illustrations show how to make the flowers and put them together.

Serve the bouquet with at least one dip and an assortment of crackers. Sauce Verte, in the Salad Dressings chapter, is an excellent dip, as is the Avocado Dip in this chapter.

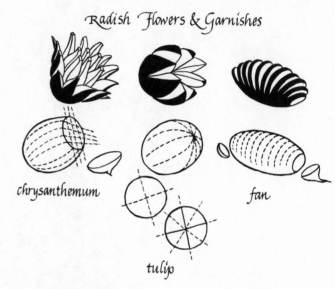

Radish Flowers & Garnishes

chrysanthemum   fan

tulip

Parsley is the easiest filler material. However, you can use any of the greens that are relatively deep in color and curly. Try mustard greens, beet greens, mint, carrot greens, watercress or curly endive. Crisp filler greens by washing, drying, and wrapping in paper towels.

Don't forget that all flowers must be crisped in ice water for several hours, or up to several days. Be sure to allow room for expansion.

For the flowers you can use:

**radishes, red and white
cauliflower
green pepper strips
snow peas
green onion flowers
green onion greens for the stems
jicama or turnips, thinly sliced and cut into
  shapes
cherry tomatoes: use whole or hollowed and
  stuffed
black or green olives
thin slices cut from the large end of carrots**
  (*Will curl when crisped. These curls can be
  put together to form the petals of a flower.*)
**onion chrysanthemums
hard-cooked egg halves with olive slices
thin slices of cheese cut into shapes with
  olive slices for the center**

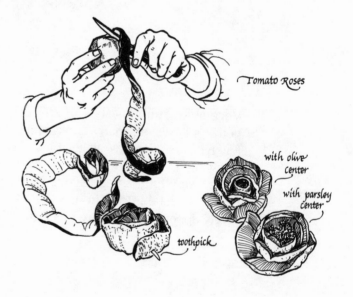

Tomato Roses

with olive center

with parsley center

toothpick

Stuffed Lettuce

This is a rather surprising appetizer or first course. The iceberg lettuce, which while bland in flavor makes up for it in crunch and texture, is a perfect foil for the creamy filling.

1 medium size, firm head iceberg lettuce
8 ounces softened cream cheese
⅓ cup bleu cheese
⅓ cup mayonnaise
⅓ cup finely chopped highly flavored
  smoked sausage
¼ cup minced green onion
a little Worcestershire sauce
a dash Tabasco

Stuffed Lettuce

Core the lettuce and hollow out the inside, using a knife and a spoon. This is easier than you may think, however you should be careful not to break through the shell, which should be about ¾ inch thick. Wash and drain the lettuce shell, letting it drain while you prepare the filling.

To make the filling, simply combine the remaining ingredients, using Worcestershire and Tabasco to taste. Mix well. Fill the lettuce shell. Any filling mixture left over will make a good sandwich spread. Wrap the filled lettuce in aluminum foil and chill well. It can be made the day before and chilled overnight. Cut into wedges to serve, arranging the wedges on a platter garnished with tomato slices and whole black olives. This will serve 6 to 8.

Mushroom Pâté

This is a light, lovely vegetable pâté with a distinctly mushroomy, lemony flavor to it. It tastes of springtime.

1 pound fresh mushrooms, cleaned and
  coarsely chopped
¼ cup butter
2 tablespoons fresh lemon juice
pinch of red pepper
a little less than a teaspoon of wine vinegar
salt to taste
freshly ground black pepper to taste
½ cup softened butter
2 large eggs, scrambled
¼ cup grated Parmesan cheese

Sauté the mushrooms in the ¼ cup butter with the lemon juice, stirring occasionally, just until the mushrooms are tender. Turn into a food processor bowl or a blender and process with quick on/off motions until nearly, but not quite, puréed. Mixture should be coarse rather than smooth. Cool slightly and then stir in the red pepper, wine vinegar, salt and pepper. Add the ½ cup softened butter and process, again with quick on/off motions, just until the butter is incorporated into the mushroom mixture. Remove from food processor and turn into a bowl.

Stir in the eggs and the cheese. Taste for seasoning, adding a little more lemon juice if necessary, or salt and pepper. It should have a *light*, not a tart, lemony flavor. Turn into a crock, or the bowl from which it will be served, and chill. This will keep for several days in the refrigerator. Serve with good crackers, Melba toast, or a crunchy bread.

Deep-fried Eggplant Pockets

This dish makes an excellent, and different, hors d'oeuvre, or a fancy vegetable dish. The dried shrimp can be bought in an Oriental grocery, as can rice wine and Oriental sesame oil. You can substitute dry white wine or dry sherry for the rice wine. There is no substitute for the Oriental sesame oil.

¼ cup dried shrimp (*optional*)
½ pound ground pork or beef
1 green onion, minced

½ teaspoon sugar
1 tablespoon soy sauce
1 tablespoon rice wine
1 teaspoon minced ginger root
1 tablespoon Oriental sesame oil
1 tablespoon cornstarch
1 medium eggplant
1 large egg, beaten
1 cup fine, dry bread crumbs
oil for deep frying

Soak dried shrimps in hot water for 30 minutes. Drain and chop. Combine shrimps, if used, with the pork, onion, sugar, soy sauce, wine, ginger, sesame oil and cornstarch. Set aside.

Peel the eggplant and cut in half lengthwise. Cut each half into ½ to ¾-inch thick slices so that you have half moon shapes. Cut a pocket in each slice (see illustration) cutting carefully so that you do not cut through the eggplant. Spread about a tablespoon of filling in each pocket. Dip each stuffed pocket first in the beaten egg and then in the bread crumbs. Set aside.

Deep fry a few coated pockets in 385°F (195°C) hot oil a few at a time for about 2 minutes on each side, or until nicely browned. Drain thoroughly, and pat dry with paper towels to remove as much oil as possible. Serve hot.

Note. These can be made ahead and then reheated in a 350°F (175°C) oven for 10 to 15 minutes.

Vegetables in Italian Beer Batter

VEGETABLES

1 9-ounce package frozen artichoke hearts, cooked and drained
1 or 2 small zucchinis, sliced
1 small cauliflower, broken into small buds
8 large mushrooms
1 green pepper, cut into strips
some broccoli flowers

BATTER

1¼ cups flat beer
1⅓ cups flour
2 tablespoons grated Parmesan cheese
1 teaspoon salt if desired
¼ teaspoon garlic powder
1 tablespoon olive oil
2 large eggs, separated
oil for deep frying

Prepare vegetables and set aside.

Whisk together the beer, flour, cheese, salt, garlic powder and oil. Add the egg yolks and whisk until smooth. Beat the egg whites until stiff and fold into the batter, folding until there are no patches of white. Now dip the vegetables in the batter and deep fry, a few at a time, in 385°F (195°C) fat or oil until vegetables are golden and crisp, 2 to 5 minutes, depending on the vegetables. Drain and serve immediately.

Deep-fried Eggplant Pockets

Antipasto

"Before the pasta" is the translation of antipasto. This dish is perfectly delicious and wonderful for entertaining as it can be prepared as much as a week in advance, and will be even better. As with most recipes of this type, it is very flexible and allows for much variation in the vegetables used, and even in the seasoning. Green beans are an excellent addition.

½ cup each: red wine vinegar, olive oil and
   lemon juice
4 stalks celery, sliced
4 to 6 carrots, cut into strips
2 medium onions, minced
8 cloves garlic, crushed
1 2 or 3-pound head cauliflower, cut into
   flowers with a little stem attached
2 or 3 medium zucchinis, sliced
1 8-ounce can tomato sauce
1 6-ounce can tomato paste
1 8-ounce jar tomato-based chili sauce
1 cup minced parsley
2 tablespoons fresh sweet basil, or 2
   teaspoons dried
2 teaspoons dried oregano
⅓ cup capers, drained and rinsed
1 20-ounce package frozen tiny onions
1 to 2 cups pitted black olives
1 to 2 cups pitted stuffed green olives
1 to 2 cups cherry peppers
1 cup button mushrooms
1 cup peperoncini
1 10-ounce package frozen artichoke hearts,
   thawed and cut into quarters
2 2-ounce cans rolled anchovies with capers
2 or 3 6½ or 7-ounce cans tuna packed in
   olive oil, undrained

Combine vinegar, oil and lemon juice. Add the celery, carrots, onions, garlic and cauliflower and cook for 8 minutes. Add zucchini and cook for 5 minutes longer. Remove from heat and stir in remaining ingredients, adding the anchovies and tuna carefully to avoid breaking them up. Return to heat and bring to a simmer. Simmer for another 5 minutes. Refrigerate for at least 3 days before serving. This will keep for a week to 10 days.

Italian Pickled Vegetables
(Giardiniera)

These easily made pickles are typically Italian and are usually served on an antipasto tray, or with cold meats. You can buy the pickle, at a premium price, at Italian delicatessens.

8 to 10 medium carrots
1 small bunch celery hearts
2 large red or green peppers
1 2-pound head cauliflower
1 pound pickling onions
1 cup salt
4 quarts cold water
¼ cup capers
2 quarts white wine vinegar
1 cup olive oil
¼ cup mustard seed
2 tablespoons celery seed
½ teaspoon dried thyme
1 or 2 small dried hot chilis
⅓ cup sugar
2 or 3 cloves garlic
about ⅓ to ½ cup each: green and black
   olives

Peel carrots and cut into long strips. You should have about 4 cups. Remove strings from celery and cut into long strips. You should have 3 cups. Remove seeds and stems from the peppers and cut into strips. Break cauliflower into small flowers with just a little of the stem. Peel the onions.

Stir salt into cold water until dissolved. Add carrots, celery, peppers, cauliflower and onions. Let stand, covered, for 12 to 18 hours. Drain and rinse in cold water, then drain again.

Combine, in a large stainless or enamel pan, the vinegar, oil, mustard seed, celery seed, thyme, chilis, sugar and garlic. Bring to a boil and boil for 3 minutes. Add vegetables and boil for 10 minutes. Vegetables should be tender/crisp. Pour into hot, sterilized jars and seal. Makes about 6 pints.

Arabic Pickles
(Torshi)

Pickling is an important method of preservation in the Middle East. Along with the pickles, called Torshi or Makboos, the liquid, either brine or oil, can be sopped up with bread.

I remember my grandmother putting up gallons of pickled cauliflower and cucumbers, turnips and zucchini, onions and carrots each year. Traditionally, she always added a small beet or two to each large jar. After a few weeks the color would leach out of the beets and everything in the jars would be a soft pink.

The pickles are put up in a simple brine with no processing of any kind, just as they have been put up for thousands of years. Home economists will tell you that pickles *must* be submerged in a boiling water bath for 5 to 15 minutes. I have never done it that way, and I have never had a bad pickle. My grandmother never boiled the pickles, and to my knowledge she never had a bad pickle.

I generally pickle vegetables raw, and rely on the brine to mellow and soften them. However, some vegetables, such as carrots or small whole onions, can be blanched in boiling water for several minutes to hasten the process. At summer's end I always put up gallons of tiny cucumbers by this pickling method, leaving out the beets.

The proportion of vinegar to water varies, with some cooks using equal parts of vinegar and water, others using all vinegar, and some using 2 parts of water to 1 of vinegar with a little oil added. The amount of salt used is usually a teaspoon to a tablespoon per cup of liquid.

BRINE

3½ cups water
1½ cups white wine vinegar
¼ cup non-iodized salt

VEGETABLES

carrots, cut in fingers or fluted slices
cauliflower in small buds
small whole cucumbers
red cabbage in thin wedges
green peppers (*or red*) in strips
whole small green beans
turnips in thin wedges
zucchini in fingers or fluted slices
small pickling onions peeled and blanched for 3 minutes
small whole beets, peeled

ADDITIONS

2 fat cloves garlic
⅛ teaspoon whole peppercorns
1 whole dried chili pod
1 grape leaf (*optional*)

Combine Brine ingredients and stir until salt dissolves.

Fill sterilized jars with any combination of Vegetables you prefer. Add to each quart jar the garlic, peppercorns, chili pod and grape leaf.

Cover vegetables completely with the Brine and seal the jars with glass lids, if possible.

These can be eaten after a few days, but are at their best in a week to 10 days. They should be used within 2 or 3 months. However, I have kept some, stored in plastic refrigerator containers, in the refrigerator, for over a year and they were crisp and good right up to the last cucumber.

Serve the pickled vegetables in a bowl surrounded by Greek olives and feta cheese, with some wedges of pocket bread.

Repickled Pickles

This mixed pickle is a simple recycling of tag ends of homemade and commercial pickles. The basic idea is very flexible and very good.

2 cups small white pickled onions with their liquid
2 cups drained and rinsed black or green olives
2 cups small garlic pickles with their liquid
2 cups sweet banana peppers with their liquid
2 cups white wine vinegar
¼ cup sugar
1 quart water

10 whole black peppercorns, crushed
10 whole white peppercorns, crushed
2 bay leaves
3 or 4 whole cloves garlic, peeled

Drain the various pickles, reserving the liquids. Combine liquids (except for the brine from the olives) with the vinegar, sugar, water, peppercorns, bay leaves and garlic. Bring to a boil.

Turn pickles, onions and olives into jars, making certain that there is an assortment of each in each jar. Pour boiling liquid over them. Cool to room temperature and then chill before serving.

Note. I very often use some leftover homemade pickles of any type. You can find your own formula.

Vegetables à la Grecque

Although I give a substantial list of vegetables that can be served this way, you can use any combination of vegetables that appeals to you. Try for contrast in shape, texture, flavor and color. The first marinade is for a typical à la Grecque. The second marinade is more typically Italian for antipasto.

MARINADE 1

½ teaspoon dried thyme
½ teaspoon coriander seeds
½ teaspoon fennel seeds
½ teaspoon dried marjoram
1 large bay leaf
12 whole peppercorns
2 whole cloves
¼ cup minced parsley
3 cloves garlic, crushed
3 cups water
¾ cup olive oil
½ cup lemon juice
¼ cup tarragon vinegar
1 teaspoon salt

MARINADE 2

3 cloves garlic, crushed
1 teaspoon dried oregano
1 teaspoon dried basil
1½ cups water
1½ cups white wine vinegar
½ cup olive oil
salt and pepper

VEGETABLES

carrots: scraped and sliced, simmer 5 minutes
celery: sliced on diagonal, simmer 5 minutes
cucumbers: sliced into rounds or sticks, do not cook
cauliflower: small flowers, simmer 3 or 4 minutes
mushrooms: whole, simmer 1 or 2 minutes
asparagus: cut on diagonal, cook 1 minute only
artichoke hearts: cook frozen ones 5 minutes only
green beans: simmer whole until tender/ crisp, about 10 minutes
red or green peppers: slice and sauté gently in olive oil
okra: whole young pods, simmer 5 or 6 minutes
pickling onions: use frozen and simmer for 2 or 3 minutes
zucchini: slice or cut into sticks and simmer just a minute or 2

For Marinade 1, tie the herbs, seeds, parsley and garlic in a cheesecloth bag. Combine all ingredients, adding the bag. Bring to a boil and cover loosely. Simmer for 15 minutes.

For Marinade 2, tie the garlic and herbs in a cheesecloth bag. Proceed as for Marinade 1.

Many of the vegetables are best if they are simmered in the marinade until just crisp/tender. The marinades are enough for 5 or 6 cups of vegetables, cooked 2 cups at a time. After cooking, remove the vegetables with a slotted spoon to a bowl. When all are cooked, remove herbs and seeds and pour the hot marinade over the vegetables. This will finish any cooking necessary. Cool, cover tightly, and chill overnight.

To serve, arrange vegetables attractively on a serving platter and drizzle with some of the marinade. Garnish and serve. Or serve as a salad platter on lettuce with tomato wedges, olives, anchovies and sliced hard-cooked eggs.

Fried Chick Peas

These make delicious nibbles, a nice addition to the appetizer tray.

1 pound dried chick peas
4 tablespoons butter
4 cloves garlic, crushed
½ teaspoon dry mustard
1 teaspoon chili powder
1 teaspoon onion salt
½ teaspoon garlic salt
1 tablespoon soy sauce
½ teaspoon powdered ginger

Soak chick peas overnight in water to cover, about 4 cups. Then cook, in the same water, for about an hour, adding more water as needed. Drain in a colander and divide into 2 equal portions.

Use 2 skillets and put 2 tablespoons butter in each. Put 2 crushed cloves garlic in each skillet and simmer gently for a few minutes. Remove garlic and add 1 portion of the chick peas to each skillet. Toast them, stirring frequently, until golden.

Combine the mustard, chili powder and onion salt in a small bowl and sprinkle over the chick peas in 1 skillet. Stir until they are evenly coated.

In another bowl mix the garlic salt, soy sauce and ginger. Stir into the second skillet and stir until chick peas are well coated.

Serve warm. These can be made ahead and reheated in a hot oven for a few minutes.

Avocado Dip

This lovely, springlike dip is an emulsion based on Hollandaise. I use the dip as a sauce over Eggs Benedict, on cooked cauliflower (the color makes a striking contrast to the white cauliflower), or simply as a dip with crackers, wedges of pocket bread and vegetables. It will keep for several days in the refrigerator.

1 large clove garlic
2 large eggs
¼ cup lemon juice
½ cup hot melted butter
1 avocado, peeled and cut up
½ teaspoon salt, if desired
pinch of red pepper or crushed pepper
  flakes

Mince the garlic in the bowl of your food processor or blender. Add the eggs and lemon juice and churn. Slowly add the bubbling hot butter. If you are using the food processor you can pour in the butter in a steady stream. With a blender you must pour in a small amount until the mixture binds, and then add the remainder more quickly. Blend in the avocado, salt and red pepper. Purée until smooth. Taste for seasoning and adjust to taste. Makes 1½ cups.

Border Dip

The border in this case is the Tex-Mex border. Some of my students say that no Sunday is complete without a large platter of Border Dip and chips.

3 avocados
2 tablespoons lemon juice
1 jalapeño pepper
salt, if desired
pepper to taste
3 green onions, minced

1 cup sour cream
½ cup mayonnaise
Tabasco, cumin powder and oregano to taste
2 cups Refried Beans *(see page 5)*
¾ cup grated Cheddar cheese

1 cup chopped green onions
2 cups chopped firm fresh tomatoes
1 cup sliced ripe olives
1 cup grated Cheddar cheese

tortilla chips

Make guacamole with the first 6 ingredients. Set aside. Combine the sour cream and mayonnaise and season rather highly with the Tabasco, cumin and oregano. Set aside.

Heat the Refried Beans with the ¾ cup cheese until the cheese is melted and the mixture softened considerably. Set aside. Prepare remaining ingredients as directed.

To assemble, spread the bean dip on a largish platter. Top with the guacamole, then with the sour cream mixture. Sprinkle with the onions, the tomatoes, the olives and cheese. Serve with hot sauce and chips.

Chick Pea Dip
(Hummus bi Tahini)

Hummus is the Lebanese word for chick peas. Bi means "with." So this recipe is for a chick pea dip made with tahini, a sesame seed paste which can be bought in health food stores. Typically Middle Eastern, it is garlicky and lemony.

    2 cloves garlic, crushed
    salt and pepper to taste
    pinch of cayenne
    2 cups drained, rinsed canned chick peas
    ½ cup tahini
    ⅓ cup lemon juice
    minced parsley and whole chick peas for
        garnish

Combine ingredients in food processor bowl. Purée. Pour into a serving bowl and drizzle with a little olive oil. Sprinkle with minced parsley and garnish with a few whole chick peas. Serve with crackers or with wedges of pocket bread.

Note. *Pomegranate seeds, used as a garnish, add a lovely touch.*

Eggplant Dip
(Baba Ghannoj)

This and the Hummus bi Tahini (*see preceding recipe*) were the only two dips I remember while growing up. My grandmother made a variation of this using avocados. This should be lemony and garlicky.

    1 1-pound eggplant
    ¼ cup or more lemon juice
    ¼ cup tahini
    2 cloves garlic, crushed
    1 or more teaspoons salt
    1 tablespoon olive oil

Grill the eggplant over charcoal, or else roast in a 450°F (230°C) oven until soft and well roasted. This will take 40 to 50 minutes in the oven.

Cool just until you can barely handle the eggplant. Then cut it open and scrape out the flesh. Turn into a food processor bowl with the remaining ingredients. Churn until puréed. Taste for seasoning, adding more lemon juice or salt if needed. Turn into a shallow serving bowl and sprinkle the top with chopped parsley. Serve with crackers or with wedges of pocket bread.

Artichoke Nibbles

This is a standard recipe, but too good to leave out.

    2 6-ounce jars marinated artichokes
    1 small onion, minced
    1 clove garlic, minced
    4 large eggs
    ¼ cup fine, dry bread crumbs
    pinch of salt
    ⅛ teaspoon each: oregano, pepper, Tabasco
    2 cups shredded Cheddar cheese
    2 tablespoons minced parsley

Drain the artichokes, reserving the marinade. Turn half of the marinade into a frying pan. (Save the other half for salad dressing.) Turn the onion and garlic into the marinade in the frying pan and simmer until tender. Set aside.

Chop the artichokes and set aside.

Beat the eggs and stir in the crumbs and seasonings. Add the artichokes, cheese, and parsley. Add the onion and garlic and the marinade in which they were cooked. Mix well and turn into a 7 by

11-inch greased baking pan. Bake in a 325°F (165°C) oven, uncovered, for 30 minutes. Cool slightly before cutting into squares. Makes 3 to 4 dozen squares.

Chutney Dip

This is actually a fresh chutney, meant to be served with all manner of Indian foods. However, we love it as a dip, sharply seasoned and delicious. When serving a dip of this type, you should also serve another, more lightly seasoned dip for those who are more cautious. Fresh coriander is also known as Chinese parsley and (in Spanish) cilantro.

**1½ cups packed chopped fresh coriander
2 fresh jalapeño peppers, sliced**

**1½ cups plain yogurt
¾ teaspoon toasted, ground cumin seeds
(*toast in a skillet until they pop, then cool and pound in a mortar or in a shirabachi*)
5 teaspoons fresh lemon juice**

Process the coriander and the peppers in a food processor or blender with 3 tablespoons of water. It won't be a smooth purée, but it will be finely mixed and chopped. Add remaining ingredients and stir to blend well. Chill until ready to use.

Note. *You can use any kind of cracker as a dipper. Try poppadums, thin deep-fried wafers of Indian origin.*

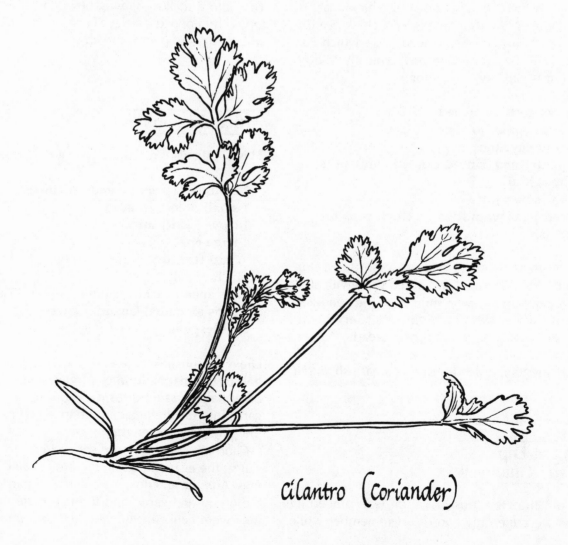

Cilantro (coriander)

Soups

Soup, once a mainstay of the American diet, has become less and less an object of fond regard. This sad state of affairs may well have been hastened by the obnoxiousness of soups served in many restaurants, tasting, as they usually do, of tin can. Or, even worse, looking and tasting as though they had been thickened with Elmer's glue.

We seem to have become convinced that soup is too time-consuming and difficult to prepare. While soup has fallen upon hard times in our country, in other countries it is as highly regarded as ever. In Mexico soup is served with all meals except breakfast. In China soup is served as the beverage with meals.

The following soups are really all quite simple. Many of them are hearty enough to be a meal. Any good soup must begin with a good stock. I am amazed at how many people think that there is something esoteric about making stocks. All you need are some bones and some of the basic items such as onions, celery, garlic and bay leaves, which you probably already have around the kitchen.

Chicken Stock

3 to 4 pounds chicken parts: wing tips, backs, necks, and gizzards (*no livers*)
1 medium size whole unpeeled onion
several cloves of garlic, unpeeled
several stalks of celery
1 to 3 bay leaves
1 or 2 carrots
leeks (*optional*)
1 teaspoon dried thyme
½ teaspoon dried sage
10 to 12 whole peppercorns

Combine all ingredients in a large pot, cover with water and bring to a boil. Reduce heat and simmer stock for 3 to 4 hours.

Strain the stock, cool, and store, covered, in the refrigerator. Or, you can reduce the strained stock to concentrate the flavor. This is a good idea if you intend to freeze it, as I generally do. Freeze some of it in ice cube trays and then turn the frozen cubes into glass jars for those times when you need only a spoonful or two of rich broth. Freeze the rest in 1 and 2-cup containers.

Note. Chicken livers impart an off flavor to stock. Use them elsewhere. If you are wondering why I do not peel the onions and garlic it is because I have never seen any need to do the extra work. The onion and garlic are going to be strained out anyway. The peel of the yellow onions will add some color to the stock, and a bit of extra flavor also.

Borscht

This is yet another basic peasant dish for which there are as many recipes as there are cooks. If you make Borscht you are bound to have firm opinions on how it should properly be made. Some good cooks use the broth from a duck or goose carcass. Still others use potato in place of the parsnips. Some use parsley root, impossible to find in a market. Still others add sausages, lovely fat garlicky sausages. Some will add cubes of ham, or pork chops, or some beef brisket cut into chunks and simmered until tender. Borscht is simply a com-bination of hardy vegetables, sometimes with whatever meat is on hand, flavored and colored with beets and served with sour cream. The following recipe, very good in its own right, can be used as a guide. You might add some chopped leeks if desired. But always cook the beets separately and use the cooking water as part of the soup liquid.

2 bunches beets, scrubbed
¼ cup butter or other fat
¾ cup grated carrots
1½ cups minced celery
2 medium onions, minced
¾ cup grated parsnips, turnips, rutabagas or potatoes
1 teaspoon marjoram
1 or 2 bay leaves
salt if desired
freshly ground black pepper to taste
beef or chicken broth and beet water to make 5 cups
1½ cups shredded cabbage
1½ cups tomatoes, seeded, peeled and diced
sour cream and fresh dill for garnish

Cook the beets in water to cover, then peel, cut into dice, and set aside. Reserve the water. Heat the fat and in it sauté the carrots, celery, onions, and parsnips just until the onion is limp. Transfer to a soup pot and add the beets. Add marjoram, bay leaves, salt and pepper and 5 cups liquid. Simmer for 30 minutes to an hour. Then stir in the cabbage and tomatoes and simmer for another 20 to 30 minutes. Taste soup and adjust seasoning. Serve in bowls garnished with sour cream and dill. Serves 8 to 10.

Note. You really do need to serve Borscht with dark bread to do it justice. A simple green salad will round out the meal.

Cabbage Soup

This is a superb cabbage soup, quite the best I have ever tasted.

2½ pounds green or Savoy cabbage
2 cups beef or chicken broth

3 cloves garlic
1 teaspoon caraway seeds
1 teaspoon peppercorns
2 bay leaves
1 teaspoon oregano
1 teaspoon basil
¼ teaspoon thyme
⅓ cup flour
⅓ cup soft butter
1 quart milk or half and half
1 cup grated Cheddar cheese

Shred the cabbage and turn it into a soup pot with 3 quarts of cold water. Add salt to taste. Bring to a boil, then reduce heat to a simmer and let simmer for 30 minutes. Keep covered.

While the cabbage is cooking, combine the broth with the garlic and all of the seasonings. Simmer for 20 minutes and then strain, reserving the broth. Discard seasonings.

At the end of the 30 minutes drain cabbage. Add the strained broth to the drained cabbage in the soup pot. Mix the flour with the soft butter to form a roux. Stir this into the cabbage soup with a whisk. Stir and simmer for 10 minutes, until soup is thickened. Now add the milk or half and half and the cheese. Cook very slowly *just* until it heats. If it comes to a boil the milk will curdle. Taste and adjust seasoning, adding salt or white pepper if needed. Some people like a little nutmeg. I don't. Serves 4 to 6.

THICKENING SOUPS

Some vegetable soups, chowders and simple cream soups require a certain amount of thickening. I dislike using flour as a soup thickener and so, with almost any soup that uses vegetables, I simply scoop out some of the vegetables, purée them and then stir them back into the soup. The taste is much fresher and the calories fewer than when flour is used.

Puréed Fresh Vegetable Soup

This is a very simple, delicious soup that uses whatever fresh vegetables you have on hand. I frequently make it to use up odds and ends of vegetables in the refrigerator. People are always surprised to find out how very good this soup is. Be sure to use a hearty chicken or beef stock.

½ cup minced onion
½ cup shredded unpeeled potato
2 cups chopped fresh vegetables
2 cloves garlic
3 cups chicken or beef stock
½ teaspoon each of basil and thyme
butter
salt and pepper to taste
some grated Parmesan cheese

Combine vegetables and stock in a saucepan with the seasonings. Bring to a boil, stirring. Reduce heat to a simmer. Cover and simmer for 15 to 20 minutes, or until vegetables are tender. Transfer vegetables, with a slotted spoon, to the bowl of a food processor or blender and purée until smooth. Return to the pot and add a little butter, salt, and pepper for flavor. Heat gently just until hot. Serve sprinkled with Parmesan cheese. Serves 6.

Basic Cream Soup

You do not need a recipe to make delicious cream soup. All you need is some good, flavorful chicken broth, half and half, and whatever vegetable or vegetables that you desire.

I especially like asparagus, broccoli, spinach, zucchini, potato and onion, spinach and avocado, lettuce.

2 to 3 cups chopped vegetable of your
    choice
2 cups chicken broth
2 cloves garlic
1 or 2 cups half and half
salt if desired
white pepper to taste
butter

Cook the vegetables in the chicken broth with the garlic until done, adding more broth or water if mixture gets too thick. Scoop out the vegetables and purée them. Return to broth and heat. Add just enough half and half to make a soup as thick or as thin as you wish it. Season to taste with salt and pepper. Heat over medium heat just until hot. It must not boil. Serve immediately with a small piece of butter on each serving. Serves 4 or 5.

Note. Avocado will become bitter if overheated. To prevent this add puréed avocado with the half and half and just heat through.

Cream of Vegetable Soup

This enticing soup is delicious. Serve it hot in the winter and cold in the summer. It's really an all-around vegetable cream soup, as the vegetables used can be varied according to availability and taste.

1 cup chopped celery leaves
2 small zucchini, thinly sliced
1 cup chopped fresh spinach leaves
1 large onion, minced
¼ cup fresh basil leaves
¼ cup minced fresh parsley
1 or 2 cloves garlic, minced
4 cups rich chicken broth
¼ cup uncooked long-grain rice
1 bay leaf
½ teaspoon thyme
2 whole cloves
salt if desired
freshly ground black pepper to taste
2 egg yolks
2 cups half and half
sour cream and minced chives, parsley or
   basil for garnish

Combine vegetables with chicken broth and rice in a large saucepan. Tie the seasonings in a square of double thickness cheesecloth and add to the pot. Bring to a boil, reduce heat to a simmer, cover, and cook for 30 to 40 minutes. Discard cheesecloth bag with the seasonings. Purée the soup. If you use a blender or food processor, scoop out the vegetables, purée them and turn them back into the broth. Bring to a bubble again. Now whisk the egg yolks together with a few spoonfuls of the hot broth. Stir back into the simmering soup and cook and stir until smooth.

Stir in the half and half and let it just heat through. If it boils it will curdle. Remove from heat and serve immediately, with a dollop of sour cream and some minced chives, parsley or basil on top. To serve it cold, chill thoroughly and serve in balloon wine glasses with a dollop of sour cream and a sprinkle of parsley or basil. Serves 4 to 6.

Gazpacho

This is Spain's noble contribution to the world of soups. One of my students invited me to dinner on a hot summer evening. She had made this soup earlier in the day and had turned it into a heavy crock which she then placed in the freezer along with the soup bowls. At serving time, she ladled the icy cold soup into the icy cold bowls and topped each with a mound of shrimp, surrounded with avocado slices and garnished with a leaf or two of fresh mint. It was marvelous. Quite the best Gazpacho I have ever had.

Another student of mine makes her Gazpacho the traditional way, but before serving it she purées 2 large ripe avocados with ½ to 1 cup sour cream and stirs this into the Gazpacho.

2 large cucumbers, peeled, seeded and
   chopped
5 or 6 medium tomatoes, peeled, seeded and
   chopped
1 large red onion, peeled and chopped
1 large green pepper, seeded and chopped
3 cloves garlic, crushed
4 cups French or Italian bread cubes
4 cups cold tomato juice
¼ cup lemon juice
1 teaspoon crushed red pepper
4 teaspoons salt if desired
freshly ground black pepper
¼ cup olive oil
garnishes: sliced stuffed green olives,
   chopped red onion, peeled and chopped
   cucumber, homemade croutons

*Gazpacho,
garnished with shrimp,
avocado & mint*

Combine everything up to, but not including, the tomato juice. Stir together thoroughly. Take half of the mixture and purée it in a blender or food processor. Stir back into the rest of the mixture and add the tomato juice and remaining ingredients. Stir together thoroughly. Chill thoroughly. Stir again just before serving. Serve in frosted bowls with small bowls of the garnishes so that each person can add his or her own.

Variation

The use of bread cubes in the soup, although traditional in certain sections of Spain, is disliked by some. They say that it detracts from the crispness of the dish. If you use the bread, make certain that it is *real* French or Italian bread, and that it is slightly stale. Others do not like to purée the soup, but prefer it as sort of soup-salad. Still others purée the entire mixture. You decide which consistency you prefer. You can add ½ teaspoon cumin to the soup. I rather like this addition myself, although I think it is more Mexican than Spanish.

Limbo Dal

Dal is the traditional lentil dish, either thin or thick, mild or spicy, that is served by both rich and poor

in India. Recipes vary enormously. This one is lemony and very, very good.

SOUP

¾ **cup olive oil**
2 **onions, minced**
3 **or 4 2-inch pieces of cinnamon bark**
2 **pounds lentils** (*red lentils are traditional,
  but any kind can be used*)
1 **or 2 slices fresh ginger root, minced**
5 **cups each: chicken stock and water**
salt to taste
1 **teaspoon red pepper**
½ **teaspoon ground cumin**
juice of 1 lemon
seeded shell of the lemon

SOUP ADDITIONS

½ **cup olive oil**
1 **medium onion, minced**
3 **cloves garlic, minced**
1 **hot green chili, minced**
4 **bay leaves**
½ **cup minced fresh coriander leaves**

To prepare the Soup, heat the oil and sauté the onion until limp. Then add the cinnamon, lentils, ginger, chicken stock and water, salt to taste, red pepper and cumin. Bring to a boil and then reduce heat and simmer for 10 minutes.

Add lemon juice and the lemon shell and simmer about 30 minutes, stirring often. While this is cooking, prepare the Additions.

Heat the oil and in it sauté the onion and garlic until limp. Add hot chili and bay leaves and heat and stir for 2 or 3 minutes.

Stir into the Soup, reheat if necessary, and pour into serving bowls. Sprinkle each with a little of the minced coriander. Serves 12.

Five Bean Soup

I have probably made this soup more than any other in my files. I can think of no finer bean soup; even though my Pinto Bean Soup (see page 119) is delicious, it can't hold a candle to this one. Just as a stew is better if you use more than one kind of meat in it, this soup benefits from the use of an assortment of dried beans. I use at least 5 kinds including blackeyed peas and dried lima beans. For the rest, I choose from pinto beans, kidney beans, navy beans, pink beans, marrow beans, or others I have on hand.

I use an assortment of meats. The ones listed are just to give you ideas. I have used leftover pork or beef roast, almost any kind of sausage, and chicken. The assortment of beans and meats blends into a most harmonious whole.

When I had a small restaurant some years ago, this was the most popular of the weekly assortment of soups that I made. My regular customers, including many farmers and ranchers, would ask for it the day after it was on the menu also, hoping there was some left.

3 pounds mixed dried beans (see above)
2 pounds ham or pork butt or chops or ham or pork hocks
a few Italian sausages
1 pound lean salt pork (optional)
2 large onions, minced
1 carrot, thinly sliced
4 cloves garlic, crushed
2 or 3 bay leaves
⅓ cup minced parsley
¼ to ½ teaspoon each: sage and thyme
salt and pepper to taste

¼ teaspoon or more Tabasco
½ cup or more dry sherry

Combine dried beans in a large pot, cover with water and let set overnight. In the morning, add more water to the beans if necessary. Let them begin cooking while you prepare the remaining ingredients.

The ham or pork can be used as is, as the bones will help to flavor the soup and the meat will fall apart. Prick the Italian sausages and brown them lightly in a skillet before adding, whole, to the soup. Cut the salt pork in small pieces and render in a skillet. Sauté the onions, carrot and garlic in the fat from the sausages or the salt pork but do not let them brown. The onion should just become transparent. When almost ready, stir the bay leaves, parsley, sage and thyme into the onion and garlic mixture and let them just heat. The heat releases the volatile oils which provide the flavor.

Add mixture to the beans, along with the meat.

Start this soup in the morning. You want it to simmer all day. Stir it occasionally, when you think of it. And taste, adding any more of anything that you think it might need. A little more salt and pepper, a little more thyme possibly. It should be a richly flavored soup. Stir in the Tabasco and the dry sherry just before serving. This amount will serve 12 easily. This soup is even better on the second or third day. It also freezes very well.

Oven Vegetable Soup

This is one of my favorites and a favorite with everyone who tastes it. A variation on the Italian *Vegetale al Forno* (baked vegetables), you can use any vegetable in season that suits you. If you don't like wine, you can use chicken broth. The addition of the cheeses and the half and half at the end of the cooking time makes the soup very rich and filling. I serve this as a meal, with nothing more than a crusty bread, some more of the wine that went into the soup, and cheese and fruit for dessert.

2 cups diced tomatoes
1 15-ounce can chick peas
2 medium zucchini, thinly sliced
2 medium onions, minced

5 fat cloves garlic, minced
1 bunch of broccoli, cut into flowers with
  some of the tender stem attached
¾ cup cauliflower flowerets
2½ cups dry white wine
1 bay leaf
1 or 2 teaspoons salt if desired
1 teaspoon basil
½ teaspoon paprika
1½ cups half and half
1 cup shredded Monterey Jack cheese
1 cup grated Parmesan cheese

Combine all ingredients up to and including the paprika. Cover and bake in a 375°F (190°C) oven for 1 hour. Test to make certain that vegetables are done the way you want them. However, they should still have some bite to them. Now add remaining ingredients and stir together. Reduce oven heat to 325°F (165°C) and bake for another 15 minutes, just to melt the cheese and heat the half and half. It is important that the soup not boil at this time, as the half and half will curdle. Serves at least 6 generously.

Minestrone

This is a thick Italian vegetable soup which varies from region to region, from cook to cook, and from season to season. In Piedmont the cook makes it with fresh white beans, cabbage, and noodles flavored with salt pork, among other things. In Naples they use more meat, combining sausage, bacon, ham and pork skin with several endives including the Belgian. In the Lombardy region they combine the white beans with salt pork and bacon and then add potatoes, zucchini, tomatoes and green peas, as well as using cabbages and rice. The Ligurians add fresh borage and some Pesto, and in Tuscany, the cook adds cauliflower, leeks and shredded lettuce as well as green peas and asparagus.

As long as you remember that Minestrone should be a combination of vegetables and starch, and that it should be thick enough to be eaten rather than drunk, any thick vegetable soup can be called Minestrone. This recipe is for one that I especially like.

¼ cup olive oil
½ pound spinach, washed, trimmed and
  chopped
¼ pound beet greens, washed, trimmed and
  chopped
¼ pound fresh or frozen lima beans
½ of a Savoy cabbage, trimmed, washed,
  shredded and blanched
2 potatoes, washed and cubed
1 small onion, minced
2 cloves garlic, crushed
1 leek, white part only, sliced
salt and pepper to taste
water as needed
½ pound small pasta
1 cup Pesto (*see page 127*)

Heat oil and to it add the spinach and beet greens and stir until just wilted. Now add everything up to and including the water. You will need about 2½ to 3 quarts of water. Simmer gently for about 2 hours. Then bring soup to a boil and stir in the pasta. Cook *just* until the pasta is cooked but still slightly firm to the tooth. Taste and adjust seasoning. Then blend in the Pesto with a whisk or spoon and cook for another 2 or 3 minutes. Serve in heated bowls with more Pesto for those who wish it. Serves 6.

Lebanese Lentil Soup

This is the soup of my childhood, a typically Lebanese-Syrian potage of beans, onions and greens. It is filling and very, very good. Different as night and day from the typically American lentil soup with franks, and my favorite way with lentils.

2 cups lentils
1 large onion, minced
⅓ cup olive oil
2 cloves garlic, crushed
½ bunch chard leaves, or 1 bunch spinach
  leaves, cleaned, trimmed and cut into
  shreds
salt and pepper to taste
⅓ to ½ cup lemon juice
lemon wedges

Combine lentils with 7 cups water and cook over low heat. Sauté the onion in the oil with the garlic until limp and then add to the lentils with the oil. (You can reduce the amount of oil used, but this amount is more traditional, as is adding it to the soup.) The lentils should be ready in about an hour. If the soup needs more liquid, add it. If the soup is too watery, you might do as traditional Lebanese cooks do and add ¼ cup uncooked rice. Simmer until rice is tender.

Add greens about 15 minutes before you plan on serving the soup. They should only simmer until done. Season to taste with salt and pepper. Stir the lemon juice in at the end, just before serving. Use the lesser amount first, and then taste. You might wish to add more. The soup should have just a mild lemony taste. Garnish with the lemon wedges. Serves 4 to 6.

Pennsylvania Dutch Rivvel Soup

The small egg dumplings called "rivvels" by the Pennsylvania Dutch enrich this soup and make it a natural with the children.

SOUP

2 cups chicken broth
2 cups milk
3 cups green peas, fresh or frozen
1 teaspoon salt, if desired
pinch of freshly ground black pepper

RIVVELS

1 cup all-purpose flour
¼ teaspoon salt
1 egg, lightly beaten
¼ cup milk
2 tablespoons butter

For the soup, combine broth and milk and heat to simmering. Add peas, salt and pepper. Cover and simmer for 10 minutes. Do not allow soup to boil.

To make the rivvels, combine flour and salt and stir together. Combine egg and milk and whisk together lightly. Stir into the flour mixture. It should make a soft dough.

The soup should be just barely bubbling. Using just the tip of a teaspoon, drop the rivvel dough into the soup, ¼ to ½ teaspoon at a time. Use a fork to stir lightly so that the rivvels don't stick together.

Cover the pot and simmer for 5 minutes. Ladle into 6 bowls and add a teaspoon of the butter to each. Serves 6.

Note. *Rivvels are good in cream soups, split pea soup and in some lentil soups.*

Peking Hot and Sour Soup

If you have never tasted this Oriental soup, it will be a real surprise. It is a delicious, hearty soup. For the preserved vegetable use any preserved vegetable that the clerk in your favorite Oriental store recommends. If necessary, you can use shredded kosher dill pickles. They taste just like the Japanese pickles that some recommend. Do use plenty of freshly ground black pepper. The soup should have a spicy, hot flavor.

¼ pound lean pork cut into thin strips
1 teaspoon Chinese rice wine or dry white wine
½ teaspoon cornstarch
4 Chinese dried mushrooms
2 tablespoons dried tree ears
4 cups chicken broth
½ teaspoon sugar
1 teaspoon soy sauce
1 tablespoon preserved vegetable, shredded or sliced (*see above*)
¼ cup shredded bamboo shoots
1 cake fresh tofu, cut into thin strips
2 tablespoons white wine vinegar
¼ teaspoon or more freshly ground black pepper
2 tablespoons cornstarch in 3 tablespoons water
1 egg, beaten
1 teaspoon Oriental sesame oil
1 green onion, minced

Prepare pork as directed and marinate in the wine and the ½ teaspoon cornstarch. Soak the mushrooms and tree ears in warm water in separate bowls for 30 minutes. Cut into small pieces and reserve.

Combine chicken broth, sugar, soy sauce and the shredded preserved vegetable in a saucepan and simmer. Stir in pork mixture. Bring to a boil and boil for 1 minute. Add the mushrooms and tree ears and the bamboo shoots. Boil another minute. Add tofu strips, vinegar and pepper. Bring to a boil once again. Stir in the cornstarch mixture and the egg and remove from heat. Garnish with the sesame oil and the green onions. Serve hot to 6.

Note. This soup can be made ahead of time, and actually gets better. However, do not add the last 4 ingredients (the cornstarch, egg, sesame oil or green onion) until ready to serve.

Pinto Bean Soup

This will keep in the refrigerator for a week and in the freezer for 2 or 3 months.

1 pound dried pinto beans, soaked
1 pound boneless ham, diced
1 quart water
1 large can *(1 pound 13 ounces)* tomatoes
1 quart chicken broth
2 medium onions, chopped
2 tablespoons butter
3 cloves garlic, crushed
¼ cup minced parsley
¼ cup minced green pepper
1 tablespoon brown sugar
1 tablespoon chili powder
1 teaspoon each of salt and dried oregano
1 bay leaf
½ teaspoon each: cumin, rosemary, thyme, basil

Soak beans overnight if possible. Then cook for an hour. At the end of an hour, add the ham, water, tomatoes, and chicken broth. Continue cooking. Sauté the onions in the butter until limp. Add the garlic and parsley and stir into the onions until warm. Then add to the soup along with the remaining ingredients. Cook until done, about

another hour or 2. Long, slow cooking improves any soup of this type. Makes 12 cups.

Winter Squash Bisque

I am always surprised at the number of people who do not know that a bisque is nothing more nor less than a thickened cream soup. This one is a winter regular, occasionally made with pumpkin instead of squash.

2 leeks, carefully washed and sliced
1 onion, minced
2 stalks celery, minced
2 green apples, peeled and chopped
⅓ cup butter
8 cups chicken or turkey broth
4 cups peeled and diced butternut squash
¼ cup flour
¼ cup soft butter
1½ teaspoons salt if desired
½ teaspoon thyme
½ teaspoon rosemary
1 cup apple cider or dry white wine
½ cup half and half
1 cup grated Gruyère cheese

In a large pot, sauté the leeks, onion, celery and apples in the butter until softened. Add broth. Simmer for 15 minutes. Then stir in the squash and cook for another 20 minutes. Combine flour and softened butter and mix together to make a roux. Stir this into the hot soup and stir and cook until thickened. Now add seasonings and stir and cook for a few minutes. Taste and adjust to taste, adding more thyme, salt or rosemary if you prefer. Stir in remaining ingredients and heat very gently just until hot. Serve to 8.

Creamy Potato Soup

This is a nice way of using up leftover whipped potatoes. This soup has been a favorite in my family for 20 years.

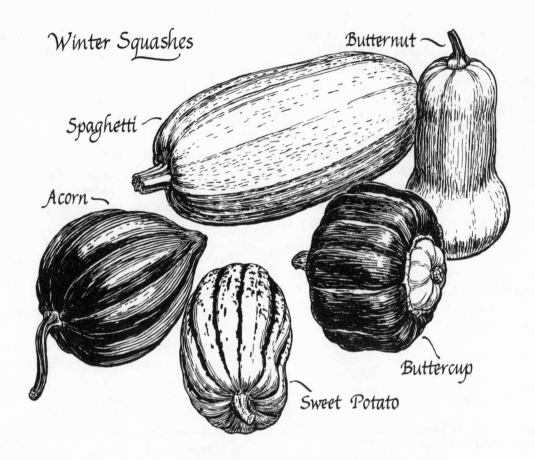

Winter Squashes

Butternut

Spaghetti

Acorn

Buttercup

Sweet Potato

1 onion, minced
2 tablespoons butter
3 cups chicken broth *(it must be a hearty broth)*
2 cups leftover whipped potatoes
1½ cups milk or half and half
chopped parsley for garnish

Sauté onion in butter until limp. Add to the broth and heat. Take some of the broth and whisk it into the potatoes, using enough to make the mixture light and soupy. Stir this back into the broth. When thoroughly blended, return to the stove and add the milk. Heat just until hot. Serve with a sprinkling of parsley on top.

Eggplant Parmesan Soup

This delicious soup is an adaptation of a recipe from a charming cookbook called *The Cabrillo Soup Festival*. It is available from the Cabrillo Music Festival in Aptos, California.

1 medium onion, minced
2 cloves garlic, minced
1 medium eggplant, peeled and diced
¼ cup olive oil
⅓ cup chopped parsley
2 tablespoons soy sauce
4 cups chicken broth
salt and pepper to taste
1 teaspoon basil
1 teaspoon oregano
1 29-ounce can Italian plum tomatoes
grated Parmesan cheese

Prepare vegetables. Turn eggplant into a colander and salt it. Let drain for 30 minutes and then rinse well.

Combine the onion, garlic and half of the diced eggplant and sauté in the olive oil until the eggplant is softened and beginning to turn golden. Add the parsley and soy sauce and stir together for a few minutes. Then turn into a soup pot and add the chicken broth, salt and pepper, basil and oregano.

Combine the remaining eggplant with the tomatoes and purée in the food processor. Add to the soup pot and stir to mix well. Simmer for at least 1 hour, more if possible. If the soup thickens too much, thin it with some more chicken broth. Taste for seasoning and adjust to taste. Sprinkle each serving with 2 tablespoons grated Parmesan cheese. Serves 8.

Potato and Onion Soup

2 medium onions, peeled and thinly sliced
3 tablespoons butter
2 medium potatoes, peeled and diced
4 cups well-flavored beef stock
2 tablespoons grated Parmesan cheese

Sauté onions in butter until limp. Add to the stock along with the potatoes. Cook until potatoes are tender. Serve with a sprinkling of the cheese. Serves 6.

Sauerkraut Soup

This wonderful Hungarian soup is occasionally called "hangover soup."

¼ cup bacon fat or butter
1 large onion, minced
2 or 3 teaspoons Hungarian paprika
3 cups chopped sauerkraut, rinsed and
**   drained**
2 cloves garlic, minced
½ pound or more of smoked sausage, sliced
salt if desired
freshly ground black pepper to taste
6 cups chicken broth
1 cup sour cream
2 tablespoons chopped fresh dill, or caraway
**   seeds**
sour cream for garnish

Heat fat and sauté the onion until wilted. Stir in the paprika, sauerkraut, garlic, sausage, salt and pepper and chicken broth. Simmer for 30 to 45 minutes. Then stir in the sour cream and dill or caraway seeds. Stir and cook gently until heated. Serve in soup bowls with more sour cream on top. Serves 6.

Pozole

One version of this dish begins with dried hominy, which must first be cooked to soften it, and is made thicker to be served as a side dish. This is made with canned hominy and is served as a soup. This is a peasant dish, originally cooked with those cuts of pork that most cooks now find objectionable—the head, ears and tail. Deluxe versions, of which the following recipe is one, add pork loin or butt and a chicken. You will love the rich flavor.

2 fresh pork hocks
1 pound pork loin or butt, cut into pieces
4 large cloves garlic, whole or minced
1 large onion, minced
1 bay leaf
4 quarts chicken broth
1 tablespoon chili powder
1 3-pound chicken, cut into pieces
2 29-ounce cans hominy, drained
salt to taste
freshly ground black pepper to taste

Simmer the pork hocks and loin with the garlic, onion and bay leaf in the chicken broth for at least an hour. Then add the chili powder and the chicken pieces and continue cooking for another 45 minutes. Stir in the drained hominy and the salt and pepper. Simmer another 30 minutes and taste for seasoning. This is usually served with an assortment of relishes to be served on the side or sprinkled on top. Use chopped lettuce, minced onions, sliced radishes or grated cheese. You can also serve with Spicy Salsa (*see below*). Serves 8 to 10.

Spicy Salsa

Chop some drained California green chilis and mix with minced garlic and salt to taste. This should be hot and spicy and delicious. Stir a spoonful into the Pozole.

Sauces

I often think that the ability to make a good sauce is the true mark of the superior cook. However, many recipes and instructions for making sauces seem so involved and complicated that they frighten some people away from serious sauce making.

The following recipes are not intended to be anything approaching the final word on sauces, but the recipes are simple enough, and varied enough, to perhaps open a door into another area of cooking expertise, and to add zip to your vegetable cookery.

Bechamel Sauce
(White Sauce)

The Italians claim that *Bechamel* is a corruption of *besciamella*, a flavorful white sauce, while the French claim the word is a corruption of *Behamiel*, the name of a 17th century gourmet. Whichever it might be, a properly made Sauce Béchamel is excellent.

MIXTURE 1

2 cups milk or half and half
1 small onion, minced
1 bay leaf
a few whole peppercorns
a pinch each of dried sage and thyme
a sprig of parsley
salt and pepper to taste

MIXTURE 2

**For a thin sauce use: 2 tablespoons flour
and 2 tablespoons butter**
**For a medium sauce use: 4 tablespoons flour
and 3 tablespoons butter**

Pour milk into a saucepan. Place the onion and herbs and peppercorns in a small muslin bag so that the herbs do not color the milk. Add to the milk along with salt and pepper. Simmer for 15 minutes. Then strain. Use the milk immediately, or prepare it ahead and cool it. Stir it frequently as it cools to keep a skin from forming, or lay a piece of waxed paper over it to prevent a skin.

When ready to prepare the sauce, reheat the milk, if necessary, and melt the butter in Mixture 2 over medium heat. Add the flour and cook gently, stirring until it bubbles. Add 1 cup of the milk and mix thoroughly. Whisk in remaining milk and cook slowly until thickened, at least 2 or 3 minutes, or until sauce is smooth and thickened. A longer cooking time, as much as 30 minutes, greatly improves the sauce. If the milk is hot, the sauce will form more quickly and there will be less chance of it lumping on you.

Sauce Mornay

To the sauce add ¾ cup grated medium or sharp Cheddar cheese. Some good cooks use a combination of grated Parmesan cheese and grated Swiss cheese.

Mushroom Sauce

Sauté ½ pound sliced mushrooms with a small clove of garlic in 2 tablespoons butter until mushrooms are tender and mushroom liquid has evaporated. Discard garlic. Add mushrooms to sauce and whisk together thoroughly.

Caper Sauce

To the sauce add 2 tablespoons chopped capers.

Soubise

Chop two or three onions and sauté in butter until limp. Purée and add to sauce. Serve with cabbage, string beans, or cauliflower.

Note. *The above sauces may be kept, refrigerated, for up to 4 days. When ready to use, heat over low heat, stirring constantly. They may also be frozen, in styrofoam cups or any freezer container. The sauce will look curdled when defrosting. Do not worry. Just reheat slowly, after defrosting, and stir constantly with a whisk.*

BUTTER SAUCES

Butter sauces are perhaps the simplest of the sauces. Garlic Butter is a sauce, as are all of the herb butters. Any of the herbed butters and garlic butter, can be made, rolled into a log, wrapped and frozen. To use, simply cut off what you will need. See Herbs in Butter, in the Salad Dressings chapter (*page 134*).

Beurre Blanc

This is good on steamed broccoli or asparagus and also on steak.

¼ cup minced shallots
½ cup dry white wine
½ cup frozen butter in small pieces

Place shallots and wine in a metal bowl and place over a pot of simmering water. Cook until liquid is reduced to about 1 tablespoon.

Now whisk in the butter, a piece at a time, whisking until each piece is thoroughly incorporated before adding another. Continue until all of the butter is used.

This can be made ahead and reheated by heating a tablespoon of butter and whisking the sauce into it.

Egg-Lemon Sauce

This is the Greek sauce which is the basis of the famous Chicken-Lemon soup. It is a quick sauce, and is superb with just about any vegetable you can think of.

>   2 egg yolks
>   2 or 3 tablespoons lemon juice
>   ½ cup hot cooking liquid from the
>   vegetable

Whisk egg yolks until thickened. Beat in lemon juice, then the hot cooking liquid. Transfer vegetable to a warm serving dish and spoon sauce over it. Serve at once.

Cold Sauce for Hot Vegetables

A tangy sauce that is excellent over steamed broccoli, asparagus or green beans.

>   1 cup sour cream
>   ⅓ cup mayonnaise
>   1 teaspoon Dijon mustard
>   1 green onion, minced
>   juice of ½ lemon
>   ¼ teaspoon seasoning salt

Combine and whisk together. Makes 1½ cups sauce.

Hollandaise Sauce

This is the basic method for making Hollandaise Sauce. See the recipe which follows for the food processor method.

>   4 egg yolks
>   ½ cup hot water
>   ½ cup hot melted butter
>   2 tablespoons warm lemon juice
>   ¼ teaspoon salt if desired
>   ⅛ teaspoon red pepper
>   ¼ teaspoon Worcestershire sauce
>   dash Tabasco

Combine the egg yolks with 2 tablespoons of the hot water, whisking all the while to keep the yolks from cooking, in a bowl placed over hot water. Once you've made this a few times, you can do it over direct low heat. When the yolks have foamed, add another tablespoon of the hot water. Then whisk in the hot melted butter, a tablespoon at a time, and the remaining hot water, a tablespoon at a time. Keep whisking until it begins to thicken. Add lemon juice in a thin stream, whisking constantly. Add remaining ingredients and whisk until thick. Makes 1½ cups.

Béarnaise Sauce

Boil ¼ cup *each* of wine vinegar and dry white wine with the following: 2 tablespoons minced shallots or green onions; 1 tablespoon fresh tarragon, or 1 teaspoon of the dried; 1 tablespoon each of minced parsley and chives; salt and pepper to taste. Boil until reduced to 2 tablespoons. Use this in place of the lemon juice in the Hollandaise recipe. Serve with vegetables, or on beef tenderloin.

Mousseline Sauce

Beat 2 egg whites until stiff and fold into the Hollandaise with a pinch of freshly ground nutmeg. Serve with cauliflower, broccoli, or asparagus.

Note. *Hollandaise Sauce can be frozen. Reheat in a double boiler over hot, not boiling, water. Stir constantly. If sauce breaks down, beat 1 or 2 tablespoons heavy cream into it. If the sauce becomes slightly curdled, turn it into a food processor bowl and churn for a few seconds.*

Hot Dressing for Vegetables

Simple, but so good. Just combine 1 tablespoon oil with 1 tablespoon butter, 1 teaspoon Dijon mustard and 2 or 3 tablespoons soy sauce. Heat gently in a small saucepan. Stir well. Pour over hot vegetables such as asparagus, green beans, broccoli, Brussels sprouts, Chinese cabbage, even barely cooked spinach.

My Favorite Food Processor Hollandaise

This is as simple as mayonnaise made in the processor.

3 egg yolks
1 tablespoon lemon juice
salt and pepper to taste
¼ teaspoon Worcestershire sauce
dash Tabasco
½ cup hot melted butter

Combine egg yolks, lemon juice, salt and pepper, Worcestershire, and Tabasco in the bowl of the food processor. Churn for several seconds. Now add the hot melted butter in a thin stream, churning until mixture thickens. Churn for about 30 seconds longer. Serve.

Persillade

To 1 cup of homemade Mayonnaise (*see page 161*) add the following: 2 crushed cloves of garlic; 2 tablespoons minced parsley; 1 tablespoon prepared Dijon mustard; ½ teaspoon Worcestershire sauce. Heat gently and serve with asparagus or other vegetables.

Rémoulade Sauce

To 1 cup homemade Mayonnaise (*see page 161*) add the following: 1 teaspoon capers; 1 teaspoon chopped sour pickle; 1 teaspoon prepared mustard; 1 minced green onion; some pepper and cayenne to taste. Serve with cold meats and fish.

Sauce Tartare

Follow the above recipe for Rémoulade Sauce and add 2 mashed hard-cooked egg yolks and 1 raw egg yolk.

Hot Wine Mayonnaise

This is an excellent alternative to Hollandaise Sauce.

1 tablespoon minced green onion
¼ cup dry white wine
¾ cup homemade Mayonnaise (*see page 161*)
1 tablespoon lemon juice
2 tablespoons minced parsley

Marinate the green onion in the white wine for 30 minutes. Then stir into the mayonnaise with the lemon juice and parsley. Turn into a bowl which will fit over a pan of hot water. You can use a double boiler, but I prefer metal or crockery bowls as I can choose any size necessary, and, since the bottom is rounded, I avoid overcooked spots. Heat over hot water until sauce is just warm. Serve over asparagus or broccoli, or wherever you use a Hollandaise Sauce.

Cream Sauce Mix

This quick mix will be a boon to the busy cook. The recipe makes 1 quart of mix which will thicken 8 cups of sauce. The mix will keep, refrigerated, for 2 months. I'm not much for mixes of any type, but this one is better tasting than most, and quite useful.

1 cup butter or margarine
1 cup flour
1 cup nonfat dry milk powder or
   2 cups instant dry milk
¼ cup onion powder
2 teaspoons seasoning salt
¼ teaspoon white pepper

Combine ingredients. Cut in butter until it resembles a fine meal. This can be done by hand, or with a food processor. Store in an airtight container.

Creamed Vegetables

Combine 2 cups vegetables with ½ cup chicken stock or water and bring to a boil. Cover pan and cook vegetables until tender/crisp. The time depends on the vegetables. Stir in 3 tablespoons of the mix and cook, stirring, until sauce thickens. Season to taste and serve.

Basic Cream Sauce

Combine ½ cup mix with 1 cup cold water in a saucepan. Cook over low heat until smooth, stirring constantly. Season to taste.

Cheese Sauce

Add ½ to 1 cup shredded Cheddar cheese to the Basic Cream Sauce after it thickens.

Basic Tomato Sauce

This is a good basic sauce. If you wish a meaty sauce, add some hot or sweet Italian sausages.

**4 cups canned Italian plum tomatoes or
    fresh plum tomatoes
½ cup olive oil
½ cup minced onion
⅓ cup minced carrots
⅓ cup minced celery
2 cloves garlic, minced
salt and pepper
basil and oregano to taste**

Chop the tomatoes. Heat the oil in a skillet or saucepan and lightly sauté the onion, carrot, celery and garlic. Stir in the tomatoes, adding salt and pepper to taste. Add herbs and simmer gently for 30 minutes. Purée if desired. Makes about 5 cups.

Note. *This is a basic sauce upon which you will build. The good Italian cook will add some chopped bacon or some kind of Italian ham, and always, of course, the wine. If it becomes too thick, thin the sauce with either a dry white or a dry red wine.*

Salsa Verde
(Green Sauce)

This is an excellent sauce to use either with or in Mexican or Tex-Mex dishes.

**1 tablespoon lard
1 medium onion, minced
2 tablespoons flour
1 cup canned stewed tomatoes, or peeled,
    seeded, chopped fresh tomatoes
1 cup chicken broth
1 cup chopped green chilis (*canned California green chilis or your own, roasted and peeled*), or more if desired
1 or 2 cloves garlic, crushed
dash of salt
¼ teaspoon powdered cumin**

Melt lard in a saucepan over medium heat. Sauté the onion until limp. Stir in the flour and mix well. Add remaining ingredients and simmer for 20 minutes. This will keep for a week in the refrigerator. Makes 2 cups.

PESTO

Used in all kinds of pasta dishes, this marvelous green sauce is redolent of summer's warm, long, lazy days. Invented by Ligurians, and traditionally used as a pasta sauce, Pesto has recently been adopted by inventive American cooks who have devised some creative ways of varying it and of using it.

Traditionalists will tell you that Pesto is best when made with a mortar and pestle, adding the oil last, until it all forms a thick, aromatic sauce. But then these same traditionalists will probably tell you to make your mayonnaise by beating the eggs with a fork, on a platter, and adding the oil drop by drop. In each case the degree of improvement is not worth the tedium of the method, especially in today's fast age.

My Favorite Pesto

I serve this marvelously aromatic sauce with lightly buttered, cooked pasta, first mixing ⅓ cup or so of the Pesto with some of the water in which the pasta was cooked. I also combine the Pesto with homemade mayonnaise and sour cream for a dip, and I frequently add several spoonfuls to a good vinaigrette to use as salad dressing. Some cooks use ½ butter (at room temperature) and ½ olive oil. Some do not use the cheese. The best basil to use is the most aromatic, which is obtainable just before the plant blooms.

from 3 to 10 cloves garlic, depending on
how garlicky you wish the final product
½ cup pine nuts (*some cooks use walnuts;*
pine nuts are much better)
½ to 1½ cups grated cheese (*use a combina-*
tion of Parmesan and Romano or Pecorino)
2 cups fresh basil leaves, packed
1 cup parsley (*optional*)
salt and pepper to taste
½ to 1 cup olive oil

I use a food processor, but you can use a blender or a mortar and pestle.

Mince the garlic with the nuts and cheese until they are fine. Then add the basil and parsley if used, the salt and pepper and enough of the oil to make a smooth paste. It should be smooth and aromatic.

This will keep, refrigerated, for up to a month. Pour a thin film of oil over the top of the Pesto to seal it.

Pesto freezes remarkably well. This is how I do it. During the summer I make as many batches of Pesto as I can get basil leaves for. I pour some into small containers and the rest into flexible ice cube trays. When frozen, I pop the frozen Pesto cubes out of the tray and put them into quart jars, seal them and place in the freezer.

Note. *Pesto does* not *have to be made with sweet basil. I have followed the above Pesto recipe and substituted any one of the following for the basil: oregano, tarragon, dill, or marjoram. Freeze as directed above. Use wherever you would use the*

individual flavors of the herbs with cheese and garlic.

curly parsley

Italian broad-leaf parsley

Cream Cheese Pesto

This is a Pesto variation which is very useful. I use it on baked potatoes as well as in the more traditional ways.

2 large cloves garlic, crushed
12 ounces cream cheese, softened
½ pound sweet butter, softened
½ cup olive oil
2 large bunches parsley, washed and
stemmed
½ teaspoon salt if desired
¼ teaspoon freshly ground black pepper

Mix all together in a food processor or blender until it is thick and creamy. This freezes perfectly, as do all of the Pestos. Just remember to freeze it in small containers, so you can defrost only what you need.

Alba's Pesto

Good cook Alba, whose family comes from northern Italy, uses the following ingredients to make her Pesto.

4 ounces cream cheese
4 ounces butter
4 ounces olive oil
½ cup grated Parmesan cheese
2 or 3 cloves garlic
2 cups packed fresh basil leaves
½ teaspoon salt (optional)

Blend all ingredients in a food processor or blender, or by hand, until mixture is a smooth paste.

Winter Pesto

This type of Pesto has its fans. However, if I have run out of Pesto before the summer's new basil is up, I much prefer the Cream Cheese Pesto.

¾ cup olive oil
2 cups fresh parsley, washed and trimmed and packed
¼ cup grated Parmesan cheese
2 tablespoons dried basil leaves
2 or 3 tablespoons pine nuts
2 cloves garlic, crushed
salt if desired
freshly ground black pepper

Place all ingredients in the bowl of a food processor or a blender. Churn until smooth. Makes about 1½ cups.

Dill Pesto

An interesting variation that goes very well with seafood, with cold boiled potatoes, or with pasta. I serve it with tuna on an antipasto tray.

2 cloves garlic
2 tablespoons pine nuts
½ teaspoon salt (optional)
¼ cup olive oil
1 cup fresh dill leaves, removed from stems and lightly packed

Blend all ingredients to make a smooth paste. This will keep for 2 weeks in the refrigerator, and it freezes well.

Italian Vegetable Sauces For Pasta

When most Americans think of pasta, they think of spaghetti and meatballs. My students are amazed to learn that most Italian pasta sauces do not use any tomatoes. After all, the tomato was not adopted by the Italians until around three hundred years ago. And pasta has been around longer than that.

Traditionally, pasta is meant to be served as a side dish, before the main course. And, as such, it is a much lighter dish.

While there are hundreds of pasta sauces, I will only give recipes here for a few of the vegetable sauces. I hope that these will give you some ideas on vegetables that you can use. Snow peas are good, as is asparagus. Try tiny green beans and cherry tomatoes. See the recipe for Pasta Primavera (page 181) and just use a few of the vegetables. My grandmother used to make a meatless pasta sauce with tomatoes and all kinds of vegetables. She always used cauliflower and cooked it first. She would then cook the pasta in the water in which the cauliflower was cooked.

These sauces can be prepared while the pasta is cooking. To serve, simply toss with the drained pasta in a serving dish or on a platter. Each of the following recipes yields enough sauce for one pound of pasta and serves 4 to 6.

Broccoli-Anchovy Sauce

1 bunch fresh broccoli, trimmed and cut into flowers with about an inch of stem attached
coarse salt
1 2-ounce tin anchovies
¾ cup olive oil

Cook broccoli in boiling salted water, or steam it, for 8 to 10 minutes. Drain and keep warm. Heat the oil in a small saucepan and add the anchovies. Mash them into the oil. Add the broccoli to the anchovies and toss to heat. Serve with your favorite pasta.

Cauliflower Sauce

An excellent sauce, and one of our alltime favorites. Make this with shells, spaghetti, fettucini or linguine.

1 small cauliflower
⅓ to ½ cup butter or margarine
1 teaspoon salt
freshly ground black pepper
½ cup grated Parmesan cheese

Break cauliflower into small flowers and cook in boiling, salted water, or steam, until just tender. Drain and toss with the melted butter. Season with the salt and pepper.

To serve, add to the pasta and toss. Add cheese and toss again.

Broccoli and Zucchini Sauce

I like this with roast chicken or with a summer barbecue. I serve it with linguine.

1 large bunch broccoli, trimmed and cut into flowers with about an inch of stem attached

½ pound zucchini, thinly sliced
¼ cup olive oil
½ cup chicken broth or water
4 cloves garlic, crushed
¼ cup butter or margarine
salt and pepper
grated Parmesan cheese to taste

Cook or steam the broccoli until tender/crisp. Keep warm. Sauté the zucchini in the olive oil for 5 minutes. Then add the broccoli, chicken broth or water, garlic and butter. Add salt and pepper to taste. Simmer for 5 minutes.

To serve, toss with linguine or your favorite pasta, add grated cheese to taste and toss again.

Zucchini Sauce

Serve this with the large pasta shells as a side dish or as the main dish of a light meal.

½ cup olive oil
1 or 2 cloves garlic, crushed
3 or 4 zucchini, sliced
1 teaspoon rosemary
salt and pepper to taste
⅓ cup minced parsley or some minced fresh chives
⅓ to ½ cup grated Parmesan cheese

Heat oil and in it sauté the garlic and zucchini until tender. Add rosemary and season to taste with the salt and pepper. Let simmer a couple of minutes to blend flavors. To serve, toss with pasta, add parsley and cheese, and toss again.

Salads

Tabooli

The first salads that I remember were those made by my mother and grandmother. Salad was considered an important part of the evening meal and was always served. My mother had a large wooden salad bowl, and in the bottom of this she would pound garlic and salt to a smooth paste. Over this she would tear assorted lettuces, one of which was always romaine. She would add tomatoes, chopped red or green onion and fluted cucumbers. The mixture was salted and peppered and the juice of a lemon or two was squeezed directly over the greens and, last, the salad would be drizzled with olive oil and then tossed. I still can't think of a better salad. Or a more simple one.

My grandmother made Tabooli, that marvelously crunchy Middle Eastern mixture of wheat, tomatoes, mint, parsley and green onions dressed with fresh lemon juice and olive oil. Sometimes she served it in a bowl lined with romaine. We would tear off pieces of the romaine to use as scoops for the Tabooli. At the huge Lebanese picnics which we attended once or twice a year there was always a contest among some of the old men to see how much Tabooli they could scoop up with a leaf of romaine and transport to their mouths without spilling any. I loved to watch.

At other times she would mound Tabooli on a leaf-lined platter, mold it as smooth as possible and then garnish with mint sprigs, tomato wedges, lemon slices and olives. A bowl of romaine leaves was placed alongside to be torn and used as scoops.

The other salad that was especially popular with the family was a Middle Eastern vegetable salad made with cooked potatoes, beets, eggs, etc., similar to an American potato salad. Traditionally it was dressed with lemon juice and oil, but sometime along the way mayonnaise was added to its preparation.

Iceberg lettuce was never used, although salad was served every day. We lived in Southern California where the produce is lovely all year and salads, and vegetables in general, tend to be used in quite imaginative ways.

SALAD GREENS

If you are going to make a tossed salad, you have a wide choice of greens. If you are just beginning to become a little adventuresome, start by combining assorted greens—use two or three types of lettuce for example. When you discover how delightful that is, you might begin branching out. Any of the following can be used in salad.

Beet Greens: Use only when young and tender.
Belgian Endive (French Endive, Witloof): See Leafy Vegetables.

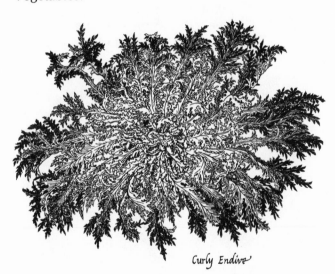

Curly Endive

Bibb Lettuce (Limestone): Soft textured and subtly sweet.
Boston Lettuce (Butterhead, Simpson): This is occasionally confused with Bibb Lettuce. However, Boston Lettuce is larger and a deeper green.
Cabbage: See The Whole Cabbage Family.
Chicory (Curly Endive): Curly head, shading from a white heart to dark green at the edges. Has a slightly bitter flavor that is good in small quantities.
Corn Salad (Lambs' Lettuce, Field Lettuce): This is a weed and grows wild in cornfields as well as in

the average garden. Small, delicate leaves are good in salad.
Dandelion Greens: The small, spring dandelion leaves are good in salad. They are tart and slightly bitter.
Escarole: Broad, curly leaves shade from a yellow heart to dark green at the edges. Texture is rough and taste is slightly bitter. Good in small amounts.
Fiddlehead Ferns: Pick these in early spring when the ferns are just appearing. Pick the tiny, white, curled babies. Wash, rubbing to remove any fuzz, and steam until tender. Toss into salad.
Iceberg Lettuce: Crisp, tightly rounded head with little flavor.
Leaf Lettuce: This includes a number of varieties of lettuce ranging in color from varying shades of

Leaf Lettuce

green, to green with red tipped leaves. Some varieties form heads, some don't. Best when young and tender. Easy to grow.
Nasturtium (Chinese Mustard): Somewhat similar to watercress with its peppery flavor. Use leaves and flowers, large as well as small.
Parsley: The flat-leafed Italian parsley is more flavorful. However, the curly variety makes a more attractive garnish.
Purslane (Miner's Lettuce): A weed. The rounded, fleshy leaves make a delightful addition to salads.

Romaine (Cos Lettuce): This is the most popular lettuce throughout the Middle East. The long heads and crisp leaves shade from pale to dark green. Excellent lettuce.

Romaine   *Romaine / Cos*

Sorrel (Sour Grass): This grows wild in some areas. The leaves have a refreshingly sour taste and are best used when young and tender.

Spinach: A current salad favorite, either alone or combined with other greens.

Swiss Chard: I love the flavor of Swiss chard. Wash the tops and tear into salad. Use in place of spinach in just about any recipe.

Watercress: If you live near a cold water stream you may be able to pick your own fresh watercress. Toss whole sprigs into salads. Use to garnish meats and poultry. Watercress does not keep well, although it will keep for several days in a jar of water in the refrigerator.

ONIONS

Mild-flavored onions are best in salads. The following are good choices.

Bermuda and **Italian (Red) Onions:** Large, mild onions. The Bermuda onions are white or yellow. The Italian onions are red.

Spanish Onions: Flatter in shape than Bermuda or Italian onions, these are also mild and delicious.

Shallots, Green Onions (Scallions), **Chives:** These all have a mild yet distinctive flavor and are excellent in salads and dressings.

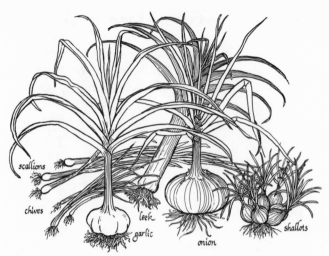

scallions *chives* *leek* *garlic* *onion* *shallots*

OTHER INGREDIENTS

You might consider any of the following, but do not use too much of any one ingredient—nor too many ingredients: Sliced avocado; marinated artichoke hearts; marinated Brussels sprouts; marinated chick peas; cucumbers, scored and sliced thin; radishes; tiny green beans, fresh from the garden and blanched; red or green pepper; raw zucchini, sliced thin; fennel; radish or alfalfa sprouts.

If you use tomatoes in your salad, add them just before serving. Tomatoes weep and will dilute the dressing. Or use small cherry tomatoes for variety.

seeding a cucumber

HERBS AND SPICES

The following herbs and spices are those that I consider best with salads. Fresh herbs are always preferable.

Basil (Sweet Basil): Called the "royal herb," this is probably the most popular herb. Basil can be added with harmonious results to virtually the entire range of foods, from soup to after-dinner cheese. Add it to *fines herbes* for egg dishes; to *maitre d' hotel* butter to be served over fish. Use it in all herb bouquets, in soups, stews, with fricassees or roasts. Chop up some fresh leaves and sprinkle over spaghetti. Use it in all tomato dishes, of course, as well as with peas, new potatoes, string beans, squash, zucchini, spaghetti squash. And don't forget to use it when making your own sausage.

Burnet (Salad Burnet): This tastes like cucumber. Add the leaves to salad, or use to make an herb vinegar.

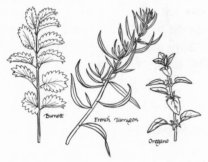

Burnett   *French Tarragon*   *Oregano*

Capers: The tiny flower buds of the caper plant. Usually available preserved in brine. When you buy a jar, drain and rinse the brine off the capers. Return to the jar and add a clove of garlic. Cover the capers with white wine and keep refrigerated.

Chervil: Use in potato salad, egg, or chicken salad, salad dressings, *fines herbes*. Try to find fresh.

Chives: A versatile plant with a mild onion flavor, the chive leaves can be used either fresh, dried, or frozen. It is easily grown and the entire plant is usable. The lovely lavender flowers are an excellent addition to some salads, either as an ingredient or as a garnish.

crushing garlic

Dill: A favorite for pickling, its flavor is magic with cucumbers. Use with any cucumber salad and with fish.

Fennel: Shred the bulbous stem and add to salads.

Garlic: One of my favorite herbs. Forget about rubbing the salad bowl with half a cut clove of garlic for flavor. This method simply does not add enough flavor. It just sounds nice. Pound garlic and salt in a wooden or marble mortar with a pestle, and add to the dressing. Or pound the garlic with salt in the bottom of a wooden salad bowl. Don't be afraid of garlic; it is delicious and adds much to any salad.

Marjoram: (Sweet Marjoram): Use with spinach, peas, lima beans or green beans. Use fresh marjoram in salads.

Curly Mint

Mint: There are at least a dozen of the "true mints" of which Spearmint, Peppermint, Apple mint and Orange mint are the most commonly used culinary mints. Spearmint is probably the one growing in your garden. Use it in salad dressings and with tomatoes, cucumbers, zucchini and peas.

Oregano (Wild Marjoram): More aggressive than sweet marjoram. Use it, preferably fresh, with tomatoes and with most salads.

Parsley: The two most common varieties are the curly leaf, most often used as garnish, and the Italian flat-leaf parsley which has a more pronounced flavor. You are missing a rich source of vitamins, minerals and flavor if you insist on using parsley only as a garnish. Keeps well in a glass jar.

Savory: Marvelous in bean salads. Use a little in some salad dressings.

Tarragon: Mince the fresh tarragon and use in place of parsley where judicious amounts are called for. Use it in tomato cocktail or salad, with fish, mushrooms, egg and chicken dishes. Steep fresh tarragon branches in a mild white wine vinegar for a subtle flavor to add to salad dressings.

Thyme: Fresh thyme, especially lemon thyme, lends a spicy flavor to pickled olives and some salad dressings. You might try sprinkling some of the fresh leaves over salads. Use thyme in meat and fish sauces and in the gravy for roast lamb.

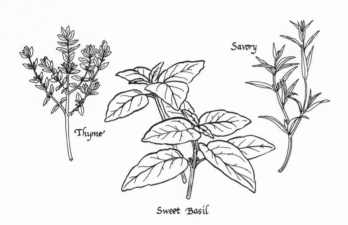

Thyme

Savory

Sweet Basil

PRESERVING SUMMER'S HERBS

My summer project one year was experimenting with the different methods of preserving the fresh flavor of herbs.

Herbs in Oil

This Italian method works very well with any leaf herb, and ended up being one of my favorite methods of preservation. I have used it with basil, oregano, sage (the whole leaf), marjoram and tarragon.

Simply wash and dry the herbs and pack into small containers. Cover with corn or peanut oil and freeze. The leaves can be removed from the oil as wanted with just a minimum of thawing. Also the oil is richly flavored and excellent for use in cooking or in salads, depending on the herb used.

Herbs in Butter

This is an excellent method, and very simple. Just melt the amount of butter that you wish to use, and to it add a lot of fresh herbs. For example, I will add a cup of fresh tarragon leaves to a pound of melted butter. Stir together and pour into small containers, or chill until it can be molded and mold into small balls. Freeze these balls on a tray and then bag them. Naturally the strength of the herb-flavored butter depends on how much of the fresh herb you have added. I frequently will add minced or crushed garlic to the herb butter, since I use garlic in many dishes.

I had some leftover tarragon butter from a baste for some roast chicken. Not knowing what to do with it I used it as part of the fat when making Ratatouille (*see page 183*). The smoky flavor of the tarragon permeated the vegetables and the dish was nothing short of divine.

Freezing Fresh Herbs

Fresh herbs are always better than dried herbs, although we must use the latter when necessary. But if you have an herb garden, or have access to fresh herbs during the growing season, you might try freezing them. Just wash and dry the herbs and lay them on a tray. Freeze and then bag the herbs.

Herbs in Vinegar

This French method was my least favorite, but you might like it more than I do. Use any leaf herb such as those mentioned in Herbs in Oil (*see above*), wash and dry and pack into a container. Cover with white wine vinegar. The vinegar becomes absolutely wonderful and a spoonful will do wonders to pick up a bland salad dressing. But I feel that the herbs themselves lose their flavor completely.

MARINATED VEGETABLES

Almost any vegetable, either raw or cooked until just crisp/tender, can be combined with a good vinaigrette (see *Basic Vinaigrette, page 159*) with happy results. For better flavor, toss with the dressing while the vegetable is still warm. Try this with cooked tiny new potatoes, green beans, slices of zucchini, or cauliflowerets, with strips of roasted green peppers, and with thick slices of raw tomato. Keep marinated vegetables in a covered container in the refrigerator. Serve separately as a side dish or use as part of a composed salad. Decorate with black or green olives and/or strips of anchovy or pimiento.

Note. If you are using home-frozen vegetables, add them to boiling water and remove them as soon as the water comes back to a boil. Do the same with baby fresh carrots. No further cooking is necessary.

Jerusalem Artichokes

Scrub and trim 2 or 3 small Jerusalem artichokes. Shred with the food processor or with a four-sided shredder. Combine with chopped green onion (for flavor and color) and some thinly sliced celery. The food processor slices the celery perfectly. Add vinaigrette to coat and salt and pepper to taste. This is another salad that tastes delicious and holds up well in the refrigerator.

My Mother's Marinated Green Peas

In the summer my mother used fresh peas which she just barely blanched. In the winter she drained a can of good peas. Either way she dressed the peas with a mixture of fresh lemon juice, olive oil and plenty of garlic, with just a little salt. I still love them and prepare them as a side dish for a buffet.

Pickled Blackeyed Peas

Drain a can of blackeyed peas, or cook up a batch of dried peas (but do not overcook) and drain. Add vinaigrette dressing and several cloves of garlic. The garlic is essential. Refrigerate for at least 24 hours before serving.

Marinated Brussels Sprouts

Buy some nice *small* Brussels sprouts and cook them in salted boiling water until just barely tender. Remove, drain and immediately pour some Basic Vinaigrette (see *page 159*) over them. Add an extra clove of garlic or two. Refrigerate overnight before using. These will keep for at least a week in the refrigerator.

Marinated Broccoli Stems

I like these tossed into a salad, or combined in a composed salad with some of the other marinated vegetables. Take the broccoli stems that are left after using the flowers. Peel them and slice thinly. Again the food processor is perfect for this step. Pour some Basic Vinaigrette (see *page 159*) over them and add an extra clove of garlic or two. Refrigerate overnight before using. These are a little different, and quite good. Add thinly sliced radishes for a colorful side dish.

Marinated Olives

Add this to your marinade file. Combine the following in a 2 or 3-quart jar: 2 cups good oil; ½ cup white wine vinegar; 3 dried hot red chilis; 8 black peppercorns; 1 tablespoon salt; 1 teaspoon dried thyme; 2 large bay leaves and 1 teaspoon dried tarragon. Add: 4 ounces anchovy fillets with their oil; 12 ounces pitted large green olives, drained; 12 ounces pitted large ripe olives, drained; 3 large cloves garlic, crushed; 3 tablespoons capers, drained. Let stand, covered, at room temperature for at least 3 days before using. Then keep in the refrigerator if you are planning on storing for any length of time.

Marinated Red Onion Rings

Pour boiling water to cover over 2 cups of thinly sliced red onion rings. Let stand for 20 minutes and then drain. Place in a refrigerator container that can be sealed and pour dressing over. Cover and chill for 2 days before serving. To make the dressing, combine ⅓ cup olive oil, 2 tablespoons lemon juice, 1 teaspoon salt, ⅛ teaspoon paprika, ¼ cup crumbled bleu cheese and some black pepper.

Marinated Zucchini

This will keep for several days in the refrigerator and makes a nice side dish. Take 3 5 or 6-inch long zucchini and cut into ½-inch slices. Heat ¼ cup good oil in a large skillet and add zucchini in a flat layer. Sauté over medium heat for 2 minutes on each side. Then add ¼ cup red wine vinegar, cover the pan and cook for 2 or 3 minutes longer. Remove zucchini to a plastic refrigerator container and pour over the oil and vinegar. Chill thoroughly and serve as a side dish.

Marinated Mushrooms

Add this to the list of marinated vegetables and you are prepared for most emergencies.

**2 pounds fresh mushrooms, wiped clean
    with a damp cloth
2 tablespoons minced garlic
1 cup white wine vinegar
1 cup olive or other oil
1 cup water
2 large bay leaves
½ teaspoon dried thyme
3 tablespoons minced fresh shallots
2 teaspoons salt
½ teaspoon freshly ground black pepper**

Prepare mushrooms and set aside. Combine remaining ingredients in a 3 or 4-quart saucepan and bring to a boil. Lower heat and simmer for 5 minutes. Then add mushrooms and simmer for an additional 10 minutes. Transfer to containers. These will keep, refrigerated, for at least 3 weeks. To serve, drain and serve with picks, or slice and add to salads. Makes about 3 pints.

Note. Save this marinade to use again, or add it to a salad dressing.

Marinated Spicy Carrots

This spicy, hot dish will keep for about 4 months in the refrigerator. It will improve with age. Take 12 medium sized carrots and peel them and slice them diagonally into ½-inch chunks. Place them in a large bowl and cover with boiling water. Let stand for 30 minutes, then drain and pour ice water over the carrots to stop any cooking immediately. Combine the following: 1 12-ounce can whole jalapeño peppers; 2 large onions, thinly sliced into rings; 1 cup good oil; 1 cup white wine vinegar and 1 teaspoon salt. Add carrots, cover and refrigerate for at least a day. They are best if they stand for several days before using.

An Array of Marinated Vegetables

Marinated Vegetable Platter

Having a variety of marinated vegetables in the refrigerator is just like money in the bank if you entertain a lot. Arrange them in decorative ways. I like to prepare a large platter with triangles (with the point of the triangle at the center of the platter and the wide part at the edge) of vegetables. Arrange them with color in mind—slices of yellow summer squash next to Brussels sprouts for example, and then some tiny new potatoes next to slices of tomato and a mound of marinated grated Jerusalem artichokes. I always drain the vegetables first (the tomatoes are not marinated) and then drizzle some of the marinade over any unmarinated vegetables. If you want to be fancy, you might make a tomato rose for the center. Otherwise, just use rings of red onion and arrange them over the top.

Fresh Marinated Salad

This can be served as a salad, or as a vegetable side dish. It holds up well and is perfect for buffets or dinner parties.

1½ cups thinly sliced mushrooms
1½ cups thinly sliced zucchini
1½ cups thinly sliced carrots, preferably tender, young carrots
1½ cups broccoli flowers
1½ cups bite-sized cauliflower florets
1 cup sliced red onion
1 cup green pepper rings
1½ cups halved cherry tomatoes
approximately 2 cups Basic Vinaigrette (*see page 159*)

Place all vegetables in a large bowl. Add dressing and toss lightly. Chill for at least several hours before serving, stirring occasionally. Drain, reserving dressing, and serve on a lettuce or spinach-lined platter, mounding nicely. Or serve on individual chilled salad plates. Serves 6 to 8.

Note. Any of the following vegetables can be substituted or added: thinly sliced yellow squash; chopped green onions; raw green peas; snow peas; sugar snaps; thin strips of jicama.

Marinated Chick Peas

Keep these in the refrigerator, and toss some in almost any salad, or serve by themselves as a side dish. Simply cook dried chick peas until tender, or drain and rinse canned ones. Turn into a plastic refrigerator container and cover with Basic Vinaigrette (*see page 159*) with some extra garlic. Chill overnight before using.

Italian Salad

This is especially good with Italian dishes.

1 medium head romaine or leafy lettuce, washed and drained
½ cup Marinated Chick Peas (*see above*)
⅓ cup diced pimiento or roasted, peeled red peppers
½ cup Italian salami, cut into narrow strips
⅓ cup diced red onion
2 medium tomatoes, seeded and diced
½ cup freshly grated Parmesan or Romano cheese
Italian Salad Dressing (*see page 162*)

Tear lettuce into pieces and place in a salad bowl. Add chick peas, pimiento, salami, onion and tomatoes. Toss with enough dressing to coat and sprinkle with the cheese. Serve to 6.

Angie's Eggplant Appetizer

Except for the eggplant, I give no specific ingredient amounts. Use whatever amount of vinegar or oil that you will need. If you like a lot of garlic you might use 4 or 5 crushed cloves. Taste and adjust seasonings to your taste.

1 or 2 large eggplants, peeled and sliced *very* thin
boiling vinegar
olive oil
crushed garlic cloves
dried red pepper
dried oregano
salt if necessary

Some people cube the eggplant. I always slice it. Dip the slices in boiling vinegar. (The vinegar can be cooled and used again.) Then drain. Layer in a container with the garlic, red pepper and some oregano. Cover with olive oil. Taste and add salt if necessary. Store for 5 or 6 days before using. This will keep for several weeks.

Marinated Beets

Cook baby beets until just tender. Peel them and place them, whole, in a jar which has a tight-fitting lid. Fill the jar with Basic Vinaigrette (*see page 159*) and add an extra clove of garlic or two. These will keep, refrigerated, for several months. They are a lovely addition to a salad tray.

Belgian Endive and Beet Salad

For this salad you should begin with homemade Marinated Beets for the best results.

1½ cups Marinated Beets (*see above recipe*), sliced
5 or 6 Belgian endives, cut into 1 inch lengths
½ cup pine nuts, toasted
¼ cup Basic Vinaigrette (*see page 159*)
¼ cup vinaigrette from the beets
1 teaspoon Dijon mustard

Combine the beets, endives and pine nuts. Combine the vinaigrettes with the mustard and shake well. Add to the salad, tossing just to mix. Turn into serving bowl. This amount will serve 6 generously.

Note. *You can vary the ingredient amounts to suit your taste. You can also used canned beets, cut into julienne, in place of the Marinated Beets.*

Italian Marinated Eggplant

About the best you will ever taste.

3 medium eggplants, peeled, cut into 1-inch thick slices and then into fingers
oil for frying
1 cup olive oil
1 cup white wine vinegar
4 teaspoons dried oregano
½ to 1 teaspoon crushed red pepper
4 cloves garlic, crushed
2 tablespoons Worcestershire sauce
¼ cup minced parsley
1 teaspoon salt

Heat enough olive oil to cover the bottom of a skillet. Add eggplant and cook, turning often, for 3 or 4 minutes. Eggplant should be lightly browned. Remove and drain. Combine remaining ingredients. Place eggplant in a serving bowl or other container and pour over the marinade. Be certain that the eggplant is well coated. Let marinate for at least several hours, but preferably overnight or even a few days before serving.

Note. *Marinated eggplant is usually served as part of an antipasto platter. (See The Vegetable as Appetizer chapter.) You can also serve it as a side dish or in a composed salad.*

PASTA SALADS

It is unfortunate that macaroni salad, that usually tasteless combination of overcooked elbow macaroni, celery, cheese and mayonnaise is the only pasta salad that the average American has any knowledge of. A good "pasta" salad, made with large or medium shells, rotelli, rigatoni, fettucini, linguine, bow ties, or the long fusilli, tossed with a well-flavored vinaigrette and some raw or blanched vegetables is a visual as well as a taste delight. The possibilities are almost endless. The most important thing is to use a good pasta. The inexpensive pastas break up in the cooking and turn to mush. You save money on the pasta and lose money by ruining the finished dish. Good pasta *is* more expensive. It is made with a good durum wheat and will hold its shape during the cooking and saucing and have a better flavor. The best pasta, of course, is that which you make yourself. However, the delightful shapes such as rotelli, rigatoni and shells and bow ties are impossible to make at home. If you are among the fortunate who have a source for fresh pasta nearby, use it.

Most, if not all pastas will cook in less time than it says on the package or box. For a thin pasta such as spaghetti, linguine or the long fusilli begin testing after about 5 minutes. For the larger, thicker shapes, begin testing after about 8 minutes. Remove from the water the minute the pasta is done. If you are using homemade pasta, the fresh will cook in seconds and the dried will cook in no more than 4 or 5 minutes.

Always remember to use at least 6 or 7 quarts of boiling water to each pound of pasta. Salt the water well and add several tablespoons oil or butter to the water. This helps to prevent sticking. The biggest mistakes that people make when cooking pasta are using too little water and overcooking the pasta.

If you make your own pasta, do not salt it. It isn't necessary to add salt to pasta. But do salt the water in which it cooks.

Do not rinse the pasta with cold water. To serve it I use two spaghetti forks for the long pasta and a large slotted spoon for the other shapes. If it is a pasta that holds liquid, such as the shells, I will generally turn it into a colander and shake it. The pasta goes directly onto hot plates if I am saucing it with a hot sauce, or into a mixing bowl if for salad. For salad I immediately toss it with some vinaigrette before adding the other ingredients. Many people rinse pasta with cold water to stop the cooking if it is to be used for salad. I toss it with vinaigrette; warm pasta absorbs the flavor of the vinaigrette better. For convenience the pasta can be cooked a day ahead and tossed with some of the vinaigrette and chilled. I prefer pasta salads served at room temperature, so I frequently make them several hours before serving and do not chill them.

Linguine Salad

A sort of flattened spaghetti, linguine is one of my favorite pasta shapes. I occasionally make this salad with rotelli, in which case I grate the mozzarella.

> **1 pound linguine**
> **Mustard Vinaigrette** (*see page 160*)
> **1 medium sized zucchini, thinly sliced or diced**

> **1 bunch broccoli, trimmed and separated into flowers** (*reserve stems for another use*)
> **1 pound mozzarella or Monterey Jack cheese, grated or cut into small dice**
> **½ cup grated Parmesan cheese**
> **½ cup pine nuts, toasted**
> **½ to 1 cup cherry tomatoes, halved**

Linguine Salad — with Rotelli

Cook the pasta as directed for Pasta Salads. Immediately dress it with some of the vinaigrette. Blanch the zucchini and broccoli for 1 or 2 minutes only. Run under cold water to stop the cooking. If desired the vegetables can be used raw. Combine them with the pasta, using a little more vinaigrette if necessary. This can be done several hours or even the day ahead.

When ready to serve, add the cheeses, pine nuts and cherry tomatoes. Use more vinaigrette as necessary as different pastas absorb different amounts of dressing. If you make the salad the day ahead you will definitely need more. Serves 4 to 6.

Pasta Salad Tonnato

Make above salad using *only* the pasta, zucchini, broccoli and cherry tomatoes. Dress with the following: 1 6½-ounce can tuna, drained; 3 anchovies; 1 cup homemade mayonnaise; 2 tablespoons capers and 2 tablespoons lemon juice that have been puréed in the blender or food processor. Delicious.

Spinach Noodle Salad

This salad can be made with any of the pastas that I discussed in Pasta Salads, but the spinach noodles are fun.

8 ounces spinach noodles
2 cups fresh small green beans, blanched for 5 minutes
Mustard Vinaigrette *(see page 160)*
¼ pound Italian salami, cut in julienne
¼ pound provolone, cut in julienne
1 small red onion, minced
2 cups chopped crisp lettuce

Cook noodles as directed. Drain and combine with the blanched beans and enough vinaigrette to moisten. Add the salami, provolone and red onion. Chill. Just before serving add the chopped lettuce and toss well. Add more dressing as needed. Serves 4 to 6.

Variations

Substitute 1 7-ounce can of good tuna, well-drained, for the salami and provolone. Add some halved cherry tomatoes.

Use 2 cups snow peas, trimmed and blanched for 1 or 2 minutes in place of the green beans.

Green and White Tortellini Salad

This was the result of an evening of unexpected company, when I grabbed what was available in the refrigerator and cupboard and put them together with what we felt was a superb result.

Cook, following directions on the box, two 7-ounce boxes of tortellini, one white and one green. (You could use all white or all green if you wish.) Open a 10-ounce box of frozen peas and place them, still frozen, in a colander. When the tortellini are done turn them into the colander over the peas. The boiling water will thaw and cook the peas *just* enough. You don't want overcooked

peas. Drain thoroughly and turn into a bowl and toss with some Basic Vinaigrette *(see page 159)*. Set aside to cool. When cooled, crumble in approximately 4 ounces of Gorgonzola cheese, toss with a little more vinaigrette if the mixture seems a little dry, and taste for seasoning. You may or may not need to add some coarse salt and freshly ground black pepper to taste. This amount should serve 8 to 10.

Pasta Primavera Salad

I especially like this with summer barbecues. For a party I barbecue whole Cornish game hens (basted with a mixture of melted butter, white wine and tarragon) and an assortment of whole sausages. With them I serve this salad, my crusty sourdough French bread with whipped butter and an assortment of cheeses and a nice white wine.

12 ounces linguine or other pasta shape
1 cup green onion slices
1 cup very thinly sliced celery *(the food processor does this perfectly)*
½ pound fresh asparagus spears
1 cup zucchini slices
1 cup broccoli flowers
1 cup snow peas
⅓ cup lemon juice
¼ cup good oil *(see page 156)*
¾ cup sour cream
½ cup homemade mayonnaise
salt and pepper to taste
16 cherry tomatoes, halved
fresh tarragon leaves

For a subtle flavor, cook the pasta in the vegetable water. First, blanch the asparagus, zucchini and broccoli in boiling water for 1 minute. Use a large scoop to remove the vegetables from the water and run cold water over them to stop the cooking process. Reserve.

Cook the pasta in the same water. Drain well. Combine pasta with the green onion slices, celery, the blanched vegetables and the snow peas. Add the lemon juice and oil. Toss to combine. Chill well.

Just before serving the salad, combine the sour cream and mayonnaise and whisk together. Add to the salad with salt and pepper to taste. Add tomato halves, toss well and turn into a bowl or onto a platter. Scatter fresh tarragon leaves over the top.

Chinese Noodle Salad

This is my version of a traditional Chinese salad. Because it holds up so well, it is great on a buffet, and I always include it with my Chinese dinners. You can use packaged egg noodles, or linguine or even spaghetti if you absolutely cannot find the thin Chinese noodles. I always serve a bowl of Hot Chili Oil with it, as with any Chinese dish, for those who wish it a little hotter.

1 pound thin Chinese egg noodles

DRESSING

1 clove garlic, crushed
¼ cup soy sauce
2 tablespoons Oriental sesame oil
2 tablespoons peanut oil
½ tablespoon Hot Chili Oil (*see below*)
2 tablespoons Chinese black vinegar, or red wine vinegar

1 bunch green onions
½ pound fresh snow peas, blanched for 1 minute, or 1 cup fresh bean sprouts
1 cup shredded chicken or pork (*optional*)

Cook the Chinese noodles exactly as directed on the package. Be careful not to overcook them. While the noodles are cooking, combine the ingredients for the Dressing.

When the noodles are done, drain them and rinse with cold water. (This is probably the only time that I recommend rinsing pasta of any kind with cold water.) Add Dressing and toss well. Chill for at least several hours, or overnight.

When ready to serve, take 2 out of the bunch of green onions and cut them into flowers (*see page 102*). Chill in ice water until curled.

Chop the remaining green onions. Add to the noodles and toss well. Add the snow peas or bean

sprouts and meat, if desired, and toss well. Turn salad out onto a platter and garnish top with the green onion flowers. Serves 4 to 6. Serves more if you are serving it Chinese style, where you are preparing one dish for each guest.

Note. If you wish, you can use both snow peas and bean sprouts.

Hot Chili Oil

I set out a bowl of this with every Chinese meal, and with a few other meals, also. Just stir a little into the dish for a spicy hotness. You can buy it in Chinese markets, but the cost is high and it is surprisingly easy and inexpensive to make. I got the recipe from Bill Slattery. Take two cups of inexpensive salad oil and place in a pot on the burner. Set the heat on low. Put a generous handful of dried cracked red pepper (red pepper flakes) into the oil and let heat for an hour. Strain and store. It will keep forever.

Spinach Salad

This is probably the most popular "tossed" salad in the United States today. It seems to be on every restaurant menu and it is served at many parties, perhaps because fresh spinach is so delicious that it is difficult, indeed, to botch the salad. A friend of mine painstakingly snips the stem out of each leaf of spinach. Her care results in a remarkably tender salad.

2 pounds spinach, stemmed and washed
3 or 4 hard-cooked eggs, peeled and sliced
salt and pepper to taste
1 large avocado, peeled and cut into wedges
6 to 8 slices bacon, cut into small pieces and cooked until crisp
Egg Vinaigrette (*see page 160*)

Tear spinach into bite-sized pieces and place in a salad bowl. Arrange eggs and avocado on top. Sprinkle with crisp bacon pieces. Just before serving toss with just enough Egg Vinaigrette to thoroughly moisten. Sprinkle with salt and pepper to taste. Serves 6.

Variations

Chopped green onions and sliced large mushrooms are a delicious addition.

Flaming Spinach Salad

This one is fun. Make the above salad omitting the Egg Vinaigrette. Reserve ⅓ cup of the bacon fat. To it add ¼ cup good wine or malt vinegar, 2 tablespoons lemon juice, 1 teaspoon sugar and ½ teaspoon Worcestershire sauce. Heat until boiling. Pour over the salad just before serving. Then heat 2 tablespoons brandy or cognac and ignite it while pouring over the salad. Toss lightly and serve immediately. To appreciate this, it should be done at the table in front of the guests.

California Spinach Salad

This is my favorite spinach salad.

DRESSING

½ cup red wine vinegar
1 teaspoon salt
½ teaspoon sugar
2 teaspoons Dijon mustard
1 teaspoon sweet pickle relish
½ teaspoon minced capers
1½ cups good oil (see page 156)

SALAD INGREDIENTS

2 or 3 hard-cooked eggs
3 pounds spinach, cleaned and stemmed
¼ pound bacon, minced and sautéed until crisp
½ red onion, minced
¼ pound mushrooms, sliced

Combine Dressing ingredients and set aside. Chop the eggs and reserve. Drain the spinach on paper towels and pat dry. Place leaves in a large salad bowl and sprinkle with the crisp bacon. Add the onion and mushrooms to the bacon drippings and sauté until tender. Stir 1 cup of the Dressing (mix well first) into the hot drippings and bring to a boil. Pour over the spinach and toss. Sprinkle with the chopped eggs. Serve immediately with the remaining Dressing on the side. Serves 6.

The Ultimate Tossed Salad

I love salads, and could easily live on salads, seafood and good wine. Even my passion for pasta and for eggplant can be satisfied with salads. So about once a week my little grandson Christopher and I have a salad for dinner. With some hot biscuits or my homemade Sourdough French Bread (see page 186) we have a good, nutritious meal.

I begin by checking the refrigerator to see what is lurking in those small pots and bowls, then decide what is to go into the salad. I begin with two or three kinds of lettuce, some fresh spinach if possible, a bunch of green onions or a red onion, chopped, and a few hard-cooked eggs, sliced. If there are some marinated chick peas, or some sliced cooked carrots, they go into the bowl. Leftover luncheon meat, cooked chicken or seafood, or cheese slices are cut into julienne and tossed in. Marinated artichoke hearts or raw or marinated mushrooms are added if available. A little bowl of leftover green peas, or pea pods? Add them, they're delicious in a salad. Bean sprouts? Yes! Sliced cooked carrots or cauliflower? Yes! Some raw or cooked asparagus? Yes! Avocado? Yes! In the spring there are probably some tender dandelion greens right in the yard, and later in the summer some sorrel. Clean them and toss them in. Whatever you have combined in that salad bowl, dress it lightly, tossing ever so gently so that every ingredient, cooked or raw, retains its identity. Serve extra dressing on the side for those who, like me, love a lot of salad dressing. The salad in the bowl however, should be just coated.

You are not going to use every ingredient I have mentioned above. But they are ideas. I have seen people throw out that spoonful or two of vegetables because they just didn't know what to do with

them—and then make a salad with iceberg lettuce, tomatoes and some chopped onion. All of the good, interesting ingredients went down the garbage disposal, or into the compost heap.

Be imaginative. Be creative. If your family doesn't like a particular ingredient, just don't use it again. But don't stop being imaginative and creative. Don't stop trying different ideas.

Jake's Salad

I borrowed this idea from my favorite eastern Idaho restaurant. This salad holds up nicely, making it a good addition to a buffet. It also goes especially well with quiche for a simple meal.

In any amounts desired, combine the following ingredients in a salad bowl: sliced crisp fresh cucumbers or raw zucchini; sliced green onions; diced seeded fresh tomatoes, or halved cherry tomatoes; bean or alfalfa sprouts. Add salt and pepper to taste. Add Basic Vinaigrette (see page 159) just to coat everything.

Italian Relish
(Scacciata)

Nice with an antipasto tray, or with any pizza or pasta dish. You might also enjoy it on sandwiches.

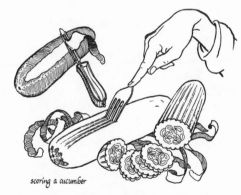

scoring a cucumber

**2 cups thinly sliced celery, including a few
  leafy ends**
⅓ cup chopped stuffed olives
½ teaspoon oregano
2 tablespoons olive oil
2 tablespoons white wine vinegar
salt and pepper to taste

Combine ingredients and cover dish. Marinate overnight if possible, or at least for 4 to 6 hours. Serve cold in lettuce cups. Serves 4.

Raw Vegetable Salad

This salad, with its bright green broccoli flowers, red tomatoes and beige mushrooms, is as colorful as it is delicious. One friend adds crab meat to it to make it a main dish salad and serves it with my crusty Sourdough French Bread (*see page 186*).

1 bunch broccoli
1 zucchini, about 5 or 6 inches long
1 cucumber, preferably the long European kind
4 large, firm mushrooms
1 bunch green onions
3 firm, medium sized tomatoes, or 12 to 15 cherry tomatoes
Basic Vinaigrette (*see page 159*) **to which you have added 1 or 2 minced shallots and 1 minced cornichon and a spoonful of Dijon mustard**

Trim the broccoli, reserving the stems for a pasta sauce. Use just the flowers and a few thin slices of the tender stem. Blanch in boiling water for 1 minute. Cool under cold running water and then drain.

Slice the zucchini, cucumber and mushrooms into thin slices. Use the food processor if you have one. Combine with the broccoli. Slice the tomatoes into wedges, or halve the cherry tomatoes. Add to broccoli mixture.

Add just enough of the dressing to coat the vegetables. Add salt and pepper to taste. I serve this in a shallow bowl because it is such a pretty dish. Serves 6 to 8.

Variation

To provide a thoroughly delicious contrast in flavors and textures, add any or all of the following: 1 7¾-ounce can hearts of palm, drained and cut into 1-inch pieces; 1 7-ounce box tortellini, cooked and drained as package directs, and then marinated in the salad dressing; 1 cup homemade or commercial marinated artichoke hearts.

Shredded Zucchini Salad

This is something a little different to do with zucchini. The texture is lovely.

2 to 3 pounds small firm zucchini
cherry tomatoes

DRESSING

¼ cup homemade mayonnaise
¼ cup sour cream
1 tablespoon lemon juice
4 teaspoons Dijon mustard
salt and pepper to taste

Wash zucchini but do not peel. Shred enough to make 4 cups. Drain in a colander, pressing lightly to extract as much water as possible without crushing the shreds. Halve enough cherry tomatoes to make one cup. Combine zucchini and tomatoes in a bowl.

Combine Dressing ingredients and whisk to blend well. Add to salad mixture and toss lightly so that the shreds do not pack down. To serve, mound on chilled lettuce leaves. Serves 4 to 6.

Middle Eastern Chick Pea Salad

This simple salad is good with cold cuts, or on a picnic, or simply as a light meal with hard-cooked eggs, cheese and good bread. You could add some sliced olives and chopped parsley to the salad.

3 cups warm, cooked chick peas
1 or 2 large cloves garlic, minced
grated rind of ½ a lemon
⅓ cup olive oil
1 or 2 tablespoons tahini (*sesame seed paste*), optional

2 tablespoons fresh lemon juice
salt and pepper

Combine all ingredients. Make certain that the chick peas are warm as they will absorb the flavor better. Cool to room temperature, stirring occasionally. Serves 4 to 6.

North Beach Broccoli Salad

A nice idea, to serve with pizza or any pasta dish. Simply thaw and drain well a box of frozen broccoli cuts. Press lightly to express as much water as possible. Then dress with olive oil, fresh lemon juice, crushed garlic and salt and pepper to taste.

Shredded Beet Salad

This marvelously crunchy and delicious salad was first suggested by Cora, Rose and Bob Brown in their *Salads and Herbs*, published by Lippincott in 1938 and long out of print. It is one of our favorites and always a surprise to those who taste it for the first time and find out that it is made with *raw* beets. It keeps well for several days as there is no lettuce to break down and become limp. Take it on picnics, and serve it with barbecues or with cold cuts. When I serve it at home, I mound individual portions on a bed of chopped lettuce.

1 pound (*3 medium sized*) raw beets, peeled and trimmed
3 carrots (*long, thin young ones are best*)
1 bunch green onions
Mustard Vinaigrette (*see page 160*)
salt and pepper

Shred the raw beets and carrots in the food processor or by hand. Slice the green onions. Combine and mix together lightly. Add just enough Mustard Vinaigrette to dress the vegetables and salt and pepper to taste. Serve to 4.

Note. *The carrots can be omitted, in which case add another beet or two.*

Tabooli

One of the most popular Middle Eastern dishes, and certainly one of the most healthful as well as delicious dishes in the world. I serve it with salad luncheons, and it is almost always part of any buffet. If you plan on making enough Tabooli for several days, add the tomatoes just before each serving. Tomatoes weep copious amounts of liquid and will ruin any dressing. The bulgur can be bought in any Middle Eastern store and in many Italian markets. It comes in three grinds. Fine, which is excellent for Kibbe and Tabooli; the medium grind and the coarse grind. The coarse grind can be cooked as you would rice for an excellent pilaf. The medium or the coarse grind can also be used for Tabooli, but the coarse grind should be soaked in boiling water for an hour. The fine grind can be soaked in cold water for 10 to 15 minutes. Any recipe that tells you to soak the fine grind in hot or boiling water for several hours is not authentic.

1 cup bulgur (*see above*), soaked in water to cover
4 cups finely chopped parsley
1 cup finely chopped fresh mint (*optional*), or ¼ to ⅓ cup dried mint soaked in the lemon juice and oil
2 large bunches green onions, finely chopped
1 or 2 cucumbers, peeled and seeded (*the peeling and seeding is not necessary if you are using the European cucumbers*)
2 or 3 large tomatoes, seeded and chopped
salt and pepper to taste
½ to ⅔ cup fresh lemon juice, approximately
½ cup olive oil, approximately
1 or 2 cloves garlic, crushed and mixed with the lemon juice and oil
romaine leaves

Soak the bulgur in the water to cover for 10 to 15 minutes for the fine bulgur and an hour or two for the coarse grind. Drain thoroughly and press to remove as much water as possible. Now fold in the chopped vegetables, excluding the tomatoes which should be added at the last minute. Fold together carefully so that the vegetables are not crushed in the process. Dress with the lemon juice and oil into which you have mixed the dried mint, if used, and the garlic. Use just enough to moisten everything. More can be added if necessary. *At this point the salad can be chilled for several hours.* Just before serving taste for seasoning and add more dressing if needed. Fold in the tomatoes.

Traditionally the Tabooli is served in a romaine lettuce-lined bowl, or mounded on a romaine-lined platter and garnished with tomato wedges and black olives and sprigs of mint. A bowl of romaine leaves is always served with the Tabooli so that it can be scooped and eaten.

Fattoush

This is a Lebanese peasant salad with a particularly pleasing variation in textures.

> 1 to 1½ cups bite sized pieces of French or pocket bread, lightly toasted
> 1 large clove garlic, crushed
> salt and pepper to taste
> ½ cup lemon juice
> ½ cup parsley
> 1 bunch green onions, chopped
> 1 cup fresh mint (*optional*)
> ½ of a European cucumber, or 1 regular cucumber, peeled, halved lengthwise and seeded
> 4 or 5 romaine leaves
> 2 or 3 medium tomatoes, seeded and diced
> ½ cup good oil (*see page 156*)

Toast the bread lightly and reserve. Crush the garlic and mix it with the salt and pepper in a salad bowl. Add the lemon juice, parsley, green onions and mint. Toss. Dice the cucumber and add to the bowl. Tear romaine leaves into bite-sized pieces and add. Then add the tomatoes. Toss gently but thoroughly. Add the oil just before serving and taste for seasoning, adding more salt and pepper if necessary. Toss with the bread pieces and serve. Serves 4 to 6.

Moroccan Carrot Salad

Scrub and thinly slice 1 pound of carrots. Boil them in salted water to cover until barely tender. Drain. Toss with the following: 1 clove garlic, crushed; 1 teaspoon paprika; ½ to 1 teaspoon cumin; 3 tablespoons lemon juice and 2 tablespoons olive oil. Toss carefully.

Tomato and Green Pepper Salad

This is one of my favorite salads. The green peppers assume a completely different character when they have been roasted and peeled. The simple dressing of cumin, garlic, paprika, olive oil and lemon juice is extremely important. *Do not substitute a lesser oil. You will have a completely different salad, and one not as good.*

> 5 large green peppers, roasted and peeled
> 5 or 6 large tomatoes, peeled and seeded
> 2 cloves garlic, crushed
> pinch of paprika
> ¼ teaspoon cumin
> 3 tablespoons olive oil
> 2 tablespoons lemon juice
> salt and pepper

Cut peppers and tomatoes into small dice. Combine in a glass serving dish. Combine remaining ingredients and whisk together lightly. Toss gently with the peppers and tomatoes. Serve at room temperature. Serves 4 to 6.

Moroccan Tomato Salad

Moroccan salads traditionally are made with very few ingredients, often only two or three, so that the dressing is extremely important. Always use a fine oil, preferably at least half olive oil, and fresh garlic and lemon juice if these two ingredients are called for.

3 or 4 large ripe tomatoes
3 or 4 inside ribs of celery
⅓ cup chopped parsley
2 tablespoons drained capers
1 or 2 hot green peppers
3 or 4 hot pickled cherry peppers
¼ teaspoon cayenne pepper
1 teaspoon paprika
¼ cup olive oil

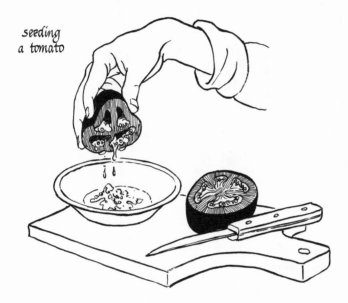

seeding a tomato

Core and seed tomatoes. Cut into small dice. Trim the celery and slice thinly—a food processor will give the perfect thickness. Combine with parsley and capers. Chop the peppers and add. Blend remaining ingredients and toss with salad. Serves 6.

Note. *This salad makes a fine filling for pocket bread.*

Hot Avocado Salad

A marvelous variation on the wilted lettuce salad, you will love the flavor and texture of this. Serve with Chili Chips (*see below*).

3 large tomatoes, cut into eighths
3 avocados, peeled, seeded and sliced
6 to 8 green onions, chopped
7 or 8 radishes, sliced
3 slices bacon, diced
2½ tablespoons white wine vinegar

1½ teaspoons chili powder
salt to taste
lettuce leaves

Prepare the vegetables as directed and set aside. Fry the bacon until crisp. Remove from skillet, drain and reserve. Add the vinegar, chili powder and salt to taste to the hot bacon fat in the pan and let it boil for 1 minute. Then add all of the vegetables and the reserved bacon to the hot fat and toss carefully so as not to crush the avocado and tomato. Serve immediately on the lettuce leaves with Chili Chips.

Chili Chips

Cut 12 corn tortillas into eighths with a scissors. Deep fry until lightly browned and crisp, just a minute or two at 375°F (190°C). Drain and toss in a paper bag with several teaspoons chili powder. Serves 6 to 8.

Hot Cauliflower Salad

Of Italian origin, this salad is a delicious surprise.

3 cups cauliflowerets
1 small green pepper, chopped
½ cup minced green onion
1 clove garlic, crushed
¼ cup Basic Vinaigrette (*see page 159*)
¼ teaspoon dried basil
3 tablespoons water
salt and pepper to taste
1 cup cherry tomatoes, halved

Steam the cauliflowerets over boiling water for 7 minutes. Add the green pepper and steam another 3 or 4 minutes. Set aside.
Cook the onion and garlic in the vinaigrette for 2 minutes. Add basil, water, salt and pepper, the steamed vegetables and the cherry tomatoes. Heat until hot and serve immediately in individual ramekins or salad bowls. Serves 6.

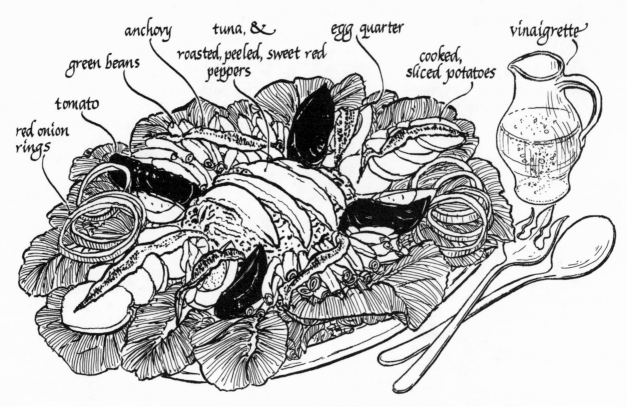

red onion
rings

tomato

green beans

anchovy

tuna, &
roasted, peeled, sweet red
peppers

egg quarter

cooked,
sliced potatoes

vinaigrette

Salade Niçoise

Salade Niçoise

In this lovely Mediterranean specialty the constants are tuna, tomatoes, green beans, olives, anchovies and, of course, greens. It makes a delicious luncheon salad served with crusty bread and a rosé wine. Traditionally it is a composed salad.

12 ounces green beans, trimmed, cooked until crisp/tender and cut into 2-inch lengths

4 medium tomatoes, cut into wedges

4 to 6 new potatoes, boiled, peeled, and cut into thick slices

1 cup Basic Vinaigrette *(see page 159)*

1 or 2 heads lettuce *(use a combination of Boston and leafy)*

1 or 2 6½ or 7-ounce cans tuna *(preferably packed in olive oil)*, **drained**

4 to 6 hard-cooked eggs, peeled and halved

8 to 12 anchovy fillets, drained and blotted

¾ cup black olives *(preferably Greek or Italian)*

rings of sliced red onion

artichoke hearts
pimiento strips

Pour some of the Vinaigrette over the green beans, tomatoes and potatoes. Set aside. Tear the lettuce into bite-sized pieces. Line a large platter or a shallow salad bowl with the lettuce. Arrange the tuna, separated into chunks, in the center.

Around the tuna arrange the green beans, tomatoes, potatoes and hard-cooked egg halves. Arrange the anchovy fillets over the egg halves. Arrange the remaining ingredients over and between, using several pimiento strips over the tuna. Just before serving, sprinkle with the remaining Vinaigrette. Serves 4 to 6.

Middle Eastern Eggplant Salad

This is a delicious, highly flavored salad made throughout the Middle East. In Algeria, the eggplant is sliced, salted and drained, then rinsed and dried. The slices are browned in hot olive oil on each side, then drained and mashed with garlic, a bit of cayenne, and cumin. This purée is fried in oil until all liquid evaporates and only the eggplant and frying oil are left. The oil is drained off and the eggplant is mixed with some fresh lemon juice and served lukewarm or at room temperature.

My mother, who is Lebanese, makes the same salad very simply. She roasts the whole eggplant until it is soft and tender and then scrapes it out of the shell and adds fresh lemon juice, some garlic that has been pounded with salt, olive oil, salt and pepper. The salad should taste rather highly of lemon juice and garlic. It keeps well. My version follows.

> 2 large eggplants with a strip of peel cut off
>   every inch or two
> 3 white onions, peeled and sliced
> olive oil for baking
> ⅓ cup fresh lemon juice
> ⅓ cup olive oil or other good oil
> 2 large cloves garlic, crushed
> salt and pepper

Slice the eggplant into ½-inch slices and place on a lightly oiled baking pan. Brush each slice lightly with oil and cover with a slice of onion. Bake in a 450°F (230°C) oven for 45 minutes, or until eggplant looks roasted. Remove from oven and cool for just a few minutes. It is important to mix with the dressing while the eggplant is warm.

Remove eggplant and onion to a cutting surface, or put into a wooden bowl. Cut into small dice with a large knife. Turn into a salad bowl and mix with remaining ingredients, adding salt and pepper to taste. Add more oil, lemon juice or garlic if you think the salad needs it. Serve at room temperature, mounded in a bowl and sprinkled with parsley, or decorated with a few black olives. Serves 6 to 8.

Three or Four Bean Salad

This is a popular salad that keeps well. It can also serve as a side dish. The kinds of beans you use are

up to you; kidney beans are the only constant. Whichever combination you choose, keep these important points in mind: cook fresh beans only until crisp/tender; drain and rinse canned beans. If you begin with dried beans (instead of canned) and cook them according to package directions, you will have a better looking and better tasting finished product. Cook the beans separately. That bit of extra care is what makes the difference between adequate and excellent.

COMBINATION 1

> 1 pound green beans, cut in 1-inch pieces,
>   cooked
> 1 pound wax beans, cut in 1-inch pieces,
>   cooked
> 1 16-ounce can blackeyed peas *or* chick
>   peas, drained and rinsed
> 1 16-ounce can kidney beans, drained and
>   rinsed

COMBINATION 2

> ⅔ cup dried chick peas, soaked, cooked,
>   and drained
> ⅔ cup dried blackeyed peas, soaked,
>   cooked, and drained
> ⅔ cup dried kidney beans, soaked, cooked,
>   and drained

REMAINING INGREDIENTS

> 1 or 2 green peppers, seeded, deribbed and
>   cut into thin rings
> 1 or 2 medium red onions, peeled and thin-
>   ly sliced and then separated into rings
> 1 cup Basic Vinaigrette *(see page 159)*
> 2 cloves garlic, crushed
> ⅓ cup minced parsley
> 2 tablespoons fresh tarragon, or ½ teaspoon
>   dried
> 1 tablespoon fresh basil, or 1 teaspoon dried

Prepare the beans in Combination 1 or Combination 2. Add remaining ingredients to the cooked bean mixture and taste for seasoning. You might want to add salt and pepper.

This amount will serve about 10, depending on the rest of the menu.

Mexican Zucchini Salad

This is a delicious salad. For best flavor and looks, use small zucchini, the smaller the better. Mound it nicely on a platter that has been lined with romaine leaves. I decorate each end of the platter with green onion flowers when I'm making the salad for a party.

2 pounds small zucchini, unpeeled
several small white onions, peeled and
    sliced into rings
4 large, California green chilis, roasted,
    peeled and cut into strips
1 6-ounce can whole black olives
¾ cup vinegar and oil dressing to which
    you have added several anchovy fillets,
    minced, and ¼ cup minced green and
    black olives
2 large avocados, peeled and cubed
½ to ¾ cup feta or Monterey Jack cheese,
    cubed or crumbled

Cook the zucchini, whole, in boiling salted water for 10 minutes, or until you can just pierce them with a fork. Remove from water, drain and then slice into ½-inch thick slices. Place in a bowl and add the onion rings, chilis, and olives. Add just enough dressing to coat well. Marinate for several hours. Just before serving, mix in the avocado and cheese. Serve as directed above. Serves 8.

Mexican Chef's Salad

Also called Taco Salad or Tortilla Salad, this combination of hot and cold is fairly new on the culinary scene. Basically it's a combination of all the ingredients commonly served in a taco shell without the shell. The crunchiness is provided by tortilla chips, either homemade or bought. Some recipes call for a side dish of vinaigrette mixed with green chili sauce and some call for heating together a can of crushed tomatoes with enough diced cheese to make a thick chili con queso type mixture when melted. To this latter one I add some green chili sauce and serve a bowl of extra hot chips on the side.

HOT MIXTURE

2 pounds ground beef
salt and pepper to taste
1 15-ounce can kidney beans, drained

SALAD MIXTURE

1 head iceberg lettuce, torn into bite sized
    pieces
1 avocado, peeled and sliced
3 medium tomatoes, seeded and diced
1 red onion, diced
2 cups crushed tortilla chips
½ pound Monterey Jack or Cheddar cheese,
    grated
1 cup sliced black olives
1 head romaine lettuce, torn into bite-sized
    pieces
1½ cups Basic Vinaigrette *(see page 159)*

First prepare the Hot Mixture. Brown the ground beef and add salt and pepper to taste and the drained kidney beans. Set aside while you prepare the salad.

For the Salad Mixture combine all salad ingredients *except* the Vinaigrette. Toss lightly and add enough of the Vinaigrette to coat the salad, but do not drench it. The best way to serve this is on individual plates. Mound the salad and spoon the hot meat mixture over the salad. Serve some extra hot chips and some hot sauce on the side. Serves 6.

Nopalitos Salad

A deliciously different salad made with the bottled cactus called nopalitos. I always serve this with Mexican meals. It is especially good with barbecues or as part of a buffet. This amount will serve 8 or 10 people but the salad halves (and also doubles) easily.

2 26-ounce jars nopalitos, drained, rinsed
    and drained
1 medium red onion, cut into thin rings
3 tomatoes, cut into wedges

3 medium avocados, peeled and sliced
about ½ cup grated Parmesan cheese

For the best effect use a straight-sided glass serving dish. Layer the nopalitos, onion, tomato and avocado. Sprinkle each layer with a tablespoon of the cheese. You should have 2 or 3 layers of each, ending with avocado and cheese. You will need no dressing and no salt or pepper. Let stand for at least 20 minutes before serving, and up to an hour, if possible. Serves 8 to 10.

Basque Green Bean Salad

This different salad is just slightly revised from a delightful little book, *From the Basque Kitchen*, published in Reno, Nevada. It is very good.

1 to 1½ pounds green beans, cooked until just tender
6 hard-cooked eggs
2 to 4 ripe tomatoes, quartered
1 clove garlic, crushed
handful of chopped parsley
wine vinegar
good oil *(see page 156)*

Place the green beans in a bowl. Remove the yolks from the egg whites and chop the egg whites, adding them to the green beans. Add the tomatoes.

Now take the egg yolks and begin mashing them, adding the garlic. Mash until smooth. Then add some of the parsley and a tablespoon of the wine vinegar and 3 tablespoons of the oil, mixing until it forms a *thin*, smooth sauce. Add more vinegar and oil as needed. What you are doing is making a mayonnaise. Pour this sauce over the other ingredients and stir gently until they are coated. Chill. Serve on a bed of chopped lettuce. Serves 4.

California Oriental Spring Salad

The fried wonton skins elevate this salad from the ordinary.

DRESSING

½ cup good oil *(see page 156)*
¾ teaspoon dry mustard
¾ teaspoon Worcestershire sauce
1 large clove garlic, crushed

SALAD INGREDIENTS

1 cup shredded lettuce
1 cup diagonally sliced celery
2 cups julienned cooked chicken
1 cup chopped green onions
2 cups bean sprouts
1 cup cherry tomatoes, halved
2½ ounces wonton skins
oil for deep frying

Combine Dressing ingredients in a jar and shake well. Set aside.

Combine the lettuce, celery, chicken, green onions and bean sprouts with the tomato halves. Toss gently. Cut wonton skins into strips and deep fry until crisp. Drain and then toss with the salad. Shake Dressing again, add to salad, and mix gently. Serves 8.

Green Bean and Mushroom Salad

This is a lovely idea. Simply cook some tiny green beans, or larger green beans cut on the diagonal, until tender/crisp. Sauté some thickly sliced mushrooms in olive oil with plenty of garlic. Let each come to room temperature. Thin some mayonnaise with wine vinegar and season to taste. Combine the beans and mushrooms and dress with the mayonnaise.

Pennsylvania Green Pea Salad

A Pennsylvania friend of mine taught me this salad. She also introduced me to fried cucumbers with breakfast, and fried green tomatoes. Lovely.

1 pound fresh green peas, cooked until just
   barely tender
1 or 2 green onions, sliced
½ cup diced Cheddar cheese
2 or 3 hard-cooked eggs, chopped
½ cup thinly sliced celery
½ cup mayonnaise
1 clove garlic, crushed
2 tablespoons white wine vinegar
6 slices bacon cut into dice and fried until
   crisp
leaf lettuce

Combine the peas, green onions, cheese, eggs and celery. Toss gently just to combine. Add the crushed clove of garlic to the mayonnaise and thin with the wine vinegar. Toss with the salad. Place in lettuce cups and top with the bacon. Serves 4.

Chick Pea Salad

Serve this with a crusty bread. It's one of my particular favorites.

2 16-ounce cans chick peas, drained and
   rinsed
2 cloves garlic, crushed
½ cup tarragon or other white wine vinegar
⅓ cup good oil *(see page 156)*
1 twist of a pepper mill
½ cup stuffed green olives, sliced
¼ pound Genoa salami, cut into thin strips
salad greens
½ cup chopped green onions
2 tomatoes, seeded and chopped
2 tablespoons minced parsley

Turn chick peas into a bowl. Combine crushed garlic with the vinegar, oil, and pepper. Add salt to taste. Add to the chick peas along with the olives and salami. Toss lightly and chill for several hours to blend flavors.

At serving time, line a shallow bowl with the greens. Add the chick pea mixture and mound slightly. Garnish with the green onions, tomatoes and parsley. Serves 6 to 8.

Celery Root Salad

In the cool months, make a salad with celery root. Peel the root and boil it in stock with some onion, salt and pepper and a bay leaf. Cook just until tender and then cool and cut into dice. Dress it with a mustardy vinaigrette and add some chopped green onions. Chill and serve in lettuce cups.

Italian Style Wilted Lettuce

Combine several varieties of lettuce with some chopped green onion and seeded, diced cucumber. (Or use the European cucumber and just slice it thinly.) Add some chopped watercress leaves if you can. Dress with some fine olive oil and wine vinegar and toss lightly. Sprinkle with ¼ cup grated Parmesan cheese. Heat ¼ cup olive oil in a small pan over low heat. Stir in 2 teaspoons anchovy paste until well blended. Add a little pepper to taste. You won't need salt. Pour this hot sauce over the salad, toss quickly and serve.

Summer Salad

Don't forget the summer beauty of a salad of sliced vine-ripened tomatoes, with slices of a good mozzarella, dressed with a drizzle of olive oil and wine vinegar and whole basil leaves. Serve with a crusty bread to sop up the flavorful juices.

Lebanese Yogurt Salad

This would more properly be called a side dish. It is one of the dishes that I grew up with, and this is the way my grandmother made it.

1 large cucumber, peeled, seeded and diced
   *(if you can get the European cucumber, the
   peeling and seeding can be omitted)*
2 cloves garlic, crushed
2 cups yogurt, beaten with a fork to
   ''loosen'' it

3 tablespoons fresh mint, or 1 tablespoon
   dried mint

Simply combine ingredients and mix together with a fork. Serve as a salad or side dish. Serves 4 to 6.

Parsley and Anchovy Salad

A pungent salad for those who like different flavors, or who at least are willing to try them. This will keep in the refrigerator for a week, and is excellent with a crusty bread. Make it at least a day ahead to give the flavors a chance to blend.

   1 2-ounce can flat fillets of anchovies
   4 or 5 fat cloves garlic, crushed
   ½ cup minced green onions
   1½ cups grated carrots
   ½ cup thinly sliced red or green pepper
   2 cups chopped parsley
   3 or 4 tablespoons red wine vinegar
   10 tablespoons olive oil
   ⅛ teaspoon crushed red pepper flakes
   salt and pepper to taste

Simply combine all ingredients and let marinate in the refrigerator overnight before serving. Serves 4.

New Potato Salad with Pesto

You probably have a favorite recipe for traditional potato salad (and for macaroni salad). If not, you can find one in almost every cookbook, most of them very ordinary. This potato salad is a little different, and quite delightful.

   8 to 12 new potatoes
   2 tablespoons dry vermouth
   ½ to ¾ cup mayonnaise
   2 or 3 tablespoons Pesto *(see page 127)*
   minced parsley for garnish

Allow 2 or 3 potatoes for each serving, depending on size. Boil potatoes until tender in boiling, salted water. Do not let them become mushy or over-

cooked. Peel them and cut into quarters. Sprinkle with the vermouth while still warm so that they will absorb the flavor. Combine mayonnaise with Pesto and stir into the warm potatoes. Turn into a serving dish and sprinkle with minced parsley. Serve immediately. Serves 4.

Hot Potato Salad

This one is different also.

   1 bunch green onions, chopped
   1 small onion, minced
   ⅓ cup butter
   ⅓ cup white wine vinegar
   2 tablespoons sugar
   2 tablespoons prepared mustard
   ¼ teaspoon dried thyme
   salt and pepper
   4 or 5 large potatoes, cooked, peeled and
      sliced into thick chunks

Sauté the onions in the butter until tender. Add the vinegar, sugar, prepared mustard and thyme. Add salt and pepper to taste. Add potatoes and toss gently so that you do not break them up. Cook over low heat for 15 minutes to blend flavors. Serves 6 hearty eaters.

THE FIRST SALAD BOOK

Early American cookbooks didn't give much attention to salads. However, those who think that our current preoccupation with salads is a new phenomenon might be interested to know that the first book devoted entirely to salads was written in 1699. Written by English horticulturist John Evelyn, it was titled *Acetaria* and the recipe for a green salad could be followed today. He stressed that the greens and herbs should be chosen so that "All should fall into their place like the notes in music, in which there should be nothing harsh or grating." He liked an oil and vinegar dressing, with not too much oil.

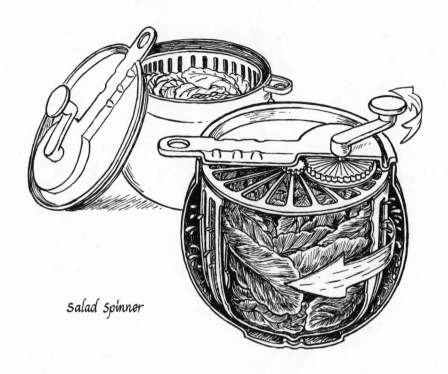

Salad Spinner

Hot Seafood Salad

I first tasted this in a restaurant and loved the dish. A simple idea, it just took a time or two to work it out to where I felt my version was even better than theirs.

½ **pound large shrimp, peeled and cut in half**
½ **pound sea scallops, cut into quarters**
1 **6-ounce jar marinated artichoke hearts, drained** *(reserve liquid)*
1 **large head leafy lettuce**
1 **or 2 tomatoes, seeded and diced**
2 **or 3 green onions, chopped**
2 **large mushrooms, sliced**
⅓ **cup olive oil**
2 **or 3 cloves garlic, crushed**
⅓ **cup white or rosé wine**
⅓ **cup lemon juice**
½ **to 1 teaspoon basil**
⅓ **cup croutons** *(optional)*
salt and pepper if desired

Prepare seafood as directed and set aside. Pour the oil from the artichoke hearts into a skillet. Tear the lettuce into a salad bowl and add the tomatoes, green onions, mushrooms and the artichoke hearts. Toss together lightly and set aside.

Pour the olive oil into the skillet with the oil from the artichoke hearts. Add the garlic and sauté until golden. Then add the seafood and stir and cook until almost cooked. Then add the wine, lemon juice and basil. Heat through and then pour over the crisp greens and toss. Sprinkle with the croutons and serve immediately. I find that this doesn't need any seasoning other than what is naturally in the ingredients themselves. However, you can add salt and pepper to taste if desired. Serves 4 to 6 depending on what else is served with it.

SALAD DINNERS

I am an inveterate party giver. Almost anything serves as an excuse to give another party for my favorite six (or 12—or 40) people. I generally begin with an earnest desire to hold this party down to a nice conversational ten or twelve people. Then I think of someone I haven't seen in ages and would love to see again. Or there is someone I just recently met, and would like to know better. And then of course there are those I would not dream of having a party without. I have great difficulty holding a party down to a reasonable number of people.

The easiest way I've found to manage my party-giving urges is to have early Sunday dinners. Since

154

most people go to work on Monday, guests don't stay late. During the summer I stick to salads. The presentation can be quite lovely, and I can begin preparing several days ahead. For a centerpiece I generally use fresh garden vegetables combined with flowers. One of the most popular centerpieces that I make is a wicker tray on which I arrange a huge cabbage with the outer leaves pressed open and mums arranged in the leaves. And the rest of the tray is filled with large purple eggplant, some small white eggplant if available, and some small zucchini and bright red tomatoes.

For the salads, different textures, flavors and colors are very important.

The following menus will give you some ideas.

MENU 1

Linguine Salad
Shredded Beet Salad
Tomato & Green Pepper Salad
Hot Cauliflower Salad

Tray of Marinated Vegetables
Spinach Salad
Sourdough French Bread with Whipped Butter

MENU 2

Moroccan Tomato Salad
Mexican Zucchini Salad
Hot Seafood Salad
Italian Salad
Tray of Marinated Vegetables
Chinese Noodle Salad
Pocket Bread

I use Pocket Bread with the second menu because the Moroccan Tomato Salad is so good in the pockets. Sometimes I add a tray of meats and cheeses to these menus, especially if I am having people who really think that it isn't a meal without meat.

Salad Dressings

A bottle—or better yet several bottles of several kinds—of a good salad dressing in the refrigerator is like money in the bank. No matter how important the salad ingredients are, the key to any salad is in the dressing.

To make a good dressing you need good ingredients. Students and guests almost always ask me about salads and their various dressings. They all know the keys to putting together good salad ingredients; it is the dressing that stumps them.

In one of the courses that I teach, we devote one evening to salads and dressings. We begin the evening with a tasting: several olive oils, a grapeseed oil, corn oil, walnut oil, my own lemon oil, a garlic oil, and a cottonseed oil. For the vinegars we taste several herb vinegars, a balsamic vinegar, white and red wine vinegar, and last, an apple cider vinegar.

Then we make two vinaigrettes, using the same recipe. We make one with a good oil and good wine vinegar, and the other with cottonseed oil and cider vinegar. The difference in flavor is amazing, and demonstrates better than words the importance of using quality ingredients.

OILS

First the oils. The best salad oil is olive oil, and the best olive oil comes from the first pressing. Somewhere on the jar or can will be the slogan "virgin," or "extra vierge." The oil may be golden or greenish depending on whether it is pressed from ripe or partially ripe olives.

Second pressings are labeled "fine" or "extra fine." Successive pressings are labeled simply "pure olive oil" and are too heavy for salad dressings.

Walnut oil is excellent for salad dressings, as is hazelnut.

The other oils—corn, safflower, sunflower, or peanut, for example—are too bland, too lacking in character to be used by themselves. *Remember that oil is, or should be, used for flavor.* Cottonseed oils are worthless. I do not even use them for deep frying.

Now, many of us simply cannot afford to use only a fine olive oil all the time. The solution is to mix your oils. I have a gallon jug in my kitchen in which I keep one of the two following mixtures:

MIX 1

½ **olive oil**
¼ **corn oil**
¼ **peanut oil**

MIX 2

⅓ **olive oil**
⅓ **corn oil**
⅓ **peanut oil**

The mixtures will have a mild olive oil flavor. I use them for mayonnaise, salad dressings and just about all cooking. For some things, of course, I reserve a small jug of pure olive oil.

Lemon Oil

Take some nice juicy lemons and cut each into 6 wedges. Place in a jar or carafe and fill with a mild olive oil. Let stand for several weeks before using. As you use this lightly flavored oil, simply keep adding more oil to the jar. This is a marvelous oil with which to dress a salad.

Use this to dress some roasted peeled peppers, along with some of the Private Stock Wine Vinegar (see below) and plenty of garlic. Serve with a hot, crusty French bread, some sweet butter and a nice cheese. Served with a small bowl of Italian or Greek olives and a nice white wine, I simply cannot imagine a better lunch or snack.

Lemon oil

Herb Oil

Take a bottle and fill it at least half full of fresh herbs—basil and tarragon, for example. Fill the bottle with oil. Cover and steep for a week or two. Strain, mark clearly and store. These various herbed oils and vinegars make fine gifts.

Garlic Oil

Add several cloves—at least 3 fat ones—to a bottle of olive or herb oil. Cover and let steep for several weeks.

VINEGAR

There is no vinegar to equal a fine wine vinegar, except perhaps an herbed wine vinegar. Wine vinegars differ widely. Some are rough and sharp. Others are as mild and mellow as aged wine, which indeed they once were. My favorite comes from a small winery out of Santa Cruz, California. I buy it by the gallon. I also like rice wine vinegar and a champagne vinegar. I always keep the following herbed vinegars on hand.

Herb Vinegar

Use any herb, or combination of herbs, such as the following: basil; tarragon; marjoram; mint; rosemary; burnet; shallot; flowers and leaves of lemon verbena; flowers and leaves of chives.

Crush the leaves lightly. This aids the infusion. Fill a bottle ½ or more full of the leaves. Add white wine vinegar. Cover and store in a warm, dark place for 2 to 4 weeks. Strain, pressing liquid out of leaves. Filter if necessary, bottle, and mark clearly.

Ravigote Vinegar

Follow method for Herb Vinegar, but use equal quantities of chervil, cress (or some other herb such as basil), burnet and tarragon. Add 2 cloves garlic and a small hot pepper per bottle. Cover with white or red wine vinegar and make as above.

Private Stock Wine Vinegar

Your own private stock wine vinegar makes marvelous salad dressings and excellent gifts for the discriminating cook.

Fill a bottle with wine vinegar. Add equal amounts of the following: basil, chives, mint, marjoram, savory, shallots and tarragon. Keep in a warm, dark place for 2 to 4 weeks. Then strain,

pressing all liquid out of the leaves. Let settle overnight. Filter and bottle. Mark clearly.

Apple Cider Vinegar

Although I prefer wine vinegar when making salads, pure apple cider vinegar is good with some salads, most generally the heartier salads. If cost is a factor, you might combine the two vinegars. When you buy vinegar, any kind, make certain that it is pure and does not say "flavored."

Note. *White vinegar is not suitable for salads.*

Lemon Juice

Lemon juice can be substituted for all or a portion of the vinegar in any salad dressing. For many salads, especially those made throughout the Middle East, a combination of equal parts of olive oil and lemon juice with a touch of garlic is the only dressing used.

Use *fresh* lemon juice only.

SEASONING MIXTURES

Along with herbs and vegetables that are used in salads and in other dishes, there are a number of homemade seasoning mixes that I always keep on hand. You might enjoy these.

My Favorite Seasoning Salt

I use this everywhere, in place of plain salt most of the time. When a dish seems to be lacking some zip, a few sprinkles of this will liven it up.

> **2 cups salt**
> **3 to 5 tablespoons onion powder**
> **1½ teaspoons each: garlic powder, curry powder, chili powder, dry mustard, black pepper**
> **2 tablespoons paprika**

1 teaspoon each: dried basil, oregano, red
   pepper, thyme, rosemary
½ teaspoon freshly grated nutmeg

Combine ingredients in food processor or blender.
Process for several seconds. Turn into a shaker
container.

Herb Salt for Meats

Use this with meats, however you cook them—
roasted, braised, barbecued, etc.

2 cups coarse salt
1 cup Homemade Garlic Salt (see below)
1 to 2 tablespoons each: dried basil and
   marjoram
1 tablespoon dried chives
2 teaspoons dried rosemary
1 teaspoon dried thyme
2 tablespoons paprika

Combine all ingredients. Use the food processor or
a blender and process for several seconds. Store in
a shaker container.

Herb Salt for Poultry

Use this with poultry. If you roast the bird, simply
rub this salt over the skin before baking, or else
add it to the basting liquid. Use in the flour mixture
for fried chicken. Add to any braised chicken
recipe or to soup or stew.

2 cups coarse salt
½ cup Homemade Garlic Salt (see below)
¼ cup dried chives
¼ cup dried parsley
⅓ cup dried tarragon leaves
1 teaspoon dried rosemary

Combine all ingredients and blend in a food processor or blender for several seconds. Store in a
shaker container.

Homemade Garlic Salt

This makes an excellent salt, better by far than any
you can buy. This will take a week to finish.

2 cups coarse salt
2 *heads* fresh garlic, separated but unpeeled

If you do not have a food processor you will need
to peel the garlic.

   Place 1 cup of the salt in the processor bowl and
add the 2 heads of unpeeled garlic cloves. Process
until the mixture is fine. Turn into a glass jar with a
tight-fitting lid and place in the refrigerator for 1
week. The salt will absorb the garlic oils during
this time, so that you have a mixture of garlic salt,
as opposed to garlicky salt. At the end of a week
turn the mix into the processor bowl again and add
the remaining cup of salt. Process until fine.

   Now turn into a shallow baking pan and spread
it out. Place in a 200°F oven to dry. This will take
about 8 to 10 hours. Then process again before
turning into shakers. Makes 2 cups.

VINAIGRETTE DRESSINGS

I make my Basic Vinaigrette by the quart during
warm weather and use it to dress fresh, raw
vegetables; cooked vegetables; leftover, cooked
beef, pork, tongue, poultry or fish; and salads. I
also use it as the base for any number of other
salad dressings.

   There are many "formulas" for Vinaigrette.
Some people like four or five times as much oil as
vinegar. Some omit the capers or pimiento, or the
garlic. As with most recipes, there is a great deal of
flexibility possible. Remember that and adjust to
your own individual taste. The following is the
way I like it.

Basic Vinaigrette

Vary the herbs according to what you like, or what
is in season. I especially love fresh sweet basil and
fresh tarragon in my salad dressings. If you use a

nice Herb Vinegar you will not need the dried herbs.

2 cups oil *(see Oils in this Chapter)*
1 cup wine vinegar *(see Vinegars)*
1 teaspoon dried tarragon
½ teaspoon dried dill
2 teaspoons salt, if desired
coarsely ground black pepper to taste
1 or 2 cloves garlic, crushed
¼ cup capers, drained
¼ cup minced pimiento

Combine and store in the refrigerator.

Basic Vinaigrette Variations

To 1½ cups Basic Vinaigrette add any of the following ingredients.
Anchovy: Mash a 2-ounce can of anchovy fillets and add to the dressing along with the anchovy oil.
Avocado: Add ¼ to ⅓ cup mashed avocado and 1 teaspoon Worcestershire sauce.
Egg: Add 4 raw egg yolks and shake together. (Add 2 to 4 teaspoons of Dijon mustard if using on a spinach salad.)
Herb: Add several tablespoons fresh herbs such as basil and chives.
Mayonnaise: Add ⅓ cup mayonnaise, preferably homemade, to dressing and shake. This makes a very popular creamy dressing. You can use it with any of the variations.
Mint: Add 2 tablespoons fresh mint leaves to dressing.
Mustard: Add a tablespoon or more of Dijon mustard to dressing.
Onion: Peel a medium onion and stud it with 4 whole cloves. Bake it at 350°F until tender. Cool. Discard cloves. Chop the onion and add to dressing.
Roquefort or Bleu Cheese: Crumble ⅓ to ½ cup cheese and add to the dressing.

Note. If using dressing on seafood salads, use lemon juice instead of vinegar.

Note. If using on meat salads, add some onion juice and a little Worcestershire sauce and grated horseradish.

Mustard Vinaigrette

5 tablespoons Dijon mustard
5 tablespoons lemon juice
¾ cup good oil
5 or 6 cloves garlic, crushed
1 bunch green onions, chopped
¼ teaspoon red pepper
salt and pepper to taste

Combine all ingredients and store, covered, in the refrigerator.

Pickled Vinaigrette

A nice dressing and a little different.

2 cups good oil *(see Oils in this chapter)*
½ cup olive oil
1½ cups white wine vinegar
juice of ½ lemon
1 cup chopped dill pickles
2 cloves garlic, crushed
1½ teaspoons black pepper
2 hard-cooked egg whites, chopped
⅓ cup minced parsley
1 tablespoon minced pimiento
2 teaspoons Worcestershire sauce
1 teaspoon hot pepper sauce
snipped chives *(optional)*
salt to taste

Combine all ingredients including chives, if used. Salt to taste. Shake well. Makes approximately 4 cups.

MAYONNAISE

Probably the most popular American salad dressing, although how some people can use it alone on a salad is beyond me. Named for the Duc de Richelieu, who was from the province of Bayonne, it was called Bayonnaise until the word became corrupted.

A fine, homemade mayonnaise is so different from the commercial variety that there is simply no comparison.

The first requirement for a fine mayonnaise is good oil. If you will remember that oil is used for flavor you will know how important it is. Your final product will only be as good as the ingredients that go into it. This rules out ballpark mustard and cottonseed oil. Use a good flavorful mustard—Dijon, homemade, hot, horseradish, German—whichever you prefer. For the acid you can use either fresh lemon juice or a good vinegar such as wine vinegar. Add salt and pepper. That is your basic mayonnaise. Begin with that and any number of additions can be made.

Food Processor Mayonnaise

**1 large egg, room temperature
1 tablespoon mustard (*see above*)
1 tablespoon lemon juice or vinegar
1 cup oil
salt and pepper to taste**

Place egg, mustard and lemon juice in bowl of food processor. Churn for several seconds. Begin adding the oil. You can pour it in in a steady stream as the mayonnaise should bind almost immediately. Salt and pepper to taste. Using the food processor, mayonnaise should take no longer than 30 or 40 seconds from start to finish.

Blender Mayonnaise

Place egg, mustard and lemon juice in blender container. Churn until well mixed. Add ¼ cup of the oil in a fine, *slow* stream until mayonnaise

161

binds. Then add remaining oil a little faster. Season to taste. This takes longer and is a little trickier.

Note. If the mayonnaise doesn't bind, simply pour off the liquidy mayonnaise into a cup. Add another whole egg to the processor or blender container. Churn, or whirl, then add liquid mayonnaise a little at a time. If using the food processor, simply pour it in steadily. It should bind almost immediately. With a blender, add ⅓ cup in a fine slow stream, then remaining mixture more quickly.

If the mayonnaise curdles: There is nothing wrong with curdled mayonnaise except for the way it looks. Simply follow instructions for mayonnaise that doesn't bind.

Note. If all else fails, don't throw it away. If it refuses to bind, simply add the liquidy mayonnaise to your salad dressing for a creamy dressing that the family will love. Adjust seasoning to taste.

Mayonnaise Variations

Mayonnaise can be made as flavorful as your imagination will allow. The following will be a help. Use with the above mayonnaise recipe.

Anchovy: Add several fillets of anchovy and the anchovy oil to the mayonnaise.

Aioli: One of the great French dips. Whirl 4 to 6 nice cloves of garlic in the processor or blender until a fine mince. Then, leaving the garlic in the bowl or container, make your mayonnaise.

Chive: One of my favorites. Begin with ½ cup or more of fresh chives. Whirl until chopped and then make the mayonnaise, leaving the chopped chives in. It turns a lovely green color and is most flavorful.

Collee: Dissolve 1 teaspoon unflavored gelatin in a little cold water and then melt over hot water. Mix into 1 cup mayonnaise. Use to coat fish or ham.

Five Spice: Add ¼ to ½ teaspoon Five Spice Powder, an Oriental seasoning.

Mock Hollandaise: Take some of the mayonnaise and heat it over gentle heat. Serve over asparagus or wherever you would serve Hollandaise.

Horseradish: Add horseradish to taste. Serve as a sandwich spread or with ham.

Herb: Add a combination of fresh chopped herbs such as basil, parsley, chives, chervil, etc.

Green Dipping Sauce

This is my favorite dip. Use half Mayonnaise and half sour cream. Chop and add 8 fresh spinach leaves (or use ½ of a 10-ounce package of frozen spinach, thawed and well drained), a teaspoon lemon juice, 3 or 4 green onions, minced, a teaspoon Worcestershire sauce and a little seasoning salt if desired. If it still needs some zip, add some chopped anchovies.

Italian Salad Dressing

Try this on mixed greens with a dash of grated Parmesan.

½ cup Mayonnaise
1 tablespoon catsup
2 cloves garlic, crushed
1 tablespoon red wine vinegar
1 tablespoon lemon juice
4 tablespoons cold water

Mix all together and chill well before tossing with salad.

The House Dressing

2 large eggs
¼ cup white wine vinegar
¼ cup red wine vinegar
1 teaspoon Dijon mustard
½ teaspoon dried tarragon
salt and pepper to taste
½ teaspoon seasoning salt
¼ teaspoon Maggi seasoning
2 cups good oil *(see Oils)*

Combine everything except the oil in the bowl of a food processor, or a blender container. Blend until smooth and then add the oil until dressing is creamy. Makes 2½ cups.

Old-fashioned Boiled Dressing

An old recipe for a salad dressing that was much used in the days before commercial mayonnaise. Some recipes call for making it with water instead of milk and some use a substantial amount of sugar. Use it with potato salad or coleslaw. If you fold in some whipped cream, it goes well with fruit salads.

    2 tablespoons flour
    1 teaspoon salt
    1 teaspoon dry mustard
    dash red pepper
    4 or 5 teaspoons sugar
    2 tablespoons melted butter
    2 egg yolks
    1 cup milk
    ¼ to ⅓ cup fresh lemon juice or apple cider
       vinegar

Combine dry ingredients. Stir well. Add liquid ingredients slowly, stirring. Pour into a heavy saucepan and cook over low heat, stirring constantly, until thickened. Strain if desired, and cool. Makes approximately 1½ cups.

Rich Boiled Dressing

This recipe, from an old book by Morrison Wood, is one I like.

    ¼ cup mild vinegar (I use a white wine
       vinegar)
    ½ cup water
    3 ounces melted butter
    ¼ teaspoon dry mustard
    1 teaspoon salt

    1 tablespoon lemon juice
    ¼ teaspoon paprika
    1 teaspoon sugar
    4 egg yolks

Mix the vinegar, water, butter, mustard, salt, lemon juice, paprika and sugar. Mix well and bring to a boil. Remove from the heat and cool for several minutes. Then beat a small amount of the dressing into the yolks, beating vigorously. Return to remaining dressing and continue cooking, over hot water, until it thickens. Approximately 1½ cups.

Creamy Cheese Dressing

A fine dressing to make in advance and keep on hand. It will keep for a month in the refrigerator. Shake well before each use.

    1⅓ cups good oil (see Oils)
    ¼ cup water
    ½ cup red wine vinegar
    1 teaspoon lemon juice
    1 or 2 cloves garlic, minced
    1 teaspoon Worcestershire sauce
    salt and pepper to taste
    1 raw egg
    ¼ cup Mayonnaise
    4 ounces bleu cheese, or Roquefort,
       crumbled

Combine ingredients and, using a wire whisk, whisk until well mixed. Refrigerate.

Sour Cream Dressing

    1 cup milk
    ¾ cup buttermilk
    2 cups homemade Mayonnaise
    3 tablespoons white wine vinegar
    ⅓ cup grated Parmesan cheese
    2 or 3 fat cloves garlic, crushed
    ⅛ teaspoon black pepper
    1 to 1¼ cups sour cream

Combine everything except the sour cream. Whisk until smooth. Fold in the sour cream, leaving the mixture somewhat lumpy. Chill. Makes about 5 cups.

Herb Dressing

1 ⅓ cups good oil
⅔ cup white or red wine vinegar
½ teaspoon dried oregano or 1 teaspoon fresh
½ teaspoon dried sweet basil or 1 teaspoon fresh
1 tablespoon parsley
3 tablespoons chopped green onion
¼ teaspoon dry mustard
1 clove garlic, crushed
1 or 2 teaspoons Seasoning Salt *(see page 158)*
pepper to taste
1 tablespoon grated Parmesan cheese
¼ teaspoon red pepper
few drops bitters *(optional)*

Combine all ingredients and shake well. Refrigerate a day before using to allow flavors to blend and mellow.

Trattoria Dressing

A lovely salad dressing which will keep for at least a month in the refrigerator. You will recognize it as a vinaigrette with additions. Try it on an Italian type salad made with assorted lettuces, hard-cooked eggs, radishes, tomatoes, olives and tuna.

1 quart good oil *(see Oils)*
1 cup red wine vinegar
1 tablespoon Dijon mustard
¼ teaspoon each: oregano and thyme
¼ cup fresh basil, or 1 teaspoon dried
1 teaspoon fresh tarragon or ¼ teaspoon dried
pinch each: nutmeg and paprika
salt and pepper to taste

2 teaspoons A-1 sauce
2 teaspoons Worcestershire sauce
a few drops of Tabasco
1 raw egg yolk

Combine ingredients and, using a wire whisk, whisk to a fine consistency. If you have a food processor you can use it. Shake well before each use.

Homemade Ranch Dressing

Commercial ranch dressing is currently one of the most popular salad dressings. This is even better and will keep for several weeks in the refrigerator. Some good cooks use milk in place of buttermilk. You can vary the proportions of the other ingredients to suit your taste.

1 cup homemade Mayonnaise *(see page 161)*
1 cup buttermilk
1 cup sour cream
⅓ cup Dijon mustard
⅓ cup grated onion
⅓ cup white wine vinegar
Worcestershire sauce
salt and pepper to taste

Combine Mayonnaise, buttermilk, sour cream, mustard, onion and white wine vinegar. Whisk until blended. Chill for at least 6 hours and then stir in the Worcestershire sauce, salt and pepper. Makes 1 quart.

Bleu Cheese Dressing

Make ½ the recipe for above dressing. Omit the mustard and Worcestershire sauce. Add 1 cup crumbled bleu cheese.

Oriental Sesame Dressing

This is especially good served over cooked, drained spinach or green beans, or over a tossed salad.

2 teaspoons toasted sesame seeds
2 teaspoons Oriental sesame oil
2 tablespoons Dashi or chicken stock
½ cup light soy sauce

Grind seeds in a mortar or suribachi. Combine all ingredients and shake well. Store in the refrigerator.

Sesame Soy Dressing

This Oriental salad dressing is good served over a salad or over any cooked vegetable you might have on hand. It keeps well.

¼ cup light soy sauce
2 teaspoons Oriental sesame oil
1 teaspoon sugar
2 tablespoons rice wine vinegar
1 teaspoon dry mustard
3 tablespoons good oil

Combine ingredients and shake well. Store, covered, in the refrigerator.

The Quiche and The Egg

Quiche with Bacon Curl Garnish

"When in doubt, whip up a quiche," could be the good cook's motto. It is as useful for utilizing odds and ends of vegetables and cheeses as is the omelet or frittata.

The quiche was first a simple peasant dish made in the Alsace-Lorraine district of France. It originally consisted of a bread base on which was baked a thin egg custard. The early recipes did not even use cheese, just seasoned eggs and cream poured over the bread base and baked in a very hot oven.

Somewhere along the culinary road cheese was added to the custard. However, it wasn't until the quiche reached our shores and made its way amongst imaginative, innovative American cooks that it reached culinary heights.

I have a great commitment to authenticity, and I hate to see it sacrificed at the altar of convenience. However, it has always seemed to me that, with foods and recipes at least, our insistence on making something the way it has "always been made" deprives us of a chance to be creative. And very often just deprives us of exciting, good food.

I know people who turn their noses up at any quiche that isn't a Quiche Lorraine, never realizing that the Quiche Lorraine as we now make it is as different from the original as some newer quiches are from Quiche Lorraine.

Good quiche is not at all difficult to make. The shells can be made in advance and even frozen. The custard is made with ingredients that are usually on hand, and the filling is made with what *is* on hand.

PREBAKING THE SHELL

It is important that the quiche shell be prebaked. "Baked blind" is the term. There is simply no other way of guaranteeing a crisp, not soggy, crust. To accomplish this, roll out the crust and place it in the pan in which it will be baked. Cover the crust with a sheet of aluminum foil and then fill it with either rice or uncooked dried beans. Bake in a preheated 375°F (190°C) oven for 12 minutes. Lift off the foil together with its dried beans or rice and set aside. Bake the uncovered crust for another 3 or 4 minutes. Any bubbles which form should be broken with the tip of a knife. After this baking the crust is ready for its savory filling and custard.

The beans or rice are reusable. Stored in a plastic container, they will keep forever. The aluminum foil used to cover the pastry can be wiped off and used again.

I do not feel that quiche can be successfully frozen; however, some of its parts can be.

FREEZING QUICHE INGREDIENTS

If you wish to freeze the crust, it is best frozen *before* baking. It can be "baked blind" while still in its frozen state.

The custard can be frozen. Simply whisk the basic custard ingredients (the eggs, half and half and seasonings) together, pour into plastic freezer containers and freeze. Allow at least 1 inch of head space for expansion. Freezing is especially handy when eggs are on sale; also when, perhaps, you have some milk or half and half which must be used quickly.

The cheese can be grated and frozen in individual quiche packets. Since several cheeses are almost always better than one, you can grate those odds and ends of "melting" cheese and store them in small freezer bags.

When ready to use, you need only thaw the custard and beat it lightly to reblend the ingredients, and thaw and add the cheese.

QUICHE FILLINGS

Within reason, anything can be used as a filling. Use bits of leftover cooked vegetables, well drained and mixed with some chopped onion and cheese. Meats can be used, or combinations of meats and vegetables.

Whatever you use as a filling, it must first be cooked and then drained, as raw meats and vegetables will not cook through in a quiche. Where possible, some or all of the cooking liquid (I am thinking of vegetables in particular) can be used as part of the custard.

Probably the single most important thing to remember is that the filling must not be too moist. Excessive moisture yields a soggy crust and a watery custard. If the filling ingredients are very moist, such as with any canned ingredient, or many cooked vegetables, simply drain them well. Leafy vegetables or grated vegetables need to be drained and then pressed lightly with the hands to extract excess liquid.

QUICHE AS AN APPETIZER

Quiche can be a main dish, a side dish, or an appetizer. Its use as a main or side dish depends on what is being served with it, and for which meal it is being served.

However, to bake as an appetizer, simply line a 10 by 15 by 1-inch jelly roll pan with the pastry. This will require a full recipe of the Basic Quiche Pastry, or enough for 2 quiches. Prebake the shell as previously directed. The shell will take filling and custard for 1 quiche. Bake quiche in a 350°F (175°C) oven for 20 to 25 minutes, or until custard is set. Cool on a rack and cut into bite size squares.

Note. *Before we get to recipes for the pastry, I will tell you that there is no salt in any of the pastry shells. It is not necessary to add salt to any pie or quiche pastry. The filling is salted. The shell provides texture more than it does flavor, and you will never notice that it is made without salt.*

Basic Quiche Shell, Food Processor Method

This is my favorite, failure-proof, quiche shell. It is simple to make, you get 2 shells out of 2 cups of flour, and it is good.

**2 cups stirred and measured white or
    unbleached white flour
¾ cup frozen butter or margarine
⅓ to ½ cup ice water**

Place flour in bowl of food processor. Cut butter into 8 pieces and add to flour. Churn until it forms a coarse meal. While churning, add the ice water, *very slowly,* using *just enough* to make a dough that will form a ball on top of the blade.

Remove dough from bowl and divide into 2 parts. Wrap each in plastic wrap and refrigerate for 1 hour. Then roll each out on a lightly floured surface. You can easily get 2 10-inch shells from this recipe. Lay pastry in pans, laying it in loosely. Cut and crimp as you would any pie. The shell *must* be "baked blind" (prebaked). (*See instructions on page 167.*)

Wine Pastry

An elegant variation for some quiches. Simply use ice-cold dry white wine in place of the water.

Basic Quiche Shell, Regular Method

If you do not own a food processor, make the shell as follows.

**1½ cups stirred and measured white or
    unbleached white flour
½ cup cold butter or margarine
¼ to ⅓ cup ice cold water**

Turn flour into a mixing bowl and cut in the butter until it forms a coarse meal, using a pastry blender.

Add water a little at a time, using just enough so that the mixture will form a ball and hold together. Form into a ball, wrap in plastic wrap and chill for 30 minutes or longer.

When ready, roll out on a lightly floured surface and fit loosely into a 9 or 10-inch quiche pan. Cut and crimp as you would any pie. Again, the shell *must* be "baked blind," or prebaked. (*See instructions on page 167.*)

Artichoke Quiche

**9-inch Basic Quiche Shell
½ to ¾ pound fresh baby artichokes, or 1
    10-ounce package frozen artichoke hearts**

CUSTARD

**5 large eggs
1½ cups half and half
3 or 4 green onions, minced
dash Tabasco
1 tablespoon minced parsley
1 tablespoon grated Parmesan cheese
salt if desired
freshly ground black pepper to taste**

Prepare and prebake Quiche Shell as directed. Set aside.

Trim the fresh artichokes, cook until just tender, and cut them in quarters. Or, cook artichoke hearts according to package directions. Drain and arrange in the bottom of the shell. (If desired you can chop up the artichoke hearts and add them to the custard.) Combine remaining ingredients and whisk together. Pour over artichoke hearts and bake in a 350°F (175°C) oven for approximately 25 minutes, or until custard is almost set. A knife inserted in the custard between the center and the edge will come out clean. Let set for 10 minutes before cutting. Serves 6.

Note. If you make this with the larger fresh artichokes, cut them in quarters before cooking and, when cooked, cut these pieces in half.

Asparagus Quiche

Ham, cheese, and asparagus make a perfect combination.

**9 or 10-inch Basic Quiche Shell
1 pound fresh asparagus or 1 10-ounce
     package frozen asparagus spears
½ cup grated Swiss cheese
½ cup chopped ham**

CUSTARD

**4 large eggs
2 cups half and half
dash of Tabasco
¼ teaspoon salt if desired**

Prepare and prebake Quiche Shell. Set aside.

Trim fresh asparagus and cook until barely tender. Or, cook asparagus spears as directed on the package. Drain. Remove 6 spears for garnish. Purée the rest. Spread cheese and ham over the bottom of the shell. Whisk together the custard ingredients and add the asparagus purée. Whisk together and then pour over ham-cheese mixture. Arrange reserved spears over the filling. Bake in a 425°F (220°C) oven for 15 minutes. Then reduce heat to 300°F (150°C) and continue baking for another 30 minutes, or until custard is barely set. Remove from oven and let set for about 10 minutes. Cut into 6 pieces to serve as a side dish.

Avocado Quiche

A lovely lime green quiche, you might garnish this with Bacon Curls.

**1 9-inch Basic Quiche Shell
1 cup grated Swiss cheese
1 large avocado**

CUSTARD

**4 large eggs
½ teaspoon salt if desired
¼ teaspoon freshly ground black pepper
1 tablespoon lime or lemon juice
1 cup half and half**

Prepare and prebake the quiche shell. Set aside.

Sprinkle the cheese over the Quiche Shell. Mash avocado until smooth. Prepare Custard by combining ingredients and whisking together. Add avocado and whisk. Pour over cheese. Bake in a 425°F (220°C) oven for 15 minutes. Reduce heat to 300°F (150°C) and continue baking for another 35 to 40 minutes, or until custard is barely set. Remove from oven and let set for 5 or 10 minutes before cutting. Garnish with Bacon Curls (*see below*) and cut into 8 pieces to serve as a side dish.

Bacon Curls

Cut 5 slices of bacon in half. Roll the halves and secure rolls with toothpicks. Broil or bake until crisp. Remove toothpicks and arrange curls on quiche. Use 1 for each serving and 2 or 3 for the center. I generally make these before I bake the quiche and then just reheat them in the oven while the quiche is setting.

Broccoli-Radish Quiche

I got this recipe from a magazine some years ago. I was intrigued by the combination of broccoli and radishes and wondered how the cooked radishes would turn out, thinking that they would burn. It turned out to be a delicious combination, and the radishes have so much moisture in them that they simply soften. This and the California Green Chili Quiche take honors as the most popular vegetable quiches that I make.

9 or 10-inch Basic Quiche Shell
2 cups broccoli flowers, steamed until barely tender
⅓ cup minced onion
2 tablespoons melted butter

CUSTARD

2 cups half and half
¼ teaspoon salt if desired
dash of Tabasco
4 large eggs

TOPPING

8 large radishes, thinly sliced
1 tablespoon butter
2 tablespoons minced parsley
⅓ cup grated Parmesan cheese

Prepare and prebake the Quiche Shell. Set aside.

Sauté the steamed broccoli and the onion in the 2 tablespoons butter for 5 minutes. Remove from skillet with a slotted spoon and turn into Quiche Shell. Combine ingredients for Custard and whisk together. Pour over broccoli and onion. Top with radish slices, dot with butter and sprinkle with the parsley and grated cheese. Bake in a 375°F (190°C) oven for 25 to 35 minutes, or until custard is barely set. Let stand for 5 or 10 minutes before cutting and serving. Will serve 8 as a side dish.

Cabbage Quiche

This is an unusual and delicious cabbage dish.

9 or 10-inch Basic Quiche Shell
1 small head cabbage (about 1 pound),
  shredded
⅓ cup butter or margarine
1 bunch green onions, minced

CUSTARD

3 large eggs
1 cup half and half
salt if desired

freshly ground black pepper
⅓ cup grated Swiss cheese
⅓ cup grated Parmesan cheese

Prepare and prebake Quiche Shell and set aside.

Melt butter in a large skillet. Add cabbage and green onions and cook slowly until they are soft and tender, stirring often. When done, remove from heat. Cool slightly and then turn into the shell.

Combine the eggs, half and half, seasonings and ¼ cup each of the Swiss and Parmesan cheeses. Whisk together until smooth and then pour over cabbage. Sprinkle top with remaining cheeses. Bake in a 425°F (220°C) oven for about 30 minutes, or until custard is barely set. Remove from oven and cool for 5 to 10 minutes before cutting. Serves 6 to 8.

Crustless Carrot Quiche

This is an especially nice way with carrots.

2 cups shredded carrots, blanched in boiling
  water for 5 minutes
1 small onion, minced
1 tablespoon butter or oil
1 clove garlic, crushed
6 large eggs
1¼ cups half and half
¼ teaspoon ground ginger
pinch of white pepper
salt if desired
freshly ground black pepper
½ teaspoon paprika
½ cup each: grated Parmesan, Monterey
  Jack and Cheddar cheese

Prepare carrots and set aside after draining thoroughly and pressing lightly to express as much liquid as possible.

Sauté onion in butter with the garlic until limp. Set aside. Now combine remaining ingredients and whisk together. Add the reserved onions, garlic

170

and carrots. Pour into a well-buttered 9-inch pie tin. Bake in a 350°F (175°C) oven until custard tests done, about 35 to 40 minutes. Test the first time after 30 minutes. Serves 6.

California Green Chili Quiche

For this quiche, one of the most popular that I make, you can use Roasted California Green Chilis that you have put up yourself (*see page 87*) or the canned ones.

**1 9 or 10-inch Basic Quiche Shell
½ to ¾ cup diced California Green Chilis,
    well drained
¾ cup ripe olives, sliced and drained
⅓ cup sliced green onions
1½ cups shredded Cheddar and/or Monterey
    Jack cheese**

CUSTARD

**2 cups half and half
¼ teaspoon salt if desired
dash of Tabasco
4 large eggs**

Prepare and prebake the Quiche Shell. Set aside.
    Combine the green chilis, olives, green onions and cheeses. Spread over the bottom of the shell. Whisk remaining ingredients together and pour over cheese mixture. Bake in a 350°F (175°C) oven for 40 to 45 minutes, or until custard is barely set. Let stand for 5 or 10 minutes before cutting and serving. This will serve 6 generously.

Onion Quiche

I have on occasion used a combination of green onions, leeks and shallots in this quiche.

**1 9 or 10-inch Basic Quiche Shell
1 cup minced green onions
1 cup leeks, carefully washed and sliced
2 tablespoons butter or oil**

¾ cup grated Swiss or Gruyère cheese

CUSTARD

**4 large eggs
2 cups half and half
dash of Tabasco
salt if desired
freshly ground black pepper**

Prepare and prebake Quiche Shell. Set aside.
    Sauté green onions and leeks in the butter until limp. Set aside. When slightly cooled turn onions into Quiche Shell and top with the grated cheese. Whisk together Custard ingredients and pour over the filling. Bake in a 350°F (175°C) oven for 35 to 40 minutes, or until custard is almost set. Remove from oven and let stand for 10 to 15 minutes before serving. Serves 6.

Green Pea Quiche

This is one of our favorite quiches. I especially like it with a roast chicken or leg of lamb.

**1 9 or 10-inch Basic Quiche Shell
1½ pounds fresh green peas, or 1 20-ounce
    package frozen
¼ cup minced green onions
⅓ cup grated Parmesan or Pecorino cheese**

CUSTARD

**4 large eggs
2 cups half and half
dash of Tabasco
salt if desired
freshly ground black pepper**

Prepare and prebake Quiche Shell. Set aside.
    Blanch green peas, fresh or frozen, in boiling water for 2 minutes only. Drain well and turn into Quiche Shell. Sprinkle with the green onions and the cheese. Whisk together the custard ingredients and pour over the filling. Bake in a 350°F (175°C) oven for 35 minutes, or until filling is set. Remove from oven and let stand for 10 to 15 minutes before cutting and serving to 6.

Chard or Spinach Quiche

You can use almost any green in this quiche, but our favorite is a combination of chard and spinach.

1 9 or 10-inch Basic Quiche Shell
1 pound chard and/or spinach, cleaned,
   trimmed and cut into slivers
2 tablespoons olive oil or butter
1 tablespoon lemon juice
2 large eggs, separated
1½ cups dairy sour cream
½ teaspoon salt if desired
pinch of white pepper
⅓ cup minced green onions
⅛ teaspoon cream of tartar
⅓ cup grated Parmesan cheese
⅓ cup fine dry bread crumbs

Prepare and prebake Basic Quiche Shell as directed.

You should have about 6 cups of slivered greens. Heat olive oil or butter in a skillet. Add greens and stir until wilted. Drain well, pressing lightly to express as much liquid as possible. Add lemon juice and stir together.

Whisk together the egg yolks, sour cream, salt, pepper and green onions. Fold in the wilted greens and lemon juice mixture. Now beat the egg whites with the cream of tartar until stiff, but not dry, and fold into the sour cream/greens mixture. Turn into Quiche Shell. Combine the Parmesan cheese and the bread crumbs and sprinkle over the top. Dot with a little more butter if desired. Bake in a 450°F (230°C) oven for 15 minutes. Reduce heat to 325°F (165°C) and continue baking another 35 to 40 minutes, or until custard is set and the quiche is a golden brown. Let stand for at least 10 minutes before cutting. Garnish with olives and tomato wedges. Serves 6.

Sauerkraut-Frank Quiche

If you like sauerkraut and nice fat franks, you will love this quiche. It incorporates everything sauerkraut lovers love. I use homemade sau-

erkraut, but any good bottled sauerkraut will do just fine. Serve it for lunch with a salad and hot rolls, and more mustard on the side.

1 10-inch Basic Quiche Shell

FILLING INGREDIENTS

4 to 6 fat or extra-large frankfurters
1 bunch green onions, chopped
2 cups sauerkraut, well rinsed and drained
1 cup grated Swiss cheese

CUSTARD

3 large eggs
1 cup half and half
2 teaspoons prepared Dijon mustard

Prepare and prebake Quiche Shell as directed. Set aside.

Cut the frankfurters into 1-inch pieces and scatter over the bottom of the pie shell. Sprinkle with the chopped green onions. Prepare the Custard by combining the eggs, half and half and mustard. Whisk together until smooth. Add the sauerkraut to the custard mixture and stir together. Then pour into the shell over the franks and onions. Sprinkle with the cheese.

Bake in a 375°F (190°C) oven for approximately 40 minutes or until set. Remove from oven and let stand for 10 minutes before cutting. Serves 6.

Note. I like to garnish the top with some onion that I have sliced into rings and sautéed in butter until limp. Drain and place in a mound in the center of the quiche.

Spring Greens Quiche

A crustless quiche that makes a marvelous luncheon dish when served with sliced tomatoes and avocados, a crunchy bread, and salad.

2½ to 3 cups steamed chopped greens (*use 2 or more of the following: spinach, chard, beet greens, sorrel or mustard greens*)

4 large eggs, beaten
2 cups grated cheese (*use a combination of Cheddar and Monterey Jack cheeses*)
1 tablespoon fresh basil, or 1 teaspoon dried
½ teaspoon salt if desired
freshly ground black pepper
⅓ cup grated Parmesan cheese

Drain the steamed greens and press lightly to express as much liquid as possible.

Generously butter an 8-inch square baking pan or a 9 or 10-inch round pie tin.

Turn the greens into a large mixing bowl and add the eggs. Mix well and then add the 2 cups cheese, the basil, salt and pepper. Mix well. Turn into prepared pan. Sprinkle top with the grated Parmesan cheese. Bake in a 350°F (175°C) oven until set, approximately 35 minutes. The edges will be lightly browned. Serves 6 to 8.

Summer Zucchini Quiche

The best zucchini quiche I have ever tasted.

1 10-inch Basic Quiche Shell, sprinkled with 1 tablespoon grated Parmesan cheese before prebaking
2 pounds fresh small zucchini, cut into ¼-inch slices
1½ cups dairy sour cream
3 large eggs, separated
½ teaspoon salt if desired
2 tablespoons minced chives
freshly ground black pepper
⅓ cup grated Swiss cheese
⅓ cup grated Parmesan cheese
⅓ cup fine bread crumbs

Prepare and prebake Quiche Shell as directed. Set aside.

Cook zucchini slices in boiling water for 3 or 4 minutes, or until tender/crisp. Drain thoroughly and set aside. To make the custard, combine sour cream with egg yolks and salt. Whisk until smooth and light. Beat egg whites until stiff and fold into the yolk mixture.

Place a layer of zucchini slices over the bottom of the prepared crust. Sprinkle with some of the chives and black pepper and some of the cheeses. Then cover with a layer of custard mixture. Continue layering until the zucchini, seasonings and custard are all used. The top layer should be of custard. There will be about 3 layers of zucchini. Combine any remaining cheeses with the bread crumbs (or use all bread crumbs if no cheese is left) and sprinkle over the top layer.

Bake in a 375°F (190°C) oven for 30 to 35 minutes, or until puffed and golden. Cool on rack for 10 minutes before cutting. Serves 6 to 8.

The Impossible Quiche

The test kitchens at Bisquik came up with this idea. You do not have to make a crust when you make a quiche. Merely add biscuit mix (you can use homemade as well as commercial) to the custard. During baking this settles, forming something like a crust on the bottom. It is not the same as using a good, crisp prebaked shell, but it is a convenient method and it works.

For that matter, if calories as well as speed are your concern, you can make any quiche without the crust. Just pour the quiche into a well-buttered pie tin or quiche pan. Quiche is just a custard poured over vegetables, fish or meats, and we bake custard without a crust all the time.

This is the original recipe as presented by Bisquik. The variations are my own. Remember that you can use the Custard with any filling, and make up your own Impossible Quiches.

CUSTARD

3 large eggs
1 cup half and half
½ cup biscuit mix
½ teaspoon salt
dash of Tabasco
¼ teaspoon pepper

FILLING

2 cups thinly sliced cauliflower
1 small onion, minced
1 cup grated Cheddar cheese

Combine Custard ingredients and whisk together. Set aside. Cook cauliflower in boiling, salted water to cover, for 10 minutes. Drain thoroughly and turn into a greased 9-inch pie tin. Cover with the onion and then with the cheese. Whisk custard again, and pour over the Filling. Bake in a 375°F (190°C) oven for 20 to 25 minutes, or until custard is set. Serves 6.

Main Dish Impossible Quiche

Use steamed broccoli in place of the cauliflower, and ⅓ cup grated Parmesan cheese in place of the 1 cup of Cheddar. Add some sliced cooked summer sausage. This bakes into a filling main-dish quiche.

Elegant Impossible Quiche

Cook 4 or 5 slices bacon until crisp and turn into the bottom of a buttered pie tin. Add a cup of crab meat and 2 cups shredded Swiss cheese in place of the Cheddar and cauliflower and onion. Pour custard on and bake as directed.

THE OMELET

Probably the most basic egg dish after fried, scrambled, poached and soft or hard-cooked eggs, the omelet is generally approached with undue reverence. Like making biscuits, it is considered very difficult to make a "good" omelet. The magazines and so many books tell us that you must have a "special" pan that is used for nothing but omelets. It must be "properly" seasoned. It must never be washed, only wiped out after each use. A "good" omelet requires special procedures and special skills. So we are told by those who have pages to fill or a mystique to market.

Most of it is hogwash. It *is* best to have a slope-sided pan in which to make omelets. But they *can* be made on a griddle if necessary. In fact I was first taught how to make a good omelet by Dick Sheets, a restaurant manager and friend. He makes all of his omelets on a griddle. He beats 3 large eggs with a spoonful of mayonnaise and some salt and pepper and Tabasco. Twenty strokes with a fork

and he pours the mixture onto the hot griddle in a long rectangle. He adds the filling and rolls the omelet up, then slides it down to the end of the griddle where it is cooler and places a lid over the omelet. The lid causes it to steam and puff while he makes another. They were good omelets. Not as fancy as some I've had in the finer restaurants, but, good, honest, legitimate omelets.

The only reason to have a pan that is used for nothing but omelets is so that it won't get nicked, thus preventing the eggs from sliding easily. I use a teflon-lined pan and I use it for all kinds of purposes.

As far as technique is concerned, there *is* a particular technique used by both amateur and professional chefs. But again, it isn't necessary. It's fun, and it's better.

It takes care to make any dish really good. And good cooking has as much to do with care as with recipes and ingredients. But you don't need to be intimidated by technique.

beating the eggs with a fork

adding mayonnaise

the butter foaming

Basic Omelet

I still use Dick Sheets' formula for an omelet. I think the addition of mayonnaise, rather than

cream or water, helps to make a moist, fluffy omelet. For each omelet use the following:

**3 large eggs
1 tablespoon mayonnaise
salt and pepper to taste
dash of Tabasco
1 tablespoon butter**

Whisk omelet ingredients together for about 20 strokes. I always use a dash of Tabasco with egg dishes to offset the blandness and add a little zip. Melt the butter in the skillet, swirling it around so that it coats the bottom and the sides. The butter should foam. When the foam has almost disappeared, the pan is hot enough. Now move quickly. Pour the eggs into the pan. Let set for a second to set the bottom. Then stir the eggs in the center as you would stir scrambled eggs, but lightly. With the other hand, shake the pan a little to keep the eggs moving. Actually, you can alternate these actions quickly for the 30 seconds or so that it will take to finish the omelet. The eggs will set on the bottom, and stirring the center assures a creamy center. Now lay the filling over the omelet and roll or fold the omelet over the filling. You can do this with a fork, or with a spatula. Or you can practice making omelets until you master that deft flip of the wrist that makes the omelet fold itself. It's fun to do and will enthrall your guests when you are cooking for company. When done, slide the omelet out of the pan and onto a warm plate. I always serve omelets with a few slices of fresh tomato.

Omelet Additions

The omelet is a great and delicious catch-all for leftovers. Use anything that is tasty, but don't forget the following ideas for omelet fillings.

Omelet Alsacienne: Drain ¾ cup sauerkraut and rinse well in cold water. Braise it in 1 tablespoon goose or chicken fat, or bacon fat, until lightly browned. Use to fill the omelet.

Denver Omelet: Sauté ¼ cup diced green pepper and 2 tablespoons chopped ham in a teaspoon of butter. Season to taste.

Gardener's Omelet: Use ½ cup of cooked vegetable of your choice. The vegetable should be cooked until tender/crisp. I like a combination of cauliflower and zucchini flavored with tomato, onion and garlic.

Herb Omelet: Combine 3 or 4 tablespoons of a variety of fresh herbs from the garden. Serve with browned butter.

Mushroom Omelet: Use ¾ cup chopped cooked mushrooms and heat in 2 tablespoons cream. Season lightly with pepper. Freshly picked morels are a real treat this way.

Ratatouille Omelet: Use several tablespoons of leftover ratatouille for each omelet.

Tomato Omelet: For best flavor use fresh summer tomatoes. Peel, seed and chop 3 small tomatoes. Sauté in 1 tablespoon olive oil until soft. Season with salt, pepper and parsley.

Vegetarian: Steam, and then sauté in butter lightly, some of the following: zucchini, broccoli, mushrooms, cauliflower, onion and pepper. The vegetables should be tender/crisp. Serve the omelet with a sauce.

A Few More Ideas

1. Sautéed onion, mushrooms and green peppers.
2. Sour cream with green chilis and cheese.
3. Avocado slices with sour cream.
4. Cooked sausage, with tomatoes, onions, garlic and green peppers. Season highly.

THE FRITTATA

The Frittata is an Italian omelet. It differs from the standard French omelet in that it is flat, rather than folded, and it is cooked slowly rather than quickly.

Any vegetable or combination used is first sautéed gently in oil. Then the egg mixture is poured over the vegetables and the Frittata is gently cooked until the bottom is set and the edges are browned. The top of the omelet is finished under the broiler.

The Frittata is a good, hearty breakfast dish. It enables you to use up odds and ends of leftover meat and vegetables, either chopped or cubed. It is also a good luncheon and light supper dish.

Basic Frittata Mixture to Serve 4

This is the egg mixture for any of the following Frittatas. The Tabasco is added to overcome the blandness of the eggs. It adds no spicy taste when used in the following amount.

**6 large eggs
dash Tabasco
salt if desired
fresh ground black pepper to taste**

Whisk together and set aside.

Frittata

You can vary this enormously. Try using some cooked ham or sausage, cut into small dice or into slices. In place of the broccoli and potato you could use any of the following: sliced mushrooms, cooked green beans, asparagus, cauliflower, artichoke hearts, small pieces of salami, roast pork, chicken or turkey. A true Frittata can have one ingredient or many.

**6 slices bacon
2 tablespoons olive oil
1 medium onion, minced
2 cloves garlic, minced
1½ cups leftover cooked broccoli flowers
1 medium potato, cooked and diced (*leave peel on for flavor and nutrition*)
salt if desired
freshly ground black pepper to taste
Basic Frittata Mixture (*see above*)
¼ cup grated Parmesan cheese**

Cut bacon into small pieces and cook slowly in a large skillet. Don't let it become too crisp. Remove bacon and measure the fat in the pan. Remove all but 2 tablespoons of it.

Add the oil to the 2 tablespoons bacon fat and sauté the onion, garlic, broccoli and potatoes until the onion and garlic are limp and the broccoli and potato lightly browned. Season to taste.

Pour Basic Frittata Mixture over vegetables and cook over low heat without stirring, until it is set on the bottom and the edges are lightly browned. Lift the Frittata occasionally to let some of the egg run underneath. Sprinkle with the cheese and slip under the broiler to brown and set the top. Slide onto a serving plate and garnish with parsley and sliced tomatoes. Cut into wedges to serve. Serves 4 to 6.

Spinach or Chard Frittata

**1 small onion, minced
1 clove garlic, minced
3 tablespoons olive oil**

¾ **pound chopped spinach or chard,
  uncooked**
Basic Frittata Mixture (*see above*)
2 tablespoons grated Parmesan cheese
sliced tomato and parsley for garnish

Cook the onion and the garlic in the oil until soft.
Add the spinach and stir and cook until wilted.
Pour on the Basic Frittata Mixture and cook over
medium heat, *without stirring*, until the bottom is
set and the edges are browned. Sprinkle with
Parmesan cheese and slip under the broiler to
brown and set the top. It should be a nice golden
brown. Slip out of the pan onto a serving plate.
Garnish with parsley and tomato slices. Cut into
wedges to serve. Serves 4 to 6.

Spinach-Cheese Frittata

Follow the above recipe, adding ⅓ cup of diced
mozzarella cheese to the spinach mixture.

Zucchini Frittata

1 pound zucchini, grated
salt
3 tablespoons olive oil
1 small onion, minced
1 clove garlic, minced
Basic Frittata Mixture (*see above*)
⅓ cup grated Parmesan cheese
parsley and tomato slices

Turn grated zucchini into a colander and sprinkle
with salt. Let drain for 15 minutes. Then rinse and
squeeze dry. Heat the oil in a skillet and add the
zucchini, onion and garlic. Sauté until vegetables
are limp. Whisk the Basic Frittata Mixture with the
cheese and pour over the vegetables. Cook over
medium heat, *without stirring*, until the bottom is
set and the edges are browned. Sprinkle with a little more cheese if desired and slip under the
broiler to set and brown the top. Slide Frittata out
of the pan onto a serving plate and garnish with
parsley and tomato slices. Cut into wedges to
serve. Serves 4 to 6.

Piperade

The Spanish and the Basques each make this dish
which is neither omelet nor scrambled eggs, but
has a little of the character of each. It is a good way
to stretch eggs to feed more people than expected.
The Basques add some hot peppers.

¼ cup bacon fat or olive oil
2 large onions, thinly sliced
**3 or 4 large green or red peppers, seeded
  and cut into thin strips**
**6 medium tomatoes, peeled and coarsely
  chopped**
salt if desired
freshly ground black pepper to taste
1 clove garlic, minced
some basil and/or thyme
6 to 8 large eggs, beaten

Heat bacon fat and cook the onions in it until they
are golden. Add peppers and let simmer for 10
minutes. Then add the tomatoes and the seasonings. Begin with ¼ teaspoon of basil or thyme and
add a little more after tasting. Simmer, covered, for
10 to 15 minutes, or until tomatoes and onions are
a thick mixture, softened almost to a purée. You
want the peppers to retain their identity.

Beat the eggs together lightly and stir into the
mixture with a fork until the eggs are just barely
set. Remove from the heat and stir again. The heat
in the vegetables will finish cooking the eggs to a
creamy consistency. The Piperade should be very
soft.

Serve immediately. Traditionally this is served
with ham. I serve it with lots of crusty bread, a
salad and some nice cheese. Serves 6.

Spaghetti Squash Frittata

The spaghetti squash can be cooked in the oven.
Puncture it in several places with a skewer to allow
steam to escape. Bake in a 350°F (175°C) oven for
45 minutes to an hour or until the outside gives
when you press it. Slice in half lengthwise, remove
and discard seeds, and scoop out the cooked
squash.

½ pound sausage meat or sliced bacon
6 eggs
⅓ cup grated Parmesan cheese
2 cups cooked spaghetti squash (see above)
3 tablespoons olive oil
½ to 1 cup mozzarella or Fontina cheese, diced

Cook sausage or bacon, drain, and reserve. Beat the eggs with the Parmesan cheese. Add the cooked squash and stir together well. Heat the oil in a skillet and pour in ½ of the egg-squash mixture. Top with reserved sausage or bacon and diced cheese. Cover with remaining egg-squash mixture. Cook slowly until set on the bottom, lifting the sides occasionally to let uncooked egg run onto the bottom.

When ready, the top can be browned under the broiler, or, and this is tricky, slide the Frittata onto a plate and place the hot skillet over it. Flip the Frittata, top side down, into the skillet to finish cooking. Serves 4 to 6.

Peas with Eggs
(Piselli con Uova)

Similar to the French Ratatouille with eggs, and the Spanish Piperade, this is Italian and a most pleasing little dish to serve for Sunday breakfast or a thrifty supper.

1 medium onion, minced
1 clove garlic, minced
2 tablespoons olive oil
1 medium green pepper, deribbed and cut into small dice
2 cups chopped fresh or canned tomatoes
1 cup fresh or frozen peas
freshly ground black pepper to taste
salt if desired
4 large eggs

Sauté the onion and garlic in the oil until limp. Add the green pepper and the tomatoes and cook over low heat, just enough to simmer, for 20

minutes. Add the peas and continue cooking gently for another 10 minutes. Season to taste. The mixture should be very thick.

Using the back of a spoon, make indentations for the eggs. Break an egg into each indentation and cook gently until the eggs are cooked through. If you place a lid on the skillet they will cook in about 4 or 5 minutes. Without a lid it will take a little longer. Makes 2 hearty servings, or 4 smaller ones.

Egg Foo Yung

Actually a Chinese omelet, this is one of the most popular Oriental dishes. I frequently make this in small rounds to serve as an appetizer. Remember that you can use shrimp, shreds of roast pork, roast beef, or chicken.

½ cup cooked shrimp, meat, or chicken (see above)
1 tablespoon oil
⅓ cup minced green onions
¼ cup minced fresh mushrooms
1 tablespoon soy sauce
½ teaspoon sugar
¼ teaspoon salt if desired
1 cup fresh bean sprouts, chopped
4 large eggs
¼ cup corn or peanut oil

SAUCE

½ cup chicken broth
1 teaspoon soy sauce
½ teaspoon salt if desired
2 teaspoons cornstarch
1 tablespoon cold water

Chop or shred the shrimp or meat used. Set aside.

With the 1 tablespoon oil, sauté the onion and mushrooms for 1 minute. Add soy sauce, sugar, salt if used and the bean sprouts. Stir and cook for another minute to partially cook the sprouts. Mix well and turn into a dish to cool.

Now make the Sauce. Bring the chicken broth to a boil in a small saucepan. Add the soy sauce and salt. Dissolve the cornstarch in the cold water and add to the sauce. Continue cooking and stirring until it thickens. Set aside.

Beat the eggs and stir into cooled sprout mixture.

Use a skillet about 4 inches in diameter and heat 2 teaspoons oil in it. Ladle in ¼ of the mixture. Cook until eggs have browned on one side. Turn over and brown the other side. Remove and keep warm. Repeat this process, using each remaining ¼ of the mixture, to form a total of 4 4-inch omelets.

Place the little omelets in a circle on the serving plate, overlapping them so that they look pretty.

Reheat the sauce and drizzle a little over the omelets. Serve the remaining sauce in a bowl in the center so that people can use the amount they wish. Serves 4.

Note. Alternatively I have cooked the little omelets on a griddle, using about ⅓ cup for each. If any of the egg mixture dribbles off to the side, you can push it back with the spatula. This way is easiest if you are making a lot of them.

Vegetables in Combination

Pasta Primavera

The people of most nations prepare at least one medley of vegetables called a vegetable "stew." The Romanians prepare Ghivech, a superbly orchestrated blend of anywhere from seven to eighteen different vegetables. Perfect for odds and ends from the garden. The Moroccans, using the lovely, practical cone-shaped casserole called a Tagine, prepare spicy vegetable stews as well as meat and poultry stews. All around the Mediterranean similar vegetable stews are made with some combination of eggplant, green and red peppers, zucchini, and tomatoes, flavored with onion and garlic. Ratatouille is the best known and possibly the most popular of these. In the American South we make Succotash and, in the Southwest, a Mexican-flavored squash stew called Colache is popular.

Many mixed vegetable dishes can be a meal in themselves, needing only a crusty bread and a light wine as accompaniments. Any of them will stretch a meal that is light on meat or seafood. All of them are good buffet dishes.

Some of the dishes are prepared in such a way that the individual vegetables retain their separate identities. Others achieve a harmonious blending. Never can eggplant or celery or even olives, on their own, achieve the sheer beauty of flavor the combination reaches in Caponata.

Pasta Primavera

Certainly one of the great vegetable dishes, this is simple and colorful and can be made with just about any vegetable in season. You can use as few as two or three vegetables (besides the onion and garlic) or as many as you wish. Pasta Primavera can serve as a main dish with some crusty bread and a nice wine or it can be served as a side dish with meat or fish.

I occasionally add some julienned ham or some cooked sausage to the sauce. An inspired addition, for special occasions, is some cooked shrimp, crab meat, or scallops. These must be just barely cooked, to keep from becoming tough, and then added to the vegetables at the last minute so that they just heat through.

½ cup olive oil, or a good mixture of vegetable oils *(see page 156)*
1 large onion, minced
2 or 3 large cloves garlic, minced
1 pound asparagus, trimmed and cut diagonally into pieces
½ pound mushrooms, sliced
½ pound cauliflower or broccoli *(or both)*, **sliced, or in small flowers**
1 medium zucchini, cut into ¼-inch rounds
1 slivered carrot
1 cup half and half
2 teaspoons fresh basil, or 1 teaspoon dried
1 cup frozen peas, or pea pods, or a combination of both
6 to 8 green onions, minced
salt and pepper
1 pound fettucini, linguine, or spaghetti, cooked al dente and drained
1 cup grated Parmesan cheese

I like to use a wok, but you can use a large skillet if you prefer. Heat the oil and sauté the onion and garlic until softened. Add the asparagus, mushrooms, cauliflower, zucchini and carrot and stir fry for two minutes.

Increase the heat to high and add the half and half and basil and simmer until slightly reduced, about 5 minutes. Test and see if the vegetables are done to your taste; they should be tender/crisp. Stir in the peas and green onions and the meat or

seafood if used. Cook 2 or 3 more minutes, just enough to heat the meat or seafood through. Season and add the cooked, drained pasta and the grated cheese. Toss together and turn onto a large platter. Garnish as desired. Serve immediately. Serves 8 to 10.

Pasta Primavera with Tomatoes

During the summertime, when you can get firm-fleshed tomatoes or plum tomatoes, take 2 or 3, chop them into small dice and add to the sauce at the very end. You want the color of the tomatoes. They do not need to cook. For a gourmet touch, peel and seed the tomatoes.

Broccoli and Onion Bake

A lovely combination of vegetables.

2 bunches broccoli, cut into flowers with some of the tender stems
1 1-pound package frozen small onions
½ to 1 cup mushroom slices *(optional)*

SAUCE

⅓ cup butter or margarine
⅓ cup flour
1 cup milk
½ cup chicken broth
½ cup dry white wine
salt and pepper

½ to ¾ cup grated Cheddar cheese
paprika

Cook the broccoli in boiling salted water for 8 minutes, or until just tender. Drain and place in a greased shallow baking dish. Do the same with the onions and when drained, layer them over the broccoli. Sauté the mushrooms in a small amount of butter for 5 minutes and then pour over the broccoli and onions.

Now make the sauce. Melt the butter in a small saucepan. Stir in the flour and add the milk and chicken broth, stirring until smooth. Cook and stir until mixture thickens. Stir constantly. When thickened, remove from heat and stir in the wine. Add salt and pepper to taste. Pour over the broccoli and onion mixture. Sprinkle with cheese and paprika. Bake in a 375°F (190°C) oven for 30 minutes or until just bubbly and lightly browned. Serves 6.

Baked Eggplant, Tomato and Chick Pea Casserole

A delicious dish that is simple to prepare and goes especially well at dinner parties.

> 2 medium sized eggplants, about 1 pound each, unpeeled, cut into cubes, then salted
> ⅓ cup olive oil
> 3 medium sized onions, peeled and cut into ¼-inch slices and then separated into rings
> salt and coarsely ground black pepper to taste
> 3 cups canned chick peas, drained and thoroughly rinsed
> 8 medium sized tomatoes, peeled, seeded and chopped
> 1 to 1½ cups water

Salt the eggplant and set aside for 20 to 30 minutes, drain it, rinse under running water and pat dry with paper towels. Heat the oil until it is hot and sauté the eggplant cubes for about 5 minutes, stirring frequently. Transfer the eggplant to a shallow 9 by 13-inch baking dish and spread out evenly.

Sauté the onions next, stirring frequently. They should be softened and golden, but not browned. Spread the onions and any remaining oil over the eggplant and pour over them an additional ⅓ cup oil. Sprinkle with salt and pepper and scatter the chick peas on top. Cover all with the chopped tomatoes and sprinkle with a little more salt and pepper.

Bring the water to a boil and pour it over the vegetables. Bake in a 400°F (205°C) oven for 35 to 40 minutes, or until the vegetables are tender. Traditionally this is served at room temperature. Serves 8.

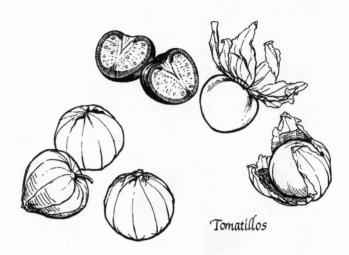

Tomatillos

Mexican Style Succotash

The following Mexican-flavored dish can be served as a main dish with hot tortillas and some extra sauce. It is also great with barbecues.

> 1 medium onion, minced
> 1 or 2 cloves garlic, minced
> ⅓ cup olive oil
> 4 zucchinis, about 5 to 6 inches long, sliced ½ inch thick
> ½ of a medium eggplant, unpeeled and cut into chunks
> 1 red or green pepper, chopped
> 4 ears of corn, scraped, or 2 10-ounce packages frozen corn
> ½ pound green beans
> 1 4-ounce can green chili sauce or fresh Salsa Verde (see page 126)
> 1 8-ounce can black olives, drained and rinsed
> 2 to 4 cups Monterey Jack cheese, grated
> ½ pound bacon, cooked until crisp, and crumbled

Sauté the onion and garlic in the hot oil until tender. Add the zucchini, eggplant, pepper, corn and green beans. Stir together to heat through. Add the sauce and the olives, cover, and steam together until almost tender, about 10 to 15 minutes. Turn vegetables into a greased 1½ to 2-quart baking dish and sprinkle with the cheese and the bacon. Bake at 350°F (175°C) for 10 to 15 minutes, or until vegetables are completely tender and cheese is melted and bubbling. Serve with more sauce. Serves 6 to 8.

Colache

A California vegetable stew of Mexican origins. As in all recipes of this type, there are infinite variations.

**4 ears fresh corn
4 cups diced summer or winter squash
¼ cup bacon fat, lard, olive oil or vegetable oil
1 large onion, minced
1 red pepper, minced** (*optional*)
**1 green pepper, minced
1 mild California green chili, chopped
4 tomatoes, peeled, seeded and chopped
½ pound fresh green beans, cut into pieces
½ cup water or chicken broth
salt and pepper to taste**

Scrape the kernels from the corn and set aside. Sauté the squash in the fat for 5 minutes. Then add all the corn and remaining ingredients. Cover and cook gently until vegetables are done, about 1 hour. Vegetables will be cooked before then, but it takes about an hour for the flavors to blend harmoniously. Serves 6 to 8.

Calabacitos con Queso

Simply add some diced Monterey Jack cheese to the Colache right at the very end, allowing it to cook just barely long enough for the cheese to begin to melt.

Variation

Some good cooks prefer to leave the corn on the cob. They simply cut each ear of corn into 3 or 4 pieces and cook with the stew. Others use green corn, left on the cob or scraped off.

Salting, weighting, & draining cubed eggplant

Ratatouille

Serve Ratatouille at room temperature, or lukewarm. It keeps well and is even better on the second day. Ratatouille lends itself well to variations. Some good cooks use an equal amount, by weight, of eggplant, zucchini, peppers, onions and tomatoes, with more garlic than I use. Any way you make it, it is delicious.

**1 eggplant, (*1 pound*) unpeeled and cut into 1-inch chunks
5 zucchinis, about 5 or 6 inches long, unpeeled and cut into chunks
salt
2 large red or green peppers, cleaned and sliced
1 large onion, minced
3 large cloves garlic, crushed
4 large, ripe tomatoes, seeded and chopped
⅓ cup olive oil
1 bay leaf
dash of Tabasco
¾ teaspoon thyme
2 teaspoons fresh basil, or 1 teaspoon dried**

Combine eggplant and zucchini in a colander and salt them. Let drain for 30 minutes. Then rinse and pat dry with paper towels. Prepare remaining vegetables and set aside.

Heat ¼ cup oil in a large skillet and lightly brown the eggplant and zucchini. Transfer to a 3 or 4-quart heavy pot. Brown the peppers lightly and add. Then lightly sauté the onion and garlic and add. Add remaining ingredients, including the rest of the oil. Simmer, covered, for 30 minutes. Remove cover and simmer another 20 minutes, or until thickened. Serves 6.

Ratatouille à la Basquaise

Mix large chunks of tuna into the vegetables. After cooking on the stove for 30 minutes, put the casserole in a 350°F (175°C) oven and bake for another 30 minutes.

To Fill Crepes

Place 1 or 2 crepes in each of as many individual ramekins as you will be needing, allowing 1 ramekin per serving. Fill crepes with Ratatouille. Sprinkle each with grated Swiss or Cheddar cheese and heat in a 350°F (175°C) oven until cheese melts and Ratatouille is hot.

Ratatouille Quiche

Spoon leftover, drained Ratatouille over the bottom of a 10-inch baked quiche shell. Sprinkle with ¼ cup grated Parmesan cheese and carefully pour on a custard of 1½ cups half and half beaten with 3 large eggs, salt and pepper and a few drops of Tabasco. Bake at 375°F (190°C) until custard is set, about 30 to 35 minutes.

For Brunch

Spoon Ratatouille into buttered, individual ramekins or into a buttered pie tin. Heat in a 350°F (175°C) oven until hot. For each serving, make an indentation in the Ratatouille with the back of a spoon. Break an egg into each indentation and pop back into the oven until the eggs are almost set, about 15 minutes. Sprinkle with grated Swiss or Cheddar cheese and bake until eggs are set and cheese is melted.

For Pizza

Add some small cubes of ham, some green olives, some mashed anchovies and some sliced mushrooms to leftover Ratatouille and use it to top pizza. Cover with cheese and bake until cheese is melted.

With Leftover Meat or Poultry

Use leftover pot roast, sliced thinly, or leftover chicken, left in pieces. Place a layer of Ratatouille in a greased baking dish. Cover with the meat or poultry and then another layer of Ratatouille. Heat in a 350°F (175°C) oven for approximately 25 minutes, or until hot throughout. Sprinkle with grated Swiss cheese, return to the oven, and heat until cheese is melted.

Vegetable Combo

1 pound fresh small mushrooms, rinsed, patted dry and stemmed
4 or 5 zucchini, cut into ½-inch slices
4 green peppers, cut into dice
1 cup minced onion
4 large tomatoes, peeled, seeded and chopped
1 cup chopped celery
2 teaspoons oregano
1½ teaspoon salt
freshly ground black pepper
⅓ cup olive oil
2 cups green beans
1 cup grated Parmesan or Romano cheese

Arrange alternate layers of the first 6 vegetables in a greased baking dish. Sprinkle each layer with seasonings. Drizzle with the oil. Bake in a 350°F (175°C) oven for 35 minutes. While vegetables are baking, parboil and then drain the green beans. These can be left whole if small; if not, cut them in pieces. Then add the beans, spooning the vegetable juices over the entire dish. Sprinkle the top with the cheese and continue baking for 15 to 20 minutes longer. Serves 8.

Vegetable Medley

**12 to 16 small whole boiling onions, peeled
and cooked in chicken broth until tender**
1 tablespoon honey
**6 small crookneck, zucchini, or pattypan
squash, cut into chunks**
1 4-ounce can sliced mushrooms
½ teaspoon salt
coarsely ground pepper to taste
2 tablespoons butter

Drain onions, reserving broth to use another time.
Pour honey over the onions and mix.

Drain mushroom liquid into skillet and add
squash. Sprinkle with the salt and pepper and dot
with the butter. Cover and cook for 5 minutes, or
until squash is almost tender. Add remaining ingredients, cover and heat until tender and cooked
through. Serves 6.

Hawaiian Vegetable Casserole

Along with some fragrant pineapples, this recipe
was a gift from a friend who had been visiting
Hawaii. It is delightfully different.

**18 to 24 small whole boiling onions, peeled
and cooked in chicken broth until tender**
1 teaspoon salt, if desired
**3 medium tomatoes, peeled, seeded and
diced**
½ cup minced green pepper
½ cup thinly sliced celery
¼ teaspoon coarsely ground black pepper
½ teaspoon sweet basil
¼ cup flour
2 tablespoons melted butter
**½ cup bread crumbs blended with another 2
tablespoons melted butter**

Drain the onions and turn them into a buttered
1½-quart casserole or large ramekin.

Combine remaining ingredients, except the
bread crumbs. Add to the onions, cover and bake
at 375°F (190°C) for 15 minutes, or until tender.

Remove from oven and cover with bread crumbs.
Bake, uncovered, for another 10 minutes, or until
crumbs are browned. Serves 6.

Caponata

Caponata

One of my favorites, Caponata can be served hot
as a rich vegetable dish, or as a side dish, or cold
as a first course or appetizer. It is also marvelous
on sandwiches. Kept at a cold enough temperature, it will keep for several weeks. It is very
often mounded on a platter and served decorated
with seafood and hard-cooked egg quarters. You
can substitute red peppers for the green, for a nice
effect.

**2 medium eggplants, partially peeled, cubed
and salted**
1 large onion, minced
2 large cloves garlic, minced
olive oil for sautéing
salt and pepper
1 cup sliced celery
3 green peppers, seeded and cut in dice
2 tablespoons minced parsley
2 tablespoons wine vinegar
1½ cups fresh or canned tomato purée
1 tablespoon capers
¾ cup green olives, rinsed and pitted
¾ cup black olives, rinsed and pitted

Salt the eggplant and allow to drain. Then rinse
and pat dry with paper towels. Sauté the onion and

garlic in olive oil until transparent. Transfer to a 4 or 5-quart heavy pot. Sauté the eggplant in oil until lightly browned all over. Transfer to pot. Salt and pepper the onion, garlic and eggplant. Then sauté the celery and peppers lightly. Add to the pot with the parsley. Toss vegetables lightly and then stir in remaining ingredients. Cook over low heat for 20 to 30 minutes. The flavor improves on standing, so it will be even better on the second or third day. Serves 6 to 8.

Note. If you do not plan to serve immediately, cook, cover and place in the refrigerator.

Holiday Version

For giftgiving, I add one or two packages of artichoke hearts, thawed, quartered and sautéed in olive oil until lightly browned. In place of the minced onion I use 1 or 1½ cups of tiny, fresh pickling onions which have first been cooked in chicken broth until tender and then dried and lightly browned in oil. I pack the Caponata in quart containers and give it with 1 or 2 loaves of my crusty Sourdough French Bread (see following recipe).

Sourdough French Bread

This is our favorite sourdough bread. It is easily made and utterly delicious.

**1½ cups sourdough starter
3 cups lukewarm water
9½ to 10½ cups unbleached bread or all-
 purpose flour
2 envelopes active dry yeast
5 teaspoons salt
cornmeal for the pans**

In a large bowl, combine the starter, 1½ cups of the water and 1½ cups of the flour. Stir until well blended, cover and set aside for 30 minutes, or up to 3 or 4 days. The sponge should be bubbly. If you let it stand for longer than the 30 minutes, stir

it occasionally. The longer standing times will result in a more sour flavor.

When ready to use, stir it and then add the remaining 1½ cups water and the yeast. Let proof for 8 minutes and then stir in 4 cups of the remaining flour and the salt. Stir well. Then gradually add the remaining flour, 1 cup at a time, until the dough is moderately soft, but not sticky.

Turn dough out onto a lightly floured bread board and knead for several minutes, being careful not to knead in too much flour. Use just enough flour to prevent sticking. Then place dough into an oiled bowl, cover and let stand until doubled in bulk, about 1 to 1½ hours.

When dough has doubled, punch it down and turn out onto a lightly floured surface. Cut into 4 equal pieces, cover with a clean towel or with paper towels, and let stand for 10 minutes.

During this time, take 2 double baguette pans (to make 4 loaves) and butter them, or spray them with Pam. Sprinkle lightly with cornmeal and set aside.

Take the dough and knead each piece into a long strand and place each in the baguette pan. Cover and let rise again until doubled in bulk. Then slash the tops decoratively with a *very* sharp knife and spray with water.

Place in a preheated 425°F (220°C) oven and bake for 30 to 35 minutes, spraying with water once during the baking. The loaves should be browned and crusty. Makes 4 loaves.

Spring or Summer Ghivech

An old Romanian recipe that is almost a meal in itself, and especially nice for using up odds and ends of vegetables. You can use from seven to eighteen different vegetables in the dish and it is as delicious to eat as it is lovely to look at.

**1 head cauliflower or broccoli, cut into
 small flowers
3 medium potatoes, peeled and diced
4 medium carrots, peeled and sliced
2 large onions, minced
4 or 5 cloves garlic, minced**

12 mushrooms, caps only *(optional)*
4 stalks celery, thinly sliced
¼ cup minced parsley
½ cup olive oil
1 cup fresh peas, or 1 10-ounce package
frozen peas *(optional)*
1 medium eggplant, cut into cubes with the
peel left on
4 or 5 large tomatoes, peeled, seeded and
diced
2 cups chicken broth *(part wine may be
used)*
¾ teaspoon sweet basil
¾ teaspoon oregano
salt and pepper to taste

Parboil the cauliflower, potatoes and carrots in boiling salted water to which you have added a bay leaf. Parboil for 8 to 10 minutes; drain. Sauté the onion, garlic, mushrooms, celery and parsley in the oil. Combine all of the vegetables in a 4 or 5-quart casserole. Combine the chicken broth with the seasonings and pour over the vegetables. Cover and bake at 350°F (175°C) for 1½ hours. Let cool for 30 minutes before serving. Serves 8.

Variation

In the spring and early summer I always add stalks of fresh asparagus, whole baby carrots, and small green beans, left whole.

Winter Ghivech

Completely different, yet the same basic recipe, this version uses the winter vegetables. The winter squash gives the dish a sweet taste.

1 medium sized acorn squash, small pumpkin, or other sweet-meated squash, peeled,
seeded and cut into cubes
3 or 4 turnips and/or small rutabagas, peeled
and cut into chunks
3 medium sized potatoes, peeled and cut into dice
3 or 4 medium sized carrots, scrubbed and
cut into slices

half a head of red or green cabbage or
cauliflower, cut into chunks
1 small eggplant, left unpeeled, cut into
cubes
several Jerusalem artichokes, peeled and cut
into chunks
1 cup thinly sliced celery
1 or 2 zucchini, cut into thick slices

———

4 or 5 tomatoes, peeled, seeded and cut into
dice
2 large onions, minced
4 or 5 cloves garlic, peeled and minced
¼ cup butter
1½ to 2 cups chicken broth *(part may be
white wine)*
½ cup olive or corn oil
salt and pepper to taste

Do not parboil any of the vegetables. Simply layer the first 9 ingredients in a 4 or 5-quart casserole. Cover with the tomatoes. Sauté the onion and garlic in the butter and add to the casserole. Combine remaining ingredients and pour over the vegetables. Cover and bake at 350°F (175°C) for 1½ hours, or until tender and done. Cool for 30 minutes before serving. Serves 8.

Ragout of Vegetables

This is a vegetable stew using fresh vegetables in season. Use any combination of the following: carrots, celery, parsnips, kohlrabi, leeks, onions, peas, potatoes, turnips, tomatoes.

½ cup diced bacon
1 large onion, minced
3 cloves garlic, minced
3 tablespoons bacon or chicken fat
1 or 2 tablespoons flour
1½ cups beef or chicken stock
2 pounds mixed vegetables in season, cleaned
and sliced or diced
1 bay leaf
½ teaspoon thyme
salt and pepper to taste
¼ cup wine vinegar

Sauté the bacon, onion, and garlic in the fat until lightly browned. Add the flour and cook and stir until smooth and golden. Add stock and stir until it comes to a boil. Add vegetables, herbs and salt and pepper. Simmer gently until vegetables are tender. The time required depends on the size and age of the vegetables, but don't let them overcook. When the vegetables are tender, stir in the vinegar, adjust seasoning to taste and serve. Serves 6.

Tian

egg~cheese~
topping

spinach~chard~zucchini

Spinach Tian

Tian is actually the name of a French baking dish, a slope-sided casserole which, like the Moroccan Tagine, lends its name to whatever is cooked in it. So this dish is Spinach Tian. It is a delicious way of serving vegetables, with the eggs and cheese forming a custard-like topping. Best served tepid, this Tian is great with barbecues or on picnics.

⅓ cup olive or other good vegetable oil
1 pound fresh spinach, cleaned and coarsely
   chopped
1 pound fresh Swiss chard, cleaned and
   coarsely chopped
2 or 3 medium sized zucchini (about 5
   inches long), cut into dice
2 medium onions, coarsely chopped
3 cloves garlic, minced
1 teaspoon basil
1 teaspoon salt
1 teaspoon coarsely ground black pepper
8 large eggs, slightly beaten
1 cup grated Parmesan cheese

Heat the oil in a large skillet and add the spinach and chard. Cook quickly just until wilted. Remove and drain, pressing out the liquid. Add the zucchini, onion and garlic to the skillet and cook until just tender.

Combine vegetables and season with the basil, salt and pepper. Turn into a well-buttered baking dish or shallow casserole. Pour the eggs over the vegetable mixture and sprinkle with the cheese and some bread crumbs if desired. Bake at 350°F (175°C) for 20 to 25 minutes, or until eggs are set and cheese is melted and bubbling. Cool before serving. Serves 6 to 8.

Summertime Pie

Similar to the Tian, this fresh vegetable pie is also good served either hot or cold. Top it with yogurt.

1 pound fresh spinach, cleaned and chopped
2 cups chopped green onions
1 cup chopped lettuce
1 cup chopped parsley
2 tablespoons flour
1 teaspoon salt
¼ teaspoon coarsely ground black pepper
⅓ cup chopped walnuts or pine nuts
   (optional)
8 large eggs, beaten
¼ cup melted butter

Combine vegetables with the flour, seasoning, nuts and eggs.

Pour the melted butter into an 11-inch pie pan. Pour vegetable mixture into the pan and bake at 325°F (165°C) for 1 hour, or until the top is browned and crisp. Serve hot or cold, topped with dollops of yogurt. Serves 6.

Layered Vegetable Casserole

Layered vegetables in a garlicky sauce, this dish is excellent with barbecues.

4 small zucchini, sliced
4 medium potatoes, peeled or unpeeled, cut
    into thin slices
2 red or green peppers, seeded and deribbed
    and cut into thin slices
2 medium onions, sliced or chopped
1 medium eggplant, cut into dice
½ cup grated Parmesan cheese
salt and pepper to taste
4 large cloves garlic, crushed
1 teaspoon oregano
6 medium tomatoes, diced
⅓ cup oil

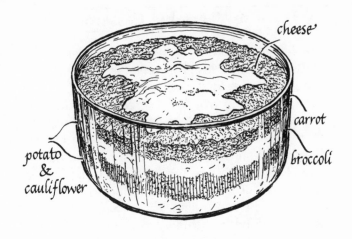

Layered Purées

Arrange layers of vegetables in a greased baking
dish. Sprinkle a little grated Parmesan between
layers, saving most of the cheese for the top.
Sprinkle with salt and pepper and then with the
garlic and oregano. Strew the top with the
tomatoes and drizzle the oil over all. Add remaining cheese. Cover the dish and bake in a 350°F
(175°C) oven for 1½ to 2 hours. Serve with a crusty bread to sop up the juices. Serves 6.

*Note. You can see by the recipes in this section
how deliciously well vegetables do when baked.
The community ovens used in earlier times determined the way dishes were cooked. And since the
dishes always had to be transported home, foods
were always served lukewarm. And indeed most
cooked dishes taste better when served at room
temperature, or just slightly warmer. The flavors
are just not as discernable when foods are very hot
or very cold.*

Layered Mixed Vegetables

This vegetable dish requires a transparent, preferably straight-sided soufflé dish to be really appreciated. It looks as good as it tastes and makes
company use of the turnips and carrots that are
usually considered homely fare.

¾ **pound white turnips, peeled and cubed**
½ **pound small potatoes, peeled and cubed**

1 head broccoli, cleaned and trimmed
1 small head cauliflower, chopped
1 bunch carrots, peeled and sliced
2 cups Bechamel Sauce *(see page 122)*
salt and pepper
1 pound Swiss cheese, grated
¾ cup buttered bread crumbs

Cook the vegetables separately in boiling, salted
water until done. Purée the turnips and potatoes
together with a small amount of the Bechamel
Sauce. Set aside. Purée remaining vegetables
separately, puréeing each with a small amount of
the Bechamel Sauce and seasoning each with salt
and pepper if desired. Set aside

Butter a 2-quart glass, straight-sided soufflé dish,
if you have one, to display the layered vegetables.
Otherwise use any 2-quart soufflé dish.

Spread the turnip-potato purée over the bottom
and sprinkle with ¼ of the cheese. Cover this
white mixture with the layer of broccoli and
sprinkle with ¼ of the cheese. Cover the green
layer with the cauliflower layer and sprinkle with
¼ of the cheese. Finish with the carrot layer and
cover this with the remaining cheese and the bread
crumbs. Bake in a 350°F (175°C) oven for 25
minutes, or until browned and heated through.

*Note. This can be prepared several hours ahead
and baked at the last minute. Serves 8.*

My Favorite Vegetable Casserole

This dish is based on the Italian Vegetables *al Forno* (Baked Vegetables). A lovely, flavorful, garlicky mixture, be sure to serve it with a crusty bread to sop up all of the wonderful juices. Occasionally, when I wish it to be a heartier dish, I will cover the vegetables with some grated mozzarella cheese about thirty minutes before the end of the baking time. The vegetables can, of course, be varied enormously. I have used a mixture of zucchini with broccoli and potatoes. Or cauliflower with peas and cubed or thinly sliced eggplant. The onion, garlic, herbs, tomato, wine and cheese are always the same. In the summertime I like to use Italian plum tomatoes, or small cherry tomatoes in place of regular tomatoes.

2 cups cauliflower in small flowerets
**2 cups broccoli flowers with some of the
   tender stems, sliced thinly**
¾ cup sliced mushrooms
1 onion, minced
3 cloves garlic, crushed
1 teaspoon basil
½ teaspoon oregano
salt and pepper
1 large tomato, diced
¾ cup white wine
½ cup grated Parmesan cheese

Combine cauliflower, broccoli, mushrooms, onions and garlic in a buttered 2-quart casserole with a lid. Sprinkle with the herbs, salt and pepper. Do not use much salt as the cheese is salty, and I have found that when you use a combination of vegetables, the natural flavors are such that you do not need much salt. Strew with the diced tomato and pour over the wine. Sprinkle with the cheese. Cover with a lid and bake in a 350°F (175°C) oven for 1½ to 2 hours, or until vegetables are tender. I like them with some bite to them, so 1½ hours does it for me. This amount will serve 4 to 6.

Note. To make a meal of this dish, simply strew over the top a cup of grated Muenster or Gruyère cheese and 6 slices of crisp cooked bacon, crumbled, about 10 minutes before baking time is over.

Vegetarian Lasagna

If I want a meatless lasagna, I usually just make a thick sauce with good tomatoes, onions, garlic and plenty of red wine, and season it with basil, oregano and rosemary, and salt and pepper. I use extra cheese and plenty of it. This makes a good side dish, or a meatless main dish. However, the following recipe is more of a luxury, a company-style lasagna with a vegetable sauce.

2 medium to large onions, minced
½ pound mushrooms, chopped
3 cloves garlic, minced
5 tablespoons olive or other oil
**3 29-ounce cans Italian plum tomatoes, or 3
   pounds ripe tomatoes, seeded and
   chopped**
1 cup dry red wine
salt to taste
1 teaspoon basil
½ teaspoon oregano
½ teaspoon thyme
1 pound zucchini, cut into ¼-inch slices
½ pound lasagna noodles
**1 pound ricotta cheese or drained cottage
   cheese**
3 cups grated Monterey Jack cheese
1 cup grated Parmesan cheese

Combine onions, mushrooms and garlic and sauté lightly in half the oil until limp. Stir in the tomatoes, wine, salt and herbs. Bring to a boil, reduce heat, and simmer for 30 minutes, or until thick.

In the meantime, sauté the zucchini slices in remaining oil until golden and partially cooked. Then add to the sauce and simmer until zucchini is tender.

Cook the lasagna noodles until just done. Do not overcook. Drain and rinse. The noodles can be cooked several hours or up to a day ahead, and drained and then rinsed and kept in cold water until needed. Then remove from the water and pat them dry just a little and use as directed.

Grease a 9 by 13 by 2-inch baking dish and in the bottom pour ⅓ of the vegetable sauce. Top with ⅓ of the noodles and then with ⅔ cup of the ricotta cheese and 1 cup of the shredded Monterey

Jack cheese. Repeat until sauce and noodles and cheeses are used. You should end with the cheese on the top. Sprinkle with ½ of the grated Parmesan. Bake in a 350°F (175°C) oven for 30 minutes, or until hot and bubbling. Serve to 8 with the remaining Parmesan on the side.

Chilaquiles

Chilaquiles is a dish of Mexican origin which has for its main ingredient leftover, stale corn tortillas. It is often cooked as a "dry soup"(meaning a thick soup) with onions, garlic, tomatoes and green chilis. This is a luxury version, which makes an excellent meatless main dish or a side dish for a buffet.

1 medium eggplant
good oil
8 corn tortillas, cut into 6 wedges each and
    deep fried until crisp
1 medium or large onion, minced
1 or 2 cloves garlic, minced
¼ pound mushrooms, chopped
2 1-pound cans tomatoes or tomato purée
1 cup California green chilis, roasted and
    peeled or 1 4-ounce can, diced
¾ cup sliced black olives
1 tablespoon chili powder
salt to taste
1 teaspoon oregano

½ teaspoon cumin powder
3 cups grated Monterey Jack and Cheddar
    cheese
1 cup sour cream

Cut eggplant into ½-inch thick slices and place in a colander, salting each layer of slices. Let drain for at least 20 minutes. Then rinse and pat dry with paper towels.

Prepare corn tortillas as directed. Reserve.

While the eggplant is draining, make the sauce as follows. Sauté the onion and garlic in 2 tablespoons good oil until limp. Add mushrooms and sauté for 2 minutes. Then stir in the tomatoes, coarsely chopped, or tomato purée, the green chilis, olives, and seasonings. Bring to a boil, lower the heat and simmer for 20 minutes or until sauce is reduced by ¼, which may take a little longer.

When eggplant has drained, and has been rinsed and dried, place the slices on a baking sheet. Brush each slice with oil and broil until golden brown. Turn the slices, brush again with oil and broil until tender and browned on the other side. Set aside.

To assemble the dish, grease a 9 by 13 by 2-inch baking dish. Place ⅓ of the sauce over the bottom of the dish. Then cover with ⅓ of the eggplant slices and ⅓ of the fried tortilla wedges. Sprinkle with ¾ cup of the grated cheese. Continue until ingredients are used. Combine the unused ¾ cup grated cheese with the sour cream and reserve.

Bake the casserole in a 350°F (175°C) oven for 30 minutes, or until hot and bubbly. Spread with reserved cheese-sour cream mixture and bake another 10 minutes. Serves 6 to 8.

Stir Frying

Stir frying is the most common method of Chinese cooking, and it is rapidly becoming a popular way of cooking vegetables with American cooks, especially those who are conscious of nutritional values.

This method of quick cooking in a small amount of liquid seals in the vitamins and also results in a crisp, colorful, flavorful mélange in which each vegetable retains its individual character and identity.

"Chow" means to "toss-fry" and ideally this is exactly the way the food is cooked. The vegetable is first tossed quickly in a small amount of very hot oil, and then finishes cooking in its own juices. The quick toss in oil coats the vegetables and makes green vegetables turn an even brighter green.

I am not going to attempt to give a short course in Oriental cooking. There are many excellent Oriental cookbooks available. What I want to do in this brief chapter is explain stir frying and present some of my favorite combinations.

THE WOK AND UTENSILS

If you are going to do much Oriental cooking, you will want to invest in a wok. A good wok is as inexpensive a piece of equipment as you can buy and its uses are far greater than those of many more expensive kitchen tools.

The most popular size wok is 14 inches in diameter. However, I much prefer a 16-inch wok and find it much more practical. You can cook a small amount of food in a large wok, but you cannot cook a large amount of food in a small one. (This is a voice of experience: I do a great deal of Oriental cooking and have, and use, 3 woks.)

*the "toss"
in Stir Fry*

When you buy your wok, be sure to buy all the parts: the ring (this is placed narrow side up on a gas range and wide side up on an electric range, enabling the wok to sit on the stove), the rack which hooks on the edge of the wok and on which you will drain fried food, the spatula and ladle and a lid. You will use all of these items.

To season your new wok, rub the inside of it all over with oil. Place on the ring over low heat and heat for 15 minutes. Remove the oil with a paper towel. Rub on more oil, reheat, and again remove the oil with a paper towel. Continue this process until the paper towel stays clean. You wok is now ready to use.

I wash the wok after each use although many chefs say that this isn't necessary. I then dry the wok over a hot burner. Then I use a couple of paper towels (with tongs, to protect my fingers) to rub some oil into the heated inside surface, using just enough so that there is a thin film of oil. The best way to store the wok is by hanging it so that air can get to it. This will prevent any off odors from the oil. Use it frequently.

STIR FRYING TECHNIQUE

Once you learn the basic technique of stir frying, you can devise combinations and recipes of your own. Remember the following points, all of utmost importance:

1. All cutting, chopping and making of sauces *must* be done in advance. There is no time to do any preparation once you have begun cooking.
2. All meats and most vegetables are cut on the diagonal as this exposes more surface to the heat, insuring quicker and more even cooking.
3. Before cutting meat on the diagonal, place it in the freezer for 15 to 20 minutes. This will firm up the meat enough to allow you to slice it with greater ease.
4. Have everything ready before you heat the pan. Make certain that oil and pan are *very* hot before you begin adding ingredients. Intense heat is necessary. It is for this reason that I do not use an

*slicing vegetables
with the
Chinese cleaver*

electric wok for Oriental cooking. As handy as they are for other types of cooking (I have two of them), they just don't get hot enough for stir frying.

5. When adding oil or a liquid ingredient to the pan after cooking has begun, pour in a circular motion around the top of the wok so that it begins to heat before reaching the cooking foods.

6. When stir frying vegetables, first add those vegetables which will take the longest time to cook. Plan ahead. Carrots, green beans, cauliflower, Brussels sprouts (cut in half), and green peppers, for example, take a longer time than asparagus, pea pods, zucchini or cabbage.

7. To give you some idea about numbers of servings, just remember that each pound of vegetables will serve 2 to 3 people. This depends, of course, on how many other dishes are being served and on whether or not there is meat in the dish.

8. Each pound of vegetables being cooked will require about 2 tablespoons of oil, although I frequently use a little more.

VEGETABLES FOR STIR FRYING

A good stir-fried dish must have the right amount of moisture. High moisture vegetables can cook in their own liquids. Hard or semi-hard vegetables will need some additional liquid. For that reason it is best to cut them, where feasible, on the diagonal so as to expose more surface to the heat.

HARD OR SEMI-HARD VEGETABLES (LOW MOISTURE)

asparagus	eggplant
bamboo shoots	lotus root
bitter melon	string beans
broccoli	snow peas
Brussels sprouts	turnips
cauliflower	green or red peppers
carrots	green peas
celery	

SOFT, OR HIGH MOISTURE VEGETABLES

bok choy
cabbage

watercress	mushrooms
bean sprouts	zucchini
lettuce	Swiss chard
spinach	onions, green
tomatoes	or regular

Fresh Ginger Root
peeled, sliced, & stored
in wine

GINGER ROOT

The ginger used in Oriental cooking is fresh ginger root. Do not use powdered ginger or preserved ginger.

Fresh ginger does not keep well. It develops mold quickly in the refrigerator and freezing changes the texture. This is what I do to store leftover ginger.

Buy a nice piece of ginger root. Peel it and cut into slices or chunks. Place in a jar and cover with a dry wine. I use a dry Chablis. However, most authorities recommend a fortified wine such as a dry sherry. I've kept ginger in this way for more than a year—in the refrigerator. It keeps beautifully. When you want to use some, remove a piece and use it just as you would if it were fresh from the market.

Basic Stir-Fry

This is a good basic recipe and one that I use all of the time. Remember to have those little bowls with all of the ingredients, properly chopped and sliced, within handy reach.

1 pound vegetable or vegetables of your choice, sliced or diced
2 or 3 tablespoons corn or peanut oil
1 large clove garlic, crushed
2 slices (⅛ to ¼ inch thick) fresh ginger root, minced
¼ to ½ cup water or chicken broth combined with 1 or 2 tablespoons soy sauce
freshly ground black pepper to taste
½ teaspoon Oriental sesame oil (optional)

Heat the wok until it is very, very hot. Add the oil as directed, drizzling it down the sides. When oil is very hot add the garlic and ginger and stir fry for 10 seconds, until pungent. Move quickly as the garlic must not burn. Add the vegetables and stir fry for 10 seconds to coat with the oil. Lower heat if necessary to prevent burning. Add the soy sauce and stock and continue stir frying until vegetables are just heated through. If vegetables need any further cooking, you may cover the wok and let the contents steam for a few minutes. Cooking time varies. Greens should be tender/crisp. Firm vegetables will take from 2 to 5 minutes. Vegetables must not lose their shape or their identity. Add the sesame oil, if desired, and toss through the vegetable mixture. This last is done for the fragrance and flavor of the dark oil.

Variations

The above is a basic recipe. You can use chicken or bacon fat in place of the oil. Diced hot peppers can be added with the ginger and garlic. This is Sichuan style. A sweet and sour stir-fry can be made by adding 1 teaspoon sugar and 1 tablespoon vinegar with the stock. You can sprinkle the stir-fry with toasted sesame seeds just before serving. You can use oyster sauce in place of soy sauce. That traditional glaze can be obtained by adding at the end a combination of ½ to 1 teaspoon cornstarch blended with 2 tablespoons of water.

Basic Stir-Fry Combinations

1. 1 cup cauliflower pieces combined with 1 cup broccoli flowers, and ½ cup each of carrot slices and red pepper pieces.
2. 1½ cups sliced mushrooms and 1 pound whole spinach leaves.
3. ¾ cup broccoli flowers combined with ¾ cup cabbage pieces, ¾ cup sliced mushrooms and ¾ cup green onion pieces.
4. 1 cup cauliflower pieces and ¾ cup asparagus pieces combined with ¾ cup green peas and ½ cup sliced mushrooms.
5. 2 green peppers, seeded and diced with 1 cucumber, peeled and diced, 2 tomatoes, peeled and diced and a small head of lettuce such as Bibb or Boston with the leaves separated.

Stir-Fried Mixed Vegetables

This stir-fry omits the ginger, although you can add 1 or 2 thin slices, minced, if you wish. I have fallen in love with that light gingery flavor.

¼ cup corn or peanut oil
1 onion, minced
2 cloves garlic, minced
1 teaspoon salt
1 red or green pepper, deribbed and thinly sliced or cut into cubes
¼ to ½ cucumber, peeled, seeded and cut into thin slices
2 stalks celery, cut into thin slices or on the diagonal
3 or 4 green onions, cut into pieces
3 or 4 romaine leaves, cut into pieces
1½ cups bean sprouts
1 teaspoon sugar
2 tablespoons soy sauce
2 tablespoons chicken broth or water

Add the oil to the wok and heat until very hot. Add the onion, garlic and salt and stir fry for about 30 seconds. Add all of the vegetables and stir fry until well coated and crisp/tender. Combine the sugar, soy sauce and broth and pour into the wok, drizzling it in from the rim. Stir fry for another minute and serve immediately. Serves 2 or 3.

Elegant Stir-Fried Vegetables

Elegant Stir-Fried Vegetables

This is definitely a party dish, and is one of the dishes most popular with my students.

**6 dried Chinese mushrooms soaked in
    lukewarm water to cover
1 medium onion, cut into 8 wedges and
    separated into its natural layers
½ cup thinly sliced bamboo shoots
⅓ cup thinly sliced water chestnuts
2 cups snow peas
1 cup bok choy
1 or 2 cloves garlic, crushed
2 thin slices ginger, minced
1 teaspoon sugar
2 teaspoons cornstarch
2 tablespoons soy sauce
½ cup chicken broth or water
liquid from the soaked mushrooms
¼ cup peanut or corn oil
2 tablespoons dry sherry
chopped green onions for garnish**

Soak the mushrooms. Prepare the vegetables and reserve. Combine garlic and ginger and set aside. Combine the sugar, cornstarch, soy sauce, chicken broth or water and liquid from the mushrooms and

set aside in a small bowl. Heat the oil in a wok until very hot. Add the garlic and ginger and stir fry for about 10 seconds. Add the onion and stir fry for 30 seconds. Add bamboo shoots and water chestnuts and stir fry for 1 minute. Then pour in the sherry, cover the wok and cook for another minute. Add snow peas and bok choy, stir, and immediately add the sugar-cornstarch mixture. Continue stir frying until sauce thickens. Turn out onto a serving dish immediately and sprinkle with the green onions. Serves 3.

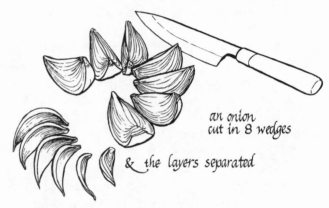

*an onion
cut in 8 wedges
& the layers separated*

HOW MANY DISHES TO SERVE

How many cooked dishes do you prepare when you are serving Oriental style? For a family dinner I prepare steamed rice and one or two stir-fried dishes. When I am entertaining, I begin with steamed rice and then prepare one dish for every two people. That would make five dishes, plus rice, for a party of 10. I do not increase the quantity of a dish, since, with so many dishes to choose from, people will take less of each. At a recent party for 14 I served the following menu. My friend Bill Slattery, who cooks Chinese style more often than most people, prepares one dish for each person.

**Egg Rolls with Mustard Sauce and a Sweet
    and Sour Sauce
Chinese Noodle Salad
Barbecued Pork with Mustard and Seeds
Steamed Rice
Beef and Broccoli in Oyster Sauce**

Shrimp Egg Foo Yung
Mock Oyster Stir-Fry
Minced Chicken in Lettuce Leaves
Sichuan Sweet and Sour Cabbage

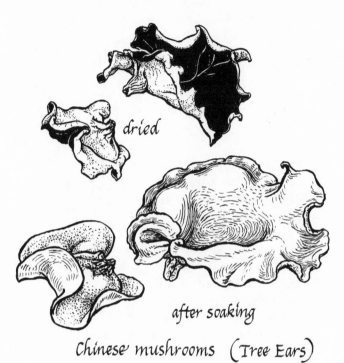

dried

after soaking

Chinese mushrooms (Tree Ears)

Chinese Egg Rolls

Egg rolls are among almost everyone's favorite Chinese dish. They're also convenient, as they can be made ahead and frozen.

¼ **pound uncooked shrimp, or 1 small can**
shrimp
¼ **teaspoon salt**
1 teaspoon dry sherry
2 tablespoons oil
2 cups minced celery
¼ **cup minced mushrooms**
1 cup fresh bean sprouts
1 egg, lightly beaten
18 egg roll skins
Hot Mustard *(see below)*

Combine shrimp, salt and wine and set aside. If you are using the uncooked shrimp, they must be

quickly stir fried until barely cooked. If you are using the canned shrimp this step is unnecessary.

Heat oil in a wok and stir fry the celery over high heat for 2 minutes. Then add mushrooms and bean sprouts and stir fry for another 3 minutes. Stir in shrimp mixture. Remove from heat and turn into a colander to drain thoroughly. Cool before using.

Place a spoonful at 1 corner of an egg roll skin. Fold skin up, over the filling. Then fold the sides towards the center and roll. Seal with beaten egg. Set aside on a plate and continue until all are filled and rolled.

Deep fry rolls at 385°F (195°C). Egg rolls should be crisp and golden. Drain on paper towels. Do not stack on top of each other as this will make them soggy.

Note. *Egg rolls freeze very well if frozen before deep frying. Or you can make them a day ahead and deep fry for 1 minute and then drain. Store in the refrigerator. When serving time comes, deep fry again until golden brown. Serve with Hot Mustard.*

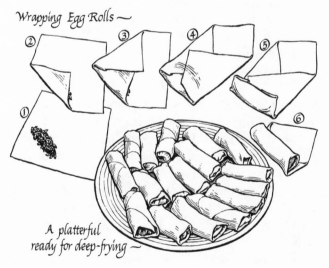

Wrapping Egg Rolls —

*A platterful
ready for deep-frying —*

Hot Mustard

I'm convinced that, served straight, this stuff can kill you. In fact I've thought of writing a mystery story wherein the murder was committed with the use of hot mustard, or the Japanese *wasabi* (green horseradish). However, when diluted, hot mustard is delightful.

All you have to do to make hot mustard is to mix some cold water and dry mustard, using just enough to make a thin or thick paste. If you wish to use the mustard as is, make the paste a little on the thin side. I always make it quite thick and then thin it with soy sauce to the consistency desired.

Some of my students use white wine or beer instead of water to thin the mustard.

Vegetable Triangles

These are extremely popular with my students, perhaps because of their similarity to egg rolls. Serve as an appetizer.

**4 green onions, minced
2 tablespoons oil
2 cups minced celery
½ cup minced or shredded bamboo shoots
½ cup chopped water chestnuts
1 clove garlic, crushed
½ teaspoon sugar
1 tablespoon soy sauce
1 tablespoon cornstarch mixed to a paste
  with a little water
40 won-ton skins**

Stir fry the minced green onions in the oil in a wok for 1 minute. Add celery, bamboo shoots and water chestnuts and stir fry another minute. Add garlic, sugar, soy sauce and cornstarch and mix well. Remove from heat and cool.

Place a teaspoon of the vegetable mixture in 1 corner of a won-ton skin. Moisten the edges and fold to make a triangle. Pinch edges together to seal.

Deep fry at 385°F (195°C) for 1 or 2 minutes, or until golden brown. Drain well on paper towels. Serve with a sweet-sour sauce, or with Barbecue Sauce, or Lemon Sauce.

Barbecue Sauce

Blend together 1 crushed clove garlic with ½ cup catsup, 1 tablespoon Worcestershire sauce and ⅛ teaspoon Tabasco.

Lemon Sauce

Combine ½ cup frozen lemon concentrate with ⅔ cup water and 1 tablespoon cornstarch. Bring to a boil. Serve hot or at room temperature.

Stir-Fried Jade Green Broccoli

This is the perfect way to cook broccoli. The color is beautiful, increasing one's appreciation of the dish.

**2 pounds broccoli flowers with some of the
  tender stems attached
1 large clove garlic, crushed
1 teaspoon sugar
1 tablespoon cornstarch
2 tablespoons soy sauce or oyster sauce
½ cup chicken broth
¼ cup corn or peanut oil
pinch of salt, if desired
2 tablespoons dry sherry
3 tablespoons minced cooked ham or crisp
  bacon**

Prepare broccoli and set aside. Reserve garlic Combine sugar, cornstarch, sauce and broth. Reserve. Heat the oil until very hot and add garlic. Stir fry quickly and then add the broccoli. Stir fry for 2 minutes. Add the sherry, cover the wok and cook for 2 minutes. Then stir in the sugar-cornstarch mixture. When sauce has thickened, turn out onto a serving dish and sprinkle with the cooked ham. Serves 4.

Stir-Fried Brussels Sprouts

Brussels sprouts are not usually thought of as a Chinese vegetable. The Chinese method of cooking, however, is the best way to prepare them.

**1½ pounds Brussels sprouts
3 or 4 tablespoons oil
1½ tablespoons soy sauce
½ teaspoon sugar
½ cup chicken broth**

Trim off the very end of each sprout and then cut the sprouts in half lengthwise. Clean and set aside.

Heat oil and stir fry the sprouts for 2 or 3 minutes, tossing until they are all well coated with the oil. This helps to keep the little sprouts bright green. Add the soy sauce and the sugar and mix well. Then add the chicken broth and cover the wok. Turn heat down to medium and cook for 5 or 6 minutes, or until sprouts are just done. Serve immediately to 3 or 4.

Note. *You can stir fry some minced garlic in the hot oil with the sprouts if desired. Add 2 thin slices of ham, cut into neat little dice, for color as well as flavor. And a few water chestnuts, thinly sliced, add color and crunch.*

Stir-Fried Romaine with Oyster Sauce

This is just an indication of how good lettuce is when it is cooked. You can also use iceberg lettuce cut into smallish squares.

2 heads romaine or iceberg lettuce
2 tablespoons corn or peanut oil
2 cloves garlic, minced
1 slice ginger root, minced *(optional)*
1 tablespoon dry sherry
½ teaspoon salt
½ teaspoon sugar
2 tablespoons oyster sauce or soy sauce

Break the romaine leaves into 2-inch pieces.

Heat the oil in a wok until very, very hot. Add the garlic and ginger if used and stir fry for 10 seconds or so. Add the wine, salt and sugar and then the lettuce leaves. Cover and cook for 1 minute. Scoop the lettuce leaves out with a perforated spoon or ladle and arrange on a serving dish. Pour the oyster or soy sauce over the lettuce and serve. Serves 3 or 4.

Variations

You can substitute Chinese cabbage for the romaine. Or use bok choy, cut on the diagonal, or broccoli which has been separated into small flowers with some of the tender stem attached. Cook bok choy or broccoli just until tender, 2 to 5 minutes.

Beef and Broccoli in Oyster Sauce

A Cantonese dish, this is very pretty and popular as well as delicious. I prefer broccoli in this dish but have used a variety of other vegetables in its place.

MARINADE

2 tablespoons oyster sauce
1 tablespoon soy sauce
1 tablespoon Chinese rice wine, or dry white wine
½ teaspoon sugar
1 tablespoon cornstarch

1 pound beef steak (*flank steak or tenderloin***)**

1 pound broccoli flowers with some of the tender stem attached

SEASONING SAUCE

2 tablespoons oyster sauce
1 tablespoon Chinese rice wine or dry white wine
1 teaspoon sugar
½ teaspoon cornstarch
1 teaspoon Oriental sesame oil

REMAINING INGREDIENTS

⅓ cup corn or peanut oil
pinch of salt if desired
1 or 2 green onions, cut into 1-inch pieces
3 thin slices ginger root, minced

Combine Marinade ingredients and stir together. Set aside. Place meat in freezer for 20 minutes to firm it up. Then remove from freezer and slice into very thin slices about ½ inch wide and 2 inches long. Add to Marinade, stir together so that meat is coated, and set aside.

Prepare broccoli and set aside. (See below for other vegetables to use.) Combine ingredients for

Seasoning Sauce and stir together. Set aside in a small bowl.

Now heat the oil in the wok until very hot. Add broccoli and stir fry for a minute, or until cooked to your satisfaction. Two minutes should be enough if your wok is hot enough. Remove broccoli to a platter. Add green onion and ginger to the wok and then add the beef with the Marinade. Stir fry until meat is almost cooked through, no more than 3 or 4 minutes if wok is hot enough and meat is thin enough. Then add broccoli and Seasoning Sauce to wok, heat thoroughly and serve immediately. Serves 4 to 6.

Vegetable Variations

Use 1 or 2 vegetables at a time, with possibly a little bit of a third for color. Use 1 pound vegetables total. Use: snow peas with 10 water chestnuts; small flowers of cauliflower; Chinese cabbage; tiny string beans combined with cauliflower are especially nice.

Sichuan Sweet and Sour Cabbage

This is one of our favorite dishes. You can control the degree of heat by the number of hot peppers you use. A delicious dish.

> **2 pounds Napa or regular (*green*) cabbage**
> **⅓ cup peanut or corn oil**
> **3 or more dried chili peppers, seeds removed**
> **1 teaspoon black pepper**
> **3 tablespoons soy sauce**
> **2 teaspoons sugar**
> **½ teaspoon salt, if desired**
> **2 tablespoons rice vinegar or white wine vinegar**
> **1 tablespoon Oriental sesame oil**

Cut cabbage into pieces about 1½ inches long and 1 inch wide. Set aside. Heat the ⅓ cup oil in a wok until very hot and stir fry the chili peppers until just browned. Add pepper and cabbage and stir fry for

3 minutes, or until cabbage is hot. Combine remaining ingredients and toss with cabbage. Serve hot or cold. Serves 4 to 6.

Mock Oyster Stir-Fry

If you like oysters, you will love this dish. If you hate oysters, don't try it. The combination of oyster sauce and tofu could fool you into thinking you were eating a dish with chunks of oysters in it.

> **2 tablespoons each: peanut or corn oil and Oriental sesame oil**
> **3 or 4 large cloves garlic, minced**
> **2 cups sliced zucchini or broccoli flowers with a little of the stem attached**
> **1 cup sliced mushrooms**
> **2 cups tofu in ½-inch dice**
> **1 or 2 tablespoons soy sauce**
> **⅓ cup oyster sauce**

Heat the oils over high heat. Add garlic, zucchini or broccoli and mushrooms. Stir fry until vegetables begin to brown. Toss in the tofu, being careful that it does not crumble or break up. Add soy and oyster sauces and toss together for a minute. Cover wok and let cook for 2 to 3 minutes. Remove cover and cook another minute until sauce thickens. Serve immediately with steamed rice. Serves 4 or 5.

Chinese Fried Rice with Chicken

Originally devised as a method of using leftover rice, there are as many recipes for Fried Rice as there are cooks. I've made it with freshly cooked rice and with leftover rice and I believe that the dish is much better if the rice has been made at least a day ahead. Fried Rice can be served as a main dish or a side dish. For a light meal, I serve it with a light soup and a tossed salad.

Chinese Fried Rice

2 large eggs
$^1/_8$ teaspoon pepper
$^1/_4$ cup soy sauce
$^1/_4$ cup oil
1 clove garlic, crushed
1 thin slice ginger, minced
$^1/_2$ cup thinly sliced celery
$^1/_4$ cup sliced mushrooms
4 cups cooked rice
4 green onions, minced
$^1/_2$ to 1 cup diced cooked chicken
1 cup bean sprouts

Combine the eggs with the pepper and soy sauce. Whisk together and set aside.

Heat the oil in a wok and in it brown the garlic and the ginger. Add the celery and the mushrooms and stir fry for 30 seconds. Then add the rice, green onions and chicken and stir fry for several minutes to heat the rice through and coat it with the oil. Add the bean sprouts and the egg mixture while stirring, so that the rice is coated with the egg mixture. Cook for another couple of minutes and serve immediately. Garnish with strips of Egg Pancake (*see below*) and green onion brushes. Serves 4 to 6.

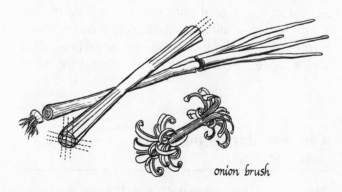

onion brush

① trim & cut green onion ~
② soak in cold water several hours ~

Note. *I often add some green peas or pea pods to the Fried Rice. These make a colorful as well as flavorful addition.*

Variations

Substitute barbecued pork, ham, cooked turkey or beef, or shrimp or crab meat for the chicken, using 1 to 2 cups.

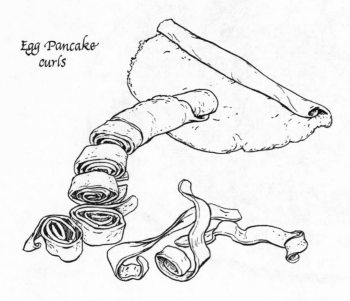

*Egg Pancake
curls*

Egg Pancake

Beat together 1 large egg with 1 tablespoon water and pinch of salt if desired. Heat 2 teaspoons oil in a skillet. Add egg and tilt the pan so that the egg mixture covers it to make a thin pancake. Let cook until set and lightly browned on the bottom. Turn out upside down, so that the lightly browned side is on top. Let it cool until you can handle it. Roll up as for a jelly roll and slice into ½-inch strips. Arrange strips on the top of the mound of Fried Rice and arrange green onion brushes around the base.

Chinese Barbecued Pork
(Char Siu)

This is always a popular dish and the pork can be used for many things. Slice it and serve warm with fried rice, egg rolls, or stir-fries, or serve cold with hot mustard and sesame seeds. Use 2 pounds of boneless pork shoulder or loin or pork tenderloin. I have, on occasion, used pork chops. Make a marinade as follows: combine ¼ cup soy sauce, 2

teaspoons 5-spice powder, 3 tablespoons dry sherry, a piece of ginger, minced, ⅓ cup sugar and 2 tablespoons Hoisin sauce. Marinate the meat in this for at least 6 hours, preferably overnight.

Preheat the oven to 425°F (220°C) and place a shallow pan of water on the bottom shelf. Place upper shelf as high as it can go. Using skewers which you have bent into hooks, hang the pork from the top rack over the pan of water. If you absolutely cannot do that, then place the pork on a cooling rack directly over the pan of water, so that it drips into the water. Roast for 20 minutes. Baste meat with marinade every 10 minutes. Reduce heat to 325°F (165°C) and continue roasting and basting for another 25 to 45 minutes. A meat thermometer inserted into the thickest part should read 180°F. The amount of time depends on how thick a piece of meat you are using. When meat is done, remove from oven and cool slightly. Slice into thin slices and place around bowls of Hot Mustard, (*see page 197*), sesame seeds and Barbecue Sauce (*see page 198*). Serves at least 8.

Minced Chicken or Pork in Lettuce Leaves
(Yook Soong)

This combination of hot chicken or pork with cold lettuce leaves is absolutely delightful. The crisp lettuce leaf is wrapped around the filling and eaten with the fingers—a Chinese taco.

**6 to 8 medium sized dried mushrooms
   soaked in warm water**

MARINADE

**1 teaspoon cornstarch
1 teaspoon soy sauce
2 teaspoons each: dry sherry, water
dash of pepper**

**1½ pounds chicken breasts, boned, skinned
   and minced, or a combination of pork and
   shrimp, or all pork**

1 thin slice ginger root, minced

2 cloves garlic, minced
2 green onions, minced
1 small can bamboo shoots, minced
1 small can water chestnuts, minced

COOKING SAUCE

1 tablespoon soy sauce
1 tablespoon dry sherry
2 tablespoons oyster sauce
2 tablespoons water
1 teaspoon Oriental sesame oil
2 teaspoons cornstarch

Hoisin sauce (*optional*)
lettuce leaves (*use iceberg or Bibb*)

Soak mushrooms in warm water for at least 30 minutes. Then drain, discard stems, squeeze mushrooms dry and mince. Reserve. Combine Marinade ingredients and add minced chicken or pork. Toss to coat the meat surfaces. Set aside. Combine the minced ginger, garlic and green onions in a small bowl. Put the minced bamboo shoots and water chestnuts in separate bowls. Combine the ingredients for the Cooking Sauce and set aside.

Heat a wok with 3 tablespoons oil. Add chicken and stir fry until opaque, about 3 minutes. Pork should be stir fried a little longer. How much longer depends on how small a dice it is cut into. Remove chicken or pork to a dish and reserve. If you use the pork and shrimp, add the minced shrimp last so that it does not overcook.

Add 2 tablespoons more oil to the wok, heat it and stir fry the ginger, garlic and green onions quickly. Then stir in the mushrooms, bamboo shoots and water chestnuts. Stir fry for 2 minutes. Add reserved chicken or pork and then the Cooking Sauce and continue cooking until sauce thickens. Serve hot.

To serve, have a bowl of cleaned, dry lettuce leaves, a bowl of the hot chicken mixture and a small bowl of Hoisin sauce. To eat, take a lettuce leaf and spread a little Hoisin sauce on it. Then spoon on some of the hot mixture, wrap and eat. Serves 6 to 8 as an appetizer.

Note. *You might also deep fry a 2-ounce package of cellophane noodles and serve them with the chicken mixture. These add still another texture to be savored.*

Microwave Cooking

*Fluffing the strands
from baked Spaghetti Squash ~*

When almost finished with this book, I decided that one really couldn't publish a vegetable cookbook in today's world without including some microwave tips and recipes. Whatever else you may think of microwave cooking, it is a marvelous way to cook vegetables. They come out bright-colored, perfectly cooked and, according to some authorities, more nutritious. Sauté onions and garlic, or mushrooms, in the microwave. Pasta, too, is easily cooked in the microwave. I also use it to blanch vegetables, as it is so simple and quick.

Cooking Fresh Vegetables in the Microwave Oven

All vegetables should be microwaved in a shallow glass casserole or pie plate. Arrange vegetables in the pie plate and add water as specified. You might add a little butter or cream, if desired, for flavor.

Cover with plastic wrap. Microwave on HIGH for the recommended time. Stir halfway through cooking time. When cooking is finished, let stand, covered, for 3 to 5 minutes before seasoning and serving. If the vegetables aren't cooked as soft as you like, just microwave another minute or two. If you cook more than the recommended amount, you must allow more cooking time.

VEGETABLES	AMOUNT	WATER	TIME
ARTICHOKES	2 trimmed, rinsed and wrapped in plastic wrap	none extra needed	8 to 9 minutes
ASPARAGUS	1½ pounds, tough ends discarded	¼ cup	7 to 9 minutes
BEANS: GREEN OR WAX	1 pound; snap or French cut	3 tablespoons	7 to 9 minutes
BEAN SPROUTS	½ pound	2 tablespoons oil	3 minutes
BEETS, WHOLE	4 medium	cover with water	15 to 17 minutes
BEETS, SLICED	4 medium	½ cup	12 to 13 minutes
BROCCOLI	1 pound flowers	2 tablespoons	7 to 9 minutes
BROCCOLI STEMS	1 pound stems cut into slices	¼ cup	7 to 9 minutes
BRUSSELS SPROUTS	½ pound (2 cups)	2 tablespoons	4 to 6 minutes
CABBAGE, WHOLE	1 medium head	2 tablespoons	13 to 15 minutes
CABBAGE, CHOPPED	1 small head	2 tablespoons	9 to 11 minutes
CARROTS, SLICED	4 medium	2 tablespoons	4 to 6 minutes
CARROTS, WHOLE	1 pound (about 6) wrapped in plastic wrap and pierced in several places	none	7 to 9 minutes or until tender
CAULIFLOWERETS	about 1 pound	⅓ cup	8 to 10 minutes
CAULIFLOWER, WHOLE	1 small head	⅓ cup	8 to 10 minutes
CELERY, SLICED	4 cups	2 tablespoons	7 to 9 minutes
CORN, KERNELS	1½ cups	2 tablespoons	3 to 5 minutes
CORN ON THE COB	2 ears placed in dish with several table-spoons of butter and covered with plastic wrap	none	4 to 6 minutes
	4 ears, same as above	none	8 to 10 minutes
EGGPLANT, CUBED	4 cups, cubes	2 tablespoons	4 to 6 minutes
MUSHROOMS	½ pound, sliced with 2 tablespoons of butter and a table-spoon Vermouth	none	4 to 5 minutes
PEAS, GREEN	2 cups shelled	2 tablespoons	4 to 6 minutes
	4 cups shelled	2 tablespoons	9 to 10 minutes
POTATOES, NEW	4, cleaned and pierced with a fork; cook uncovered	none; place potatoes on paper towels	8 to 9 minutes or until tender when squeezed
	6, same as above	same as above	10 to 12 minutes
RUTABAGA OR TURNIPS	3 cups cubed or sliced	2 tablespoons with same of butter	7 to 9 minutes
SPINACH OR CHARD	4 cups	water that clings to leaves	4 to 5 minutes
SQUASH: ACORN OR BUTTERNUT	1 medium	pierce skin in several places and place on paper towels	4 to 6 minutes
SUMMER SQUASHES	3 cups sliced	2 tablespoons	7 minutes

Blanching Vegetables

I much prefer freezing vegetables to canning them, and I find the microwave a great help in blanching. One doesn't have to spend the day in a steamy kitchen with pots and pots of boiling water.

1. Prepare vegetables by peeling, slicing, dicing or whatever, as you would for regular cooking. Place in a casserole or microwave-proof dish, add water as directed in the following Blanching Chart, cover, and microwave on HIGH.

2. Microwave for half the minimum time and then stir. Cover again (plastic wrap is perfect), and cook for remaining time. Stir at the end of the cooking time.

3. Vegetables should be evenly bright in color. Drain and place casserole or baking dish in ice water, or in a pot of ice cubes to stop the cooking.

4. Blot the vegetables dry and package in freezer bags or other freezer containers. Label carefully and freeze.

5. For some vegetables, like peas, I prefer loose-packing them. To do this, I spread them out on baking sheets, cover them with plastic wrap and freeze. When the vegetables are frozen, just pour into bags or containers. Place back in the freezer. These are nice because you can pour out what you need.

Blanching Chart

VEGETABLES	AMOUNT	WATER	TIME
ASPARAGUS	1 pound	¼ cup	3 to 4 minutes
BEANS (GREEN)	1 pound	¼ cup	4 to 6 minutes
BROCCOLI FLOWERS	1 pound	½ cup	4 to 5 minutes
CARROTS	1 pound sliced	¼ cup	4 to 6 minutes
CAULIFLOWER	1 head, divided into flowers	⅓ cup	4 to 6 minutes
PARSNIPS	1 pound sliced	¼ cup	3 to 4 minutes
PEAS	2 pounds shelled	¼ cup	3 to 4 minutes
SPINACH OR OTHER GREENS	1 pound washed	none	2 to 3 minutes
SUMMER SQUASH	1 pound sliced	¼ cup	3 to 4 minutes
TURNIPS	1 pound cubed	¼ cup	3 to 4 minutes

Hot Potato Salad

1 pound medium potatoes (*about 3*), peeled and thinly sliced
½ cup water

DRESSING

5 slices bacon, chopped
¾ cup minced onion, either red or green
2 tablespoons flour
½ cup white wine vinegar
salt and pepper to taste

2 tablespoons sugar
2 tablespoons minced parsley

Combine potatoes and water in a 2-quart glass baking dish. Cover and microwave on high for 8 to 10 minutes, stirring once at 3 or 4 minutes. Drain. Turn potatoes into another dish and reserve.

Add bacon and onion to the baking dish, cover with paper towels and microwave on high for 3½ to 4 minutes, stirring once during cooking. Then stir in the flour. Combine the vinegar with salt and pepper and the sugar and add ⅓ cup water. Add to the baking dish and stir. Microwave on high, uncovered, until bubbly, about 1½ minutes. Stir at least once during cooking. Add potatoes, cover and microwave on high until hot, about 2 minutes. Stir once during cooking. Sprinkle with parsley and serve to 4.

Wilted Lettuce Salad

The greens should stay just slightly crisp.

6 slices bacon

DRESSING

¼ cup reserved bacon drippings
¾ cup sliced green onions
⅓ cup white wine vinegar
⅓ cup water
2 teaspoons sugar
salt as desired

SALAD

4 cups torn leafy lettuce
4 cups torn fresh spinach
5 or 6 radishes, thinly sliced
2 or 3 hard-cooked eggs, chopped

Place bacon slices on plate and cover with paper towels. Microwave on high until bacon is crisp, about 4 or 5 minutes. Drain, reserving ¼ cup of the drippings. Crumble bacon and reserve.

Microwave the onion in the reserved drippings on high for 3 minutes. Add remaining Dressing ingredients and microwave on high, uncovered, until boiling, about 1½ minutes. Stir. Add lettuce and spinach to the dressing and toss well. Microwave on high, uncovered, for 1 minute, tossing once during cooking.

Serve in a regular salad bowl garnished with the radish slices and chopped hard-cooked eggs. Serves 6.

Note. You can use all lettuce or all spinach, if desired. The eggs can be hard-cooked in the

microwave as follows: grease a small individual baking dish and break the 2 eggs into it. Puncture the yolks. Cover with plastic wrap and microwave on high for 1½ to 2 minutes. Let stand for 2 or 3 minutes. The eggs will turn right out of the baking dish and can be chopped for the salad.

Tortellini Soup

The addition of the tortellini (you can also use the tiny raviolini) adds body and flavor.

4½ cups beef or chicken broth
¾ cup diced carrot
¾ cup diced potato
⅓ cup minced green onion
**1 cup tomato juice, or chopped fresh
    tomatoes**
1 cup chopped fresh spinach or other greens
**1 7-ounce box dried tortellini, cooked as
    directed on package, drained, and set
    aside**
salt and pepper to taste
grated Parmesan cheese

Heat the broth. Combine the carrot and potato with 1 cup of the broth in a 3-quart soup tureen or casserole. Cover and microwave on high for 10 minutes, or until vegetables are tender. Add the onion, tomato juice or chopped tomatoes, another 1½ cups of the broth, and the spinach. Microwave on high for 2 minutes, or until liquid is boiling.

Stir in the remaining 2 cups broth and the cooked tortellini and add salt and pepper to taste. Microwave on high for another 2 or 3 minutes, or until the soup is piping hot. Serve with cheese to sprinkle over the top. Makes 2 quarts, which will serve 6 to 8.

Fresh Corn Casserole

This is pure and delicious western cooking. The casserole freezes well; it should be defrosted before reheating. It can also be made a day ahead of serving and just reheated.

2 cups fresh corn kernels
½ cup melted butter
2 large eggs, beaten
1 cup sour cream
1 cup diced Monterey Jack cheese
½ cup cornmeal
½ to 1 cup canned or fresh roasted peeled
   California green chilis, chopped
salt to taste

Purée 1 cup of the corn kernels with the butter and eggs in a food processor or blender. Combine with remaining ingredients and mix well. Turn into a greased 2-quart shallow casserole. Microwave, on high, uncovered, for 10 minutes. Rotate casserole once during cooking. Let rest for another 10 minutes before serving to 6.

Note. You can substitute 2 10-ounce packages of frozen corn kernels for the fresh corn.

Green Rice Casserole

This makes a colorful dish, nice for buffets or with summer barbecues.

3 cups cooked long-grain rice
1 10-ounce package frozen chopped spinach,
   thawed and drained, or 1 pound fresh
   spinach, steamed and chopped
¾ cup minced green onions
½ cup minced parsley
¼ cup butter or margarine
2 teaspoons fresh lemon juice
1 teaspoon salt *(optional)*
1 clove garlic, crushed
2 large eggs
1 cup milk or half and half
2 cups grated Cheddar cheese

Butter a 2 or 2½-quart casserole and in it combine the rice, spinach, onion, parsley, butter, lemon juice, salt and garlic. Stir well. Beat the eggs with the milk and add to the rice along with 1½ cups of the grated cheese. Cover the casserole and microwave on high for 6 minutes, stirring twice. Sprinkle the top with the remaining ½ cup of

cheese and cook, covered, another 4 minutes on high. Let rest for 5 to 10 minutes before serving to 8.

Broccoli Parmesan

This makes an excellent vegetable dish for a luncheon or an evening buffet.

4 cups broccoli flowers with some of the
   tender stem attached
2 large eggs, beaten
1 cup mayonnaise, preferably homemade
1 small onion, minced
¼ cup minced green or red pepper
1 cup freshly grated Parmesan cheese
salt and pepper to taste
2 teaspoons melted butter or margarine combined with 3 tablespoons fresh bread
   crumbs

Microwave the broccoli as directed on page 205. Drain thoroughly. Beat the eggs into the mayonnaise and stir in the onion, pepper, cheese, salt and pepper. Add the broccoli and stir together. Turn into a greased shallow baking dish. Sprinkle with the buttered bread crumbs. Microwave on high for 5 minutes, or until bubbly. Serves 6.

Zucchini Parmesan

Follow the above recipe using sliced zucchini instead of broccoli.

Southern Squash Casserole

4 cups sliced summer squash
1 cup chopped green or red pepper
1 cup coarsely chopped onion
¼ cup melted butter
½ cup coarsely crushed crackers
2 large eggs, beaten
salt and pepper to taste
½ cup grated Cheddar cheese

Turn squash, pepper and onion into a 1½-quart glass casserole and add several tablespoons of water. Cover with plastic wrap and microwave on high for 8 to 10 minutes, or until vegetables are tender. Drain.

Stir together the melted butter, crackers, eggs and salt and pepper. Stir into the vegetables. Taste for seasoning and adjust to taste. Spread out until level and sprinkle top with the grated cheese. Microwave on high, uncovered, for 8 to 10 minutes, rotating once during cooking. Let stand for 5 minutes before serving to 4.

Baked Spaghetti Squash Combo

This makes a lovely side dish or light main dish.

1 medium size spaghetti squash
¼ cup olive oil
1 cup ham, cut in thin slivers
¾ cup fresh or thawed frozen peas
½ cup sliced fresh mushrooms
2 egg yolks, beaten
¾ cup half and half
1 cup grated Parmesan cheese

Pierce the squash in many places with a fork or skewer. Place it on a paper towel or in a shallow glass baking dish. Microwave, uncovered, on high for 15 minutes, turning over at least twice during this time. Let stand for 4 minutes. Press surface. If it does not give, microwave another 3 or 4 minutes.

Split squash lengthwise, discard seeds, and fork the strands free from the shells. Reserve shells. Combine 6 cups of the squash with the remaining ingredients and toss together gently. Pile mixture into the reserved shells and place them in a shallow baking dish. Cover with plastic wrap and poke several holes in the wrap. Microwave on high for 8 to 10 minutes, or until piping hot. Serve immediately to 6.

Microwaved Dried Beans

When your recipe calls for cooked dried beans, by far the best and easiest method of cooking them is with the microwave.

A pound of dried beans measures 2 cups. Place the washed and sorted beans in a 4 or 5-quart casserole with 8 cups of water. Add any seasonings that you will be using in the finished dish. Microwave on high for 8 to 10 minutes, or until boiling. Then cover and let stand for 1 hour. This is the equivalent of an overnight soaking.

When the hour is up, check the beans and add boiling water if needed to keep the beans covered with liquid. Cover—*this is important as the beans might explode and you don't want beans all over the oven*—with the lid or with plastic wrap and microwave on high for 10 minutes. Then reduce the power to 50% and cook until the beans are tender, about another 20 to 30 minutes, depending on the type of beans used and how old they are.

At this point you will have 5 to 6 cups of cooked beans for use in salads, casseroles or other dishes.

Desserts

Bibb Lettuce

Vegetables are used as an ingredient in many cakes, pies and puddings, as well as in some cookies. They add moisture as well as flavor and increase the keeping qualities.

Lettuce Tea Bread

This makes a delicately flavored, slightly lemony loaf. The bright green shreds of lettuce stay green, giving the baked loaf a speckled look, as well as added moisture. This recipe is from my most recent book, *The New Book of Breads*, and is worth repeating.

2 cups sugar
1 cup vegetable oil

4 large eggs
4 teaspoons baking powder
1 teaspoon baking soda
1 teaspoon salt
¼ teaspoon cinnamon
¼ teaspoon powdered ginger
3 cups stirred and measured white or
    unbleached white flour
1 tablespoon fresh lemon juice
2 cups finely chopped lettuce
1 cup chopped walnuts

Beat the sugar with the oil and eggs. Stir the baking powder, soda, salt, spices and flour together and add to the oil mixture. Then stir in the lemon juice, lettuce and nuts. Turn batter into 2 well-greased 8-inch loaf pans and bake in a preheated 350°F (175°C) oven for 1 hour. Begin testing the loaves, by poking a toothpick of cake tester in the center, at 45 minutes. If it comes out dry, the loaves are done. If it is moist, the loaves require more baking.

When done, remove from oven and turn out on a rack to cool. Cool for several hours, or overnight, before cutting into thin slices. Serve with whipped cream cheese or butter to which some grated lemon rind has been added. Makes 2 loaves.

Carrot Cake

There are many recipes for carrot cake, most of them pretty similar. This one is different—a cross between a pudding and a cake.

   1 cup stirred and measured white or
      unbleached white flour
   1 teaspoon cinnamon
   1 teaspoon freshly ground nutmeg
   1 teaspoon salt
   1 teaspoon baking soda
   2 cups golden raisins, soaked in boiling
      water for 30 minutes and drained
   1 cup coarsely grated carrots
   1 cup coarsely grated raw potatoes
   ½ cup vegetable oil
   1 cup sugar

Combine flour with the spices, salt and baking soda. Stir. Add the remaining ingredients and stir well to mix. Pour batter into a greased 9 by 5 by 3-inch loaf pan and level the top.

Use a covered roasting pan with a rack and pour 1 quart of boiling water into it, or enough to cover the rack with 1 inch of water. Put the loaf pan on the rack. Cover with roasting pan lid and steam in a 350°F (175°C) oven for 2 hours. Cool in pan for 15 minutes before turning out onto cooling rack. Cool completely and then frost as desired.

Mississippi Potato Cake

This is an old, old recipe that makes a fine cake. With the exception of the potatoes, which should be hot, have all ingredients at room temperature.

   2 cups sifted pastry or cake flour
   1 tablespoon baking powder
   1 teaspoon cinnamon
   ½ teaspoon nutmeg
   ½ teaspoon salt
   ¼ cup cocoa (Dutch cocoa is preferred)
   ¾ cup butter or margarine
   2 cups sugar
   4 large eggs, separated
   1 teaspoon vanilla extract
   ⅔ cup milk
   1 cup hot unseasoned mashed potatoes
   1 cup chopped nuts
   sifted powdered sugar

Sift flour with baking powder, spices, salt and cocoa. Set aside. Cream the butter or margarine, adding the sugar gradually and beating until mixture is light and fluffy. Add the egg yolks and beat in until thoroughly blended. Combine vanilla and milk. Fold the sifted dry ingredients and the milk into the creamed mixture alternately, beginning and ending with dry ingredients. Then stir in the potatoes, blending thoroughly. Beat the egg whites until stiff, and fold into the batter along with the chopped nuts.

Turn batter into a buttered and floured loaf pan (9 by 5 by 3 inches) and bake in a 350°F (175°C) oven for 50 minutes, or until cake tests done. Cool in pan for 5 minutes before turning out on a rack to cool. Sprinkle with sifted powdered sugar.

Note. If desired, batter may be baked in 2 9-inch round layer pans that have been buttered and floured. Bake at 350°F (175°C) for about 25 minutes.

Baked Pumpkin Pudding

Similar to pumpkin pie, this delicious pudding is just different enough to make a welcome change, and because you flame it, it adds the same festive note to a holiday dinner as the heavier plum puddings. Superfine granulated sugar carmelizes more quickly and easily than does regular granulated sugar and for this reason is strongly recommended. Once the sugar is carmelized it must be poured into the bowl immediately and tipped to coat both bottom and sides. Carmelized sugar hardens in mere minutes.

1¼ cups superfine granulated sugar
2 teaspoons water or lemon juice
2 cups canned pumpkin
⅓ cup sugar
⅓ cup light brown sugar
½ teaspoon salt
1 teaspoon cinnamon
½ teaspoon ginger
½ teaspoon nutmeg
6 large eggs
2 extra egg yolks
3 cups half and half, scalded and cooled
¾ cup rum or brandy
whipped cream

Put the superfine granulated sugar in a heavy skillet and stir in the water or lemon juice. Cook over moderate heat, stirring constantly, until the sugar melts and becomes a golden color. Pour immediately into a buttered 2-quart bowl with a rounded bottom and turn until the bottom and sides are coated with a layer of the carmelized sugar. The bowl must be one that you can bake in. Set aside, or chill, until the carmelized sugar hardens.

Combine the pumpkin, sugars, salt, spices and eggs. Beat with a whisk, or with an electric mixer, until thoroughly blended. Stir in the half and half and blend well, and then add ½ cup of the rum or brandy. Pour the pudding over the carmelized sugar and set the bowl in a pan of hot water. Bake in a 350°F (175°C) oven for 1 hour to an hour and 20 minutes, or until the pudding tests done. Test as you would a pumpkin pie. Cool at room temperature.

When ready to serve, place a serving plate over the bowl and invert the carmelized pudding onto the plate. If you let it stand for 5 to 10 minutes the

pudding will come out more easily. Pipe whipped cream onto the serving plate around the pudding. Warm the remaining ¼ cup of brandy or rum, set it aflame and pour it over the pudding. Serves 12.

Simple Sweet Potato Pudding

An ideal dessert for a simple winter meal, this is easily made and seems to be especially enjoyed by the children. It makes a filling dessert, so I always serve it with a light meal.

⅔ cup butter or margarine
1 cup white or light brown sugar
2 large eggs
2 cups grated raw sweet potatoes
1 tablespoon grated orange rind
1 teaspoon grated lemon rind
½ teaspoon each: ginger and cinnamon

Cream the butter and sugar until light and fluffy. Add the eggs and the sweet potatoes and blend. Then stir in the grated rinds and spices and beat until mixture is thoroughly blended. Turn pudding into a well buttered 9-inch square baking pan. Bake in a 350°F (175°C) oven for 1 hour, or until the pudding tests done. Serve hot with sweet cream.

Deep South Sweet Potato Pudding

An iron skillet is considered a necessity when making this delicious pudding, to produce the nice dark crust which is traditional. However, I've used other pans; the most important thing is to use a heavy one.

½ cup butter
4 cups grated raw sweet potatoes
1 cup honey or cane syrup
½ cup light brown sugar
1 cup chopped walnuts

1 cup raisins or chopped dates
1 teaspoon each: allspice and cinnamon
½ teaspoon each: salt and ginger
3 large eggs

Melt the butter in a heavy skillet. Combine the rest of the ingredients and blend well. Turn into the skillet and stir and mix over low heat until the mixture is heated throughout. Smooth the top of the pudding, place in a 350°F (175°C) oven and bake for about 40 minutes. Watch the pudding and when it has crusted around the edges and on top, turn the crusted part under and let the crust form again. Do this twice, the last time allowing the newly formed crust to remain. Serve hot with sweet cream. Serves 8.

Steamed Carrot-Potato Pudding

This is an old-fashioned pudding that is simpler, lighter and less rich than a plum pudding. It keeps well, and can be made several days, or even a week, ahead. If keeping the pudding, remove it from the mold to cool, then wrap well and store in the refrigerator. Return to the mold and resteam for an hour before serving. Serve with any hard sauce, brandy sauce, a lemon sauce, or with vanilla ice cream.

1½ cups all-purpose flour, stirred and measured, or ½ cup all-purpose flour mixed with 1 cup coarse, dry bread crumbs
1 cup granulated or light brown sugar
1 teaspoon baking soda
1 teaspoon cinnamon
1 teaspoon nutmeg
½ teaspoon salt
1 cup dark or golden raisins
¾ cup chopped walnuts
1 cup shredded raw potato
1 cup shredded raw carrot
1 cup chopped green apple (optional)
1 large egg
½ cup softened butter or margarine

Place all of the dry ingredients in a bowl and stir to blend. Then add remaining ingredients and blend

thoroughly. Prepare a 2-quart mold by buttering it thoroughly and then dusting it with sugar. Pack the batter into the mold. Cover with a lid, or with waxed paper and aluminum foil, securing the lid with a string. This is necessary to assure proper steaming. Place the mold on a trivet in a large pot. Add boiling water to the pot to come halfway up the sides of the pudding mold. Cover the pot and steam for 3 to 4 hours. Serve warm, topped with sauce. Serves 8.

Sauerkraut Surprise Cake

This is from my book, A World of Baking, and is a very good recipe. The recipe makes a moist, delicious cake with absolutely no sauerkraut flavor. Have all ingredients at room temperature.

2¼ cups sifted pastry or cake flour
1 teaspoon baking powder
1 teaspoon baking soda
¼ teaspoon salt
½ cup cocoa (Dutch cocoa is preferred)
⅔ cup sauerkraut
⅔ cup butter or margarine
1½ cups sugar
3 large eggs
1 teaspoon vanilla extract
1 cup water

Sift the flour with the baking powder, soda, salt and cocoa. Set aside. Rinse and drain the sauerkraut. Snip it into smaller pieces with kitchen scissors. Cream the butter or margarine until fluffy. Gradually add the sugar and cream until light. Add the eggs, 1 at a time, and beat in well. Add the vanilla and blend. Now stir in the flour mixture alternately with the water, beginning and ending with dry ingredients. Fold in the sauerkraut last.

Turn batter into 2 8-inch round layer pans that have been buttered and floured. Tap pans lightly on a counter top to release excess air. Bake in a 350°F (175°C) oven for 30 to 35 minutes, or until cake tests done. Cool in pans for 5 minutes before turning out onto racks to cool. Use your favorite chocolate frosting with this.

Sweet Potato and Pineapple Pudding
(Camote y Piña)

This is one of the famous and delicious "pastes" that the Mexicans make out of a variety of fruits and squashes. Traditionally this is cooked until it is firm enough to mold and slice. However, we prefer it cooked just until thick and served with a topping of whipped cream—more pudding than paste.

1¼ cups light brown sugar
½ cup water
2½ cups mashed sweet potatoes
1 15-ounce can crushed pineapple, well drained
1 teaspoon cinnamon (optional)
½ cup chopped almonds
sweetened whipped cream

Combine sugar and water in a heavy saucepan and cook over medium heat until sugar is dissolved. Add the sweet potatoes and cook, stirring occasionally, for 10 minutes. Then stir in pineapple and cinnamon and cook, stirring almost constantly now, to keep it from burning, until very thick. Remove from heat and stir in chopped almonds. Serve warm or chilled with whipped cream. Serves 6 to 8.

Favorite Pumpkin Pie

This can be made with pumpkin or with any cooked and puréed winter squash. It is delicious.

3 large eggs, beaten
½ cup sugar
1 cup light or dark brown sugar
¼ cup melted butter
1 cup puréed pumpkin (see above)
1 teaspoon vanilla extract
1 cup chopped pecans or sliced toasted almonds
1 9-inch pie shell
whipped cream

Combine and beat together the eggs, sugar, brown sugar, butter, pumpkin, and vanilla. Spread the nuts over the bottom of the pie shell and pour the pumpkin mixture carefully over the nuts. Bake in a 350°F (175°C) oven for 1 hour, or until done. Garnish with whipped cream.

Impossible Pumpkin Pie

Whip this up for the children, or for a quick family dessert.

1⅓ cups milk
3 tablespoons melted butter or vegetable oil
4 large eggs
½ cup white or brown sugar
½ cup buttermilk baking mix
1 cup canned pumpkin or cooked, puréed winter squash
½ to 1 teaspoon ginger
½ to 1 teaspoon cinnamon
¼ to ½ teaspoon nutmeg

Combine and beat together all the above ingredients. Pour into a well-greased 9-inch pie tin and bake in a 400°F (205°C) oven for approximately 35 minutes, or until a knife inserted in the center comes out clean. Cool. Serve topped with whipped cream.

Note. You can vary the spices, using less (or more) to suit your taste.

Potato Pudding Pie

This is from my book, A World of Baking, and makes a surprisingly good pie. Not so surprising perhaps, if we recognize its similarity to a pumpkin pie.

9-inch pie shell, unbaked
1 cup hot, unseasoned mashed potatoes
¼ cup butter
½ cup half and half
3 large eggs, separated

1 to 1½ cups sugar
1 tablespoon grated lemon rind
⅓ cup lemon juice

Combine hot mashed potatoes and the butter. Stir until butter is melted. Add half and half and blend in. Now add the egg yolks, sugar, lemon rind and juice. Beat the egg whites until stiff and fold into potato mixture. Pour into pie shell. Bake in a 450°F (230°C) oven for 10 minutes. Reduce heat to 350°F (175°C) and continue baking for 35 to 40 minutes, or until custardlike mixture tests done. Sprinkle with powdered sugar while hot. Cool on a rack.

Green Tomato Mincemeat

Over the years this has remained one of my favorite ways of using green tomatoes.

1½ pounds green tomatoes
1½ pounds corned beef or plain brisket
1½ pounds green apples
1 pound brown sugar
½ pound seedless raisins
½ pound golden raisins
1 pound candied mixed fruits, left in rather large pieces
½ cup suet
½ cup plus 1 tablespoon apple cider vinegar
1 tablespoon cinnamon
1 teaspoon cloves
1 teaspoon nutmeg
1 tablespoon grated lemon rind
1 tablespoon grated orange rind
⅓ cup brandy, whiskey, rum or cream sherry (optional)

Wash the tomatoes and chop them up fine in a food processor or by hand. Grind the corned beef or brisket and then chop the apples fine—again either by hand or with a processor. (This is a perfect example of a recipe that used to be tedious but can now be whipped up in minutes with a processor.)

Turn into a large pot and add the remaining ingredients except the liquor. Cover with water, bring to a boil, reduce heat and simmer for 2 to 4 hours. Then turn into clean containers adding, if desired, from 2 tablespoons to ⅓ cup liquor per pint of mincemeat.

This recipe makes enough for 5 pies. Mincemeat will keep in the refrigerator for 4 to 6 weeks, or 4 to 6 months in the freezer.

Index

Vegetable marrow, 67
  see Zucchini
Vegetable oyster, 64
Vegetable pear, 67
Vegetable platter, marinated, 136
Vegetable stew
  South Pacific squash and coconut, 75
Vegetarian
  lasagna, 190
  omelet, 175
Velvet Stem mushroom, 99
Venetian rice and peas, 13
Vinaigrette dressings, 159-160
Vinegar, 157-158
  apple cider, 158
  herb, 158
  lemon juice for, 158
  private stock wine, 158
  ravigote, 158
  See also Rice wine vinegar

Walnut oil, 157
Walnuts
  Deep South sweet potato pudding, 213
  lettuce tea bread, 210
  my favorite pesto, 127
  steamed carrot-potato pudding, 213
Water chestnuts
  beef and broccoli in oyster sauce, 199
  Chinese pickled garlic, 54
  jicama as substitute, 52
Watercress
  as greens, 33
  as salad greens, 131
Wax beans
  to microwave, 205
  three or four bean salad, 149
  See also Green beans
West Coast Cook Book, 62
Whipped potatoes, 62
Whiskey
  green tomato mincemeat, 215
White beans
  homemade baked beans, 3
White pepper
  Arabic spices, 35
White sauce, 122
White vinegar, 158

White wine vinegar
  Arabic pickles, 106
  Chinese pickled garlic, 54
  Dutch hot lettuce and potatoes, 45
  hot avocado salad, 147
  Peking hot and sour soup, 118
  South Pacific squash and coconut, 75
Wilted lettuce salad, 207
Wine
  mayonnaise, hot, 125
  pastry, 168
Wine vinegar, 106, 157-158
  herb, 158
  Italian marinated eggplant, 138
  marinated mushrooms, 136
  marinated olives, 135
  marinated spicy carrots, 136
  preserving herbs in, 134
  private stock, 158
  ravigote, 158
  repickled pickles, 106
  See also Rice wine vinegar
Winter ghivech, 187
Winter squash, 74-76
  bisque, 119
  colache, 182
  to cook, 74
  favorite pumpkin pie, 214
  impossible pumpkin pie, 214
  mashed, 76
  to microwave, 205
  pinto bean soup, 119
  See Acorn, Butternut, Hubbard
    See also Pumpkin
Witloof, 131
Wok and utensils, 192-3
Wolfert, Paula, 146
  Won-ton skins
    California Oriental spring salad, 151
    vegetable triangles, 198
Wood, Morrison, 163

Yams, 64-65
Yellow wax beans, *see* Green beans
Yogurt
  chutney dip, 110
  molded moussaka, 82
  moussaka, 82

salad, Lebanese, 152
summertime pie, 188

Zucchini, 67, 68-71
  antipasto, 105
  artichokes al forno, 96
  casserole, layered, 188
  cauliflower with tomatoes, 26
  -cheese pie, 70
  cream of vegetable soup, 114
  cream soup, 113
  deep-fried cauliflower, 26
  eggplant Parmigiana, 68
  to freeze, 68
  fresh marinated salad, 137
  frittata, 177
  hors d'oeuvre, 68
  layered moussaka, 68
  loaf, 71
  marinated, 135, 136
  Mexican style succotash, 182
  to microwave, 205
  mock oyster stir-fry, 200
  moussaka, 82
  Niçoise, 68
  in omelet, 175
  oven vegetable soup, 116
  Parmesan, 208
  pasta primavera salad, 140
  pie, Tomato-, 70
  pizza, 69
  quiche, summer, 173
  ratatouille, 183
  raw vegetable salad, 144
  salad, Mexican, 150
  salad, shredded, 144
  as salad ingredient, 132
  sauce, 129
  sauce, broccoli and, 129
  spinach tian, 188
  stuffed, 69
  twice-fried potatoes, 60
  vegetable combo, 184
  vegetable medley, 185
  vegetables à la Grecque, 107
  vegetables in Italian beer batter, 104
  vegetarian lasagna, 190
  winter ghivech, 187